AMERICAN FOLKWAYS

High Sierra Country

OSCAR LEWIS

HIGH SIERRA
COUNTRY

DUELL, SLOAN AND PEARCE
New York

LITTLE, BROWN AND COMPANY
Boston   Toronto

DUELL, SLOAN AND PEARCE—LITTLE, BROWN
BOOKS ARE PUBLISHED BY
LITTLE, BROWN AND COMPANY
IN ASSOCIATION WITH
DUELL, SLOAN & PEARCE, INC.

*Published simultaneously in Canada
by Little, Brown & Company (Canada) Limited*

PRINTED IN THE UNITED STATES OF AMERICA

Contents

CONTENTS

CONTENTS

High Sierra Country

I

Something for Everybody

THE SIERRA NEVADA RANGE, for all its bulk and majesty, is but a link in a vastly greater mountain chain that arises on the southernmost tip of South America, deep in the storm-lashed Antarctic, and extends with scarcely a break up the west coasts of both South and North America until it eventually terminates in a series of fog-bound islands of the outer Aleutians, almost within hailing distance of the headlands of Asia.

Of this mighty mountain line, the segment known as the Sierra occupies a position about midway between the chain's northernmost beginnings and the Isthmus of Panama. Paralleling the eastern border of California, and almost wholly within the boundaries of that state, it links up with the Cascade Range to the north, and, extending southward some four hundred miles, terminates at Tehachapi Pass at the lower end of the great central valley.

The precise points at which the Sierra Range begins and ends have long been a matter of wordy — and sometimes acrimonious — debate among geologists, both amateur and professional, as well as others who, for one reason or another,

have felt themselves qualified to get in on the hassel. The
chief bone of contention has been the fixing of the northern
boundary of the range. A few years ago, the authorities at
Washington sought to settle the matter by choosing a point
a few miles to the south of Mount Lassen; the result was
pleasing to practically nobody. For by arbitrarily placing
the dividing line at that spot, they assigned to the Cascade
Range two of the most spectacular peaks in the entire chain:
Lassen and Shasta, one the only active volcano on the continent, and the other the lofty 14,161-foot cone that dom-
inates the northern end of the Sacramento Valley.

This matter of drawing an imaginary line across the range,
and assigning all the mountains on one side to the Cascade
Range and all those on the other to the Sierra, is of little
concern to the public at large — however desirable it might
seem to the tidy minds of geodesists. For, since gold rush
times and earlier, the Californians have logically enough
looked on the succession of snowy peaks walling them in on
the east as one single unit, extending from Mount Whitney
on the south to Shasta on the north. To them, and to their
descendants today, the entire range was — and is — universally called "the Sierra."

However, even with Shasta and Lassen officially declared
out of bounds, the range in its abbreviated state is by no
means devoid of points of interest, embracing as it does some
430 miles of the most stupendous mountain scenery in the
nation, with the crests of its summits rising to heights of
14,000 feet or more above sea level and much of its upper
regions a maze of granite peaks and spires and buttresses,
interspersed with mountain meadows, jewel-like lakes, and
swift-flowing, snow-fed streams.

Among the great mountain areas of the world, the Sierra

is unique in that, for all its immensity, it is over almost its entire length a single, compact unit, its width from base to base measuring a scant forty to seventy-five miles. To explain its unusually homogeneous structure, geologists theorize that it is composed of a single mass of rock that was dislodged from its normal position and tilted upward during a mighty cataclysm, when the earth was young.

Substantial support is given this hypothesis by the topography of the range — in particular, by the marked difference in the contours of its two sides. For, as anyone who has crossed the barrier is aware, its eastern and western faces are almost startlingly unlike. The rise to the summit from the great central valleys of California is in the main a gradual one, from thirty to sixty miles separating the beginning of the foothills from the lofty crests; whereas, on the Nevada side, the range drops away much more abruptly, slanting down in a series of steep inclines to the sage-covered plains below. Hence it is by no means difficult to picture the range as having been formed by a section of the earth's crust that was violently dislodged from its horizontal position and tilted upward, its new-risen, clifflike face pointing toward the east.

Whatever its origin, the uptilted mass forms a barrier that for uncounted centuries has had a potent influence on many phases of life over much of the area that now constitutes the Western third of the United States.

To many, so sweeping a statement might seem a gross exaggeration — merely another example of the hyperbole that they are accustomed to hear in connection with all things relating to California. Before reaching that conclusion, however, it might be well to consider this single fact:

that over its entire length the range rises to heights of from 6000 to 14,000 feet; that, on meeting this barrier, the winds sweeping in from the ocean are forced upward, causing so much of the moisture they carry to condense and fall that very little passes over the crest to the parched plains beyond.

Thus a multitude of streams flow down the western side of the Sierra, fed throughout the rainless summer months by melting snowcaps high above, and provide the unfailing supply of the water on which so much of California's economy depends: for the irrigation of tens of thousands of valley farms, for the generation of hydroelectric power; for the use of populous urban centers as far distant as San Francisco and Los Angeles.

Moreover, through the ages, the towering wall of the Sierra has prevented the passage, east or west, of many forms of vegetable and animal life, with the result that the two areas, though separated by only two- or threescore miles, exhibit wide differences in their indigenous flora and fauna — a circumstance of which present-day travelers can hardly fail to become aware on their passage from the lush California valleys to the barren central plateau.

Finally, for years without number the towering range prevented any widespread intermingling of the aboriginals, confining each tribe to its own region, and resulting in two distinct — and quite different — cultures, flourishing, as it were, side by side, separated by no more than a day or two of travel. This was often remarked on, by the first parties of whites to make the journey from the Rockies to the sea. For they learned — often to their cost — that the natives of the waterless plains to the east were a wily, resourceful lot, inured to hardships and not averse to plundering the intruders should an opportunity present itself. On the other

hand, the California tribes, rendered indolent and unenter-
prising by generations of easy living, were in the main a
docile and submissive people who needed to be watched,
not for any warlike proclivities, but because of a marked
tendency toward petty theft.

That since the dawn of history the range has wielded a
profound influence on the way of life of the inhabitants of
a vast area of Western America is undeniable. This, however, is by no means its only claim to fame. Far more important, in the eyes of those of the present day, is the fact
that within its borders are an infinite variety of features
pleasing to the mountain lover whatever his particular interests or enthusiasms might be. For the Sierra truly has,
in the words of an advertising folder put out by a Feather
River resort, "something for everybody." Within its borders
are to be found the facilities for virtually every form of recreation fancied by the vacationist. Each season huntsmen and
fishermen by the thousands make their way up through the
foothills, many leaving their automobiles at the road-ends
and, carrying their camping equipment on their backs, head
for the hunting grounds or trout-filled streams and lakes
of the high back country.

Devotees of skiing and other winter sports — and their
total increases year by year — are able to indulge their hob-
bies at numberless spots from one end of the range to the
other. Within the past decade or two, the number of such
recreational areas has multiplied rapidly, each offering runs,
lifts, and food and shelter for hordes of week-end guests who
head mountainward all through the winter months. Accommodations, ranging from simple housekeeping cabins to
plush resort hotels, are to be found at many points along
the route of the Southern Pacific as it approaches Donner

Summit, in the Yosemite and Sequoia National Parks, at Mount Rose on the eastern side of the range, and various other places.

For those less strenuously inclined — vacationists who prefer to enjoy the beauty and serenity of the mountains without partaking of their austerities — there are a variety of picturesquely located resorts the length of the chain: hotels, lodges, and clusters of log cabins offering accommodations and services designed to fit virtually every taste or purse.

Finally, for the numerous group who look on themselves as simon-pure mountaineers, and who regard with polite disdain the sybarites who spend their days lounging on the terraces of the swank hotels, the range offers hundreds of square miles of solitude and magnificent distances where one may, for weeks on end, commune with nature uncontaminated. For despite more than a century of road building, which has each year opened up new regions to vehicular traffic, there still remain vast areas of the high country that can be reached only on foot or on the backs of mountainwise horses or mules.

It is into such remote, "unspoiled" districts that the part-time sons — and daughters — of the wilderness delight to penetrate. For only thus, as they rarely fail to point out to their less adventurous fellows, can one leave behind the cares and artificialities of civilization and for a few days or weeks live the austere, richly rewarding lives of our pioneer ancestors, cut off by miles of mountain trails from newspapers, telephones, TV programs, and similar distractions.

There are, indeed, many who look on their annual pilgrimage into the Sierra fastnesses as a means of restoring their perspective, affording them an opportunity, in a setting of unparalleled beauty and grandeur, to partake of the curative qualities said to abide in Mother Nature. Such, at any rate, is the reason they most frequently cite for their return, again and again, to the high and rugged back country. For only thus, they maintain, can a true appreciation of the peerless attractions of this range be gained.

II

Trail Breakers

Explorers, Missionaries, and Horse Thieves

ALTHOUGH, so far as is known, the first white man to set foot on what is now California was Hernando de Alarcón — who in the summer of 1540 explored the lower reaches of the Colorado River — and although two years later Captain Juan Rodriguez Cabrillo, a Portuguese navigator in the service of Spain, while sailing up the coast, sighted snow-clad mountains in the interior and bestowed on them the name "Sierra Nevada," the lofty range that today bears that name remained unknown to the world for more than two centuries longer. For the mountains so christened by Cabrillo could not have been a part of the present Sierra chain, since even its tallest peaks would have been invisible from the deck of his little craft. The snowy heights that he observed were a part of the present-day Coast Range — in all probability either those now called the Santa Cruz Mountains or else the Santa Lucias.

So, in a sense, our mighty Sierra was christened "sight unseen," for 230 years were to pass before the first European laid eyes on its lofty, serrated outline. It was not until 1772 — only three years, be it observed, before the American colonists on the far side of the continent began their fight for independence — that the existence of this great range became known to the world. In the spring of that year, a Franciscan priest, Father Juan Crespi, set off on an overland trek from Monterey, accompanied by Captain Pedro Fages and a group of Spanish soldiers. Having gained the crest of the Coast Range, Crespi, under date of March 20, wrote in his diary that he had sighted in the broad valley spread out below "a very large river, a league in width at least, which descended from some high mountains to the southeast, very far distant. . . ."

Before the decade of the 1770's was out, however, this passing remark about "high mountains to the southeast" was supplemented by more detailed descriptions. By then, the Franciscan fathers were founding their chain of missions along the coast from San Diego northward, and on occasion making forays into the interior, both to explore the country and to gather in neophytes to instruct in the ways of Christianity. On one such expedition was Father Pedro Font, who, after accompanying Juan Bautista de Anza's party of colonists on their long overland trek from Mexico in the fall of 1775, in the following spring proceeded inland to a point overlooking the central valley. There, on April 2, he recorded in his journal that "at the opposite end of this extensive plain, about forty leagues off, we saw a great, snow-covered mountain range, which seemed to me to run from the south-southeast to north-northeast."

In the same year that Font thus observed the range from the hills adjacent to San Francisco Bay, another Spanish missionary, Father Francisco Garcés, was gaining a far closer view by making his way, in company with a group of mission

Indians, northward from the San Gabriel Mission, over Tehachapi Pass into the lower end of the San Joaquin Valley,
and then proceeding northward to the vicinity of the Tulare
Lake before turning back. On his wilderness journey, the
good father carried with him, as an object lesson to the
savages encountered along the way, a colorful banner, one
side of which pictured the beauties of Christianity, and the
other the evils of paganism.

In general, however, the Spanish priests and civil authorities were too much occupied with the establishment and
conduct of their coastal missions and pueblos to give much
thought to exploring the unknown country that lay to the
east. The consequence was that another three decades passed
before, so far as is known, their sketchy knowledge of the
geography of the interior was extended. And this further
knowledge came, not because of any scientific curiosity as to
the nature or resources of the back country, but for other
more immediate reasons. For from time to time their Indian
converts, having found mission life irksome, were in the
habit of deserting and fleeing to ancestral hunting grounds
in the interior. Moreover, bands of savages that had not
come under the civilizing influence of the padres occasionally
made raids on mission herds — especially horses, for the
flesh of which they had a particular fondness — driving the
pilfered animals across the central valley and into the Sierra
foothills, before slaughtering them and holding protracted
banquets. It was by parties sent out in pursuit of these rene-
gades and horse thieves that the Spaniards' first on-the-spot
knowledge of the Sierra was gained.

One of the earliest of such punitive expeditions was that
of Gabriel Moraga and Father Pedro Moñoz, which in the
fall of 1806 crossed to the east side of the San Joaquin Valley

and skirted the foothills of the range from the Mokelumne River southward as far as the Kern, conferring names on many of the streams encountered and on several occasions penetrating some little distance into the mountains in search of the fugitives. Two years later, in 1808, Moraga returned and followed the base of the mountains toward the north, proceeding as far as the American and Feather Rivers and possibly reaching the Yuba as well.

That about completes the annals of Sierra exploration, as it was carried on by the Spaniards and Mexicans — surely a meager accomplishment, considering the fact that for more than half a century they had maintained numerous fairly populous establishments spaced along the more than six hundred miles of coastline, from San Diego to Sonoma.

It was not until the second quarter of the nineteenth century that the first white men trod the lofty upper reaches of the Sierra, and the trail breakers then were not of the nationality that ruled the province, but members of a far-roving breed: American fur-trappers.

A Man Named Smith

The man to whom belongs the distinction of having first made his way over the range was Jedediah Strong Smith. Authorities are quite generally agreed on that point, but on practically nothing else in connection with his memorable crossing. The result is that the question of what route he followed on his west-east passage over the crest has intermittently engaged the attention of Western historians and geographers for close to a century; and, although much has been written on the subject, the answer remains in doubt even today.

The reason for this uncertainty is not hard to explain. Smith, having entered the fur trade in 1822 at the age of twenty-three, had risen rapidly in the then flourishing beaver-trapping industry, becoming by the summer of 1826 a partner in the firm of Smith, Jackson & Sublette, one of the leaders in the field. Later that same year, in search of new trapping grounds, he led a party into unexplored territory to the southwest of Great Salt Lake. Some five months later, after a long, hard and sometimes hazardous journey, his bedraggled group wound up at the San Gabriel Mission in southern California, the first to travel from United States territory to the West Coast's Spanish province. Smith and his companions were hospitably received by the priest in charge of the mission — but less so by the Governor of the Province, José Echeandía. The latter, alarmed by the appearance of this party of Yankee trappers, denied them permission to proceed northward up the coast, and ordered them to leave by the same route by which they had come.

Smith, determined not to face a second time the barren, arid country through which they had struggled — and curious to learn if beaver were numerous in the California streams — chose to ignore Echeandía's orders. Instead, he and his party pushed into the San Joaquin Valley and, giving a wide berth to the coastal missions and towns, pressed northward, his route paralleling the towering Sierra and close to its foothills. After proceeding a distance he later estimated to be three hundred miles, he turned toward the east, planning to cross the range and continue on to rejoin his partners at Salt Lake.

However, on this first attempt, made in the spring of 1827,

he was forced to turn back. "I found the snow so deep . . . [he later wrote] that I could not cross my horses, five of which starved to death; I was compelled therefore to return to the valley. . . ." Undeterred by this first rebuff, he, after tarrying in the lowlands for several weeks waiting for the snows in the upper regions to melt, began a second try on May 20. This time he left most of his party behind and, with two companions, seven horses, and two mules, re-entered the mountains. Of this journey he reported, in the same letter quoted above, that they "succeeded in crossing . . . in eight days, having lost only two horses and one mule. I found the snow on the top of this mountain from 4 to 8 feet deep, but it was so consolidated by the heat of the sun that my horses only sunk from half a foot to one foot deep."

The above few sentences constitute, so far as is known, almost the only existing documentation of that historic first crossing. For although during most of his travels through the Western wilds Smith kept a day-by-day journal, the part bearing on this phase of his wanderings has dropped from sight. Missing, too, is a map he made shortly before he, in 1831, set off from St. Louis on what proved to be his last penetration of the frontier. For on May 27 of that year, the indomitable pathfinder — who was only thirty-two years old at the time — was set on by a band of Comanche Indians in the vicinity of the Cimarron River, and slain. The disappearance, both of the map on which he had traced the course of his travels and of his journal covering the first part of 1827, has ever since left in doubt the question of by precisely what route he and his two companions made their way over the towering range.

Over the years, however, there has been no lack of conjecture on that point. Those who have sought to fix his trail

have come up with a wide variety of answers, some placing
it as far north as the present Donner Pass in the Lake Tahoe
area, while others have favored the Kings River Canyon at
the lower end of the Sierra. In recent years, however, a number of historians, having familiarized themselves both with
the topography of the high Sierra country and the meager
documentary material bearing on Smith's movements, have
tended to agree that the crossing was made at some point
near the middle of the range.

In support of that view, present-day authorities cite two
primary sources. One of these is the evidence contained in
certain early maps of the Western frontier: specifically, those
of Brué, Gallatin, Burr and Wilkes, which appeared respectively in 1834, 1836, 1839, and 1845, all of which were apparently based in some degree on the missing chart Smith
himself drew shortly before his death in 1831. In addition is
the important "Frémont-Gibbs-Smith" map, discovered as
recently as 1953. The second source on which their hypothesis
rests is the few references Smith made to that phase of his
journey in his later writings. These include two letters
written by him in 1827, the year the crossing was made. One,
to the Spanish missionary, Fray Narciso Durán at the Mission
of San José, dated May 19, tells of his first unsuccessful attempt
to scale the heights and states that he planned "to wait a few
weeks until the snow melts so that I can go on."

The second is the more lengthy message quoted from
earlier, in which, soon after his return to the Salt Lake area,
Smith gave William Clark — the Clark of Lewis and Clark
— a resumé of his experiences in California and of his long
trek over the Sierra and across the plains beyond. Smith's
final writing bearing on this much-debated point is a single
reference in the journal he kept during his second visit to

California. For, several months after reaching Salt Lake, he again made his way to the coast, where he rejoined those of his party who had been left behind and led them on another trail-breaking journey, this time northward from the head of the Sacramento, over the rugged, heavily forested Cascade Range, to the Columbia River.

In mid-February of 1823, while encamped in the central valley, at a point where some twelve years later Captain John A. Sutter was to build his fort, he wrote in his journal that on a recent trapping expedition he had passed within a mile of the spot from which, ten months earlier, he had set off on his first fruitless attempt to get over the mountains, a circumstance that, so he stated, "brought fresh to my remembrance . . . the unpleasant times I had passed there when surrounded by the snow which continued falling, my horses freezing, my men discouraged and our utmost exertion necessary to keep from freezing to death."

The focal point of the long-drawn-out controversy revolves about the identity of the river where Smith had left the bulk of his party when he set off on his second, successful attempt, and to which he returned the following September. In his letter to William Clark he referred to the stream as the "Appelamminy," and in the journal covering his second California stay he stated that from there he had visited the Mission of St. Joseph, "a distance of about 70 miles SW."

From this widely scattered and by no means conclusive evidence, most present-day experts, while differing on minor points, are agreed that on Smith's first essay to cross the range he and his companions made their way up one or another of the forks of the American River, and that, having been forced back by the heavy snows, they retraced their route southward and encamped for some weeks beside the Stanislaus, and that on his second and successful attempt he followed the course of that stream through the foothills into the mountains themselves. Precisely what route he took thereafter is pure guesswork, but his own statement that he made the crossing in eight days indicates that the trail he broke must have been a fairly direct one, avoiding unscalable cliffs, and other natural barriers that would have necessitated time-consuming detours.

This, those most familiar with the terrain of that part of the Sierra believe, narrows the spot where he crossed the summit to one of three points; that is, to either the Relief-Emigrant Meadow Pass, the Ebbetts Pass, or the Carson Pass. They believe too that, starting at the point where the Stanislaus emerges from the foothills, he and his two companions lay a course to the north of that stream, crossed the uppermost ridge at or near Ebbetts Pass, made their way down the eastern side to the headwaters of the East Carson River, and followed its course to the sage-covered plains below. Such is the conclusion most widely held today, nor is it likely to be either proved or disproved save in the event that Smith's journal and map, both missing for well over a century, are someday brought to light.

To some this prolonged and sometimes caustic debate over what route Jedediah Smith followed on his first crossing of the Sierra has seemed a tempest in a teapot. However, students of the early West take the stand that the first passage over the mighty range by a party of white men was a feat of genuine historic significance, and that consequently it is desirable to learn all that can be learned about its details.

First Winter Crossing

The second Sierra crossing, this time from east to west, took place some six years later, and although once again much uncertainty exists as to the route followed, the annals of this expedition are far more complete than are those of Jedediah Smith. This is mainly because a member of the party, Zenas Leonard, in 1839 published an account of his five years as a fur trapper on the Western frontier — one of the most graphic sections of which describes the hardships he and his companions endured on their passage over the lofty, snow-mantled Sierra ridges.

Like Smith's party, this one, headed by Joseph Reddeford Walker, was in quest of beaver furs; and, again like the earlier group, its starting point was Great Salt Lake. However, instead of swinging far to the south and entering California at its lower end, as Smith had done, Walker headed toward the west, following the course of the Humboldt River across present-day Nevada, and thereby breaking trail on what was soon to be the most heavily traveled emigrant route to the Pacific.

In the late fall of 1833, Walker and his men reached the eastern base of the range at a point near the present town of Bridgeport, some sixty miles to the southeast of Lake Tahoe. The season was far advanced when they began their ascent of the steep eastern flank, with bitingly cold winds and the formation of ice beside the streams giving warning of the winter storms to come. The probabilities are that the company, numbering some fifty mounted men with additional horses carrying their supplies, made their way to the summit by following one of the branches of the river that now bears the name of its leader. On reaching the crest they — trained mountainmen all — were appalled by the nature of the country spread out before them: a maze of jagged granite peaks interspersed with canyons and snow-rimmed mountain lakes, extending westward as far as the eye could reach.

Into this unknown, inhospitable area the group made their way, aware that their only hope of survival lay in somehow finding a means of gaining the lowlands below. While they were futilely searching for such a passage, the supply of jerked buffalo meat that constituted their only food ran dangerously low and Walker gave his men permission to kill one of the horses whenever the pangs of hunger grew unsupportable. In all, seventeen animals were slain for that purpose; however, their meat, black and stringy and extremely tough, was far from appetizing, Leonard pronouncing it "fit only for a dog to chew on." After many days of wandering through the snowy upper ridges in search of a feasible route downward, some members of the party mutinied and demanded that they turn back and try to make their way out of the mountains by the route they had come. With difficulty did their leaders convince them that by then they had progressed too far to retrace their steps; that their only hope was to push on westward.

The point they had chosen to make their crossing was one of the wildest and scenically most spectacular of the entire range. The cold, half-famished wanderers were, however, in no mood to admire the grandeur of the country. Making their way across the high, broken area that lay between the Merced and Tuolumne Rivers, they presently came to a region where the swift, snow-fed streams leaped over the edge of a mighty chasm, falling in long plumes to the floor of a valley a half-mile or more below. In their desperate plight, even this natural phenomenon — for they were, in all probability, looking into the Yosemite Valley, the first white men ever to glimpse its wonders — aroused no more than passing curiosity, Leonard dismissing it with a few sentences in his narrative.

By then, however, they were nearing the end of their ordeal. For the descent presently grew easier, the snowfields less frequent and deep. Soon they regained the timberline, where progress was relatively fast and, more important, the hunters were able to bag both deer and grizzly bear and thus bring to a welcome end their weeks-long diet of horse meat. On this part of their long Odyssey, they stumbled on yet another of the major wonders of the Sierra, passing through a grove of huge trees, "16 to 18 fathoms round the trunk at the height of a man's head from the ground." These were, of course, one of the Sierra's famous groves of *Sequoia sempervirens,* either those of the Tuolumne or those of the Merced.

The Walker party's long and perilous crossing of the range ends on a note of irony. Having at length made their way down through the foothills onto the floor of the San Joaquin Valley, the men complained bitterly because, although its plain abounded in antelope, elk, and game birds of many sorts, it was lacking in their favorite delicacy: buffalo meat.

The Pathfinder and His Cannon

As the decade of the 1840's opened, evidence began to accumulate that Mexico's hold on its West Coast province could not be much longer maintained. Moreover, glowing reports of the climate and productivity of the region — brought back by Yankee whaling and trading ships that annually visited the coastal ports — kindled widespread interest on the far side of the continent, and it was not long until parties of emigrants were heading westward from the trans-Mississippi frontier, bent on trying their luck in the new Elysium.

One of the earliest of these was a group of thirty-two men, plus one woman and one child, who made the crossing in the fall of 1841. This party, under the leadership of John Bartelson, included in its number John Bidwell, Josiah Beldon, and several others who later rose to eminence in the affairs of the territory.

It was, however, not until three years later that there passed over the Sierra the man who was mainly responsible for setting in motion the brisk westward migration that was soon to get under way. This was none other than John Charles Frémont, the doughty thirty-year-old pathfinder who was already something of a national figure because of an expedition he had led the previous year to explore the South Pass, the Wind River Mountains, and other points in the Rocky chain.

Frémont — a lieutenant in the United States Topographical Engineers and, far more important, son-in-law of Thomas Hart Benton, the powerful United States Senator from Missouri — was, early in 1843, put in command of an exploring expedition numbering some forty men, which was charged with making a scientific survey of the still virtually unknown area that lay between the Rockies and the Pacific. On this welcome assignment, he set off from the Kansas frontier at the end of May. His departure into the wilds was a bit hasty, mainly because, along with supplies, sidearms, and a cart filled with scientific instruments he carried with him a small brass cannon, of the mountain howitzer type.

Frémont's purpose in taking along this piece of armament was, he maintained, merely to provide additional means of defense against attacks by hostile Indians. However, when word that he was so armed reached Washington, it precipitated something of a sensation in Congress where one faction claimed that for a government expedition bound on a peaceable surveying mission to carry so warlike a weapon into the lands bordering on the Pacific would constitute an affront to the two friendly nations — England and Mexico — having territorial rights there. This crisis had been mainly stirred up by those opposing a group of Senators, headed by Benton, who were more or less openly advocating the extension of the nation's boundaries to the shores of the Pacific. Frémont, having received word that the controversy had developed, and fearing that as a result he would be recalled to Washington, made haste to put himself out of reach of any such summons.

Lugging the fieldpiece, which the leader had placed in charge of one Louis Zindel, formerly an artilleryman in the Prussian army, the group made their way westward by easy stages, reaching Salt Lake in early September. From there they pushed on to Oregon Territory, arriving at the Hudson's Bay Company settlements on the Columbia two months later. During all that time, the little howitzer, mounted on its two-wheeled carriage, was fired only twice — both times as a means of informing detached groups of the whereabouts of the main party. Frémont, however, remained convinced of the wisdom of transporting his cherished weapon thus far into the wilderness. In his report, he cited two occasions when imminent Indian attacks had been warded off because the savages had caught sight of the cannon trained upon them. Moreover, the fears of the noninterventionist group at Washington that the appearance of the little weapon on the West Coast would cause international complications proved groundless. Officials of the British-held fur and trading posts on the Columbia gave no evidence that they saw in it any serious threat to their hold on the territory.

The subsequent history of the cannon is interesting. Having, on reaching the Oregon settlements, completed the mission to which he had been assigned, Frémont was free to turn eastward again and retrace the route by which he had come. However, he chose instead to swing far to the south and explore the region that lay between Salt Lake and the Mexican settlements in California, vast areas of which were unknown to the geographers of the day. His primary purpose was to locate and explore two features of the region that had appeared on the maps of certain early cartographers. One was an extensive body of water known as Mary's Lake, which supposedly lay in a rich, wooded valley and was fed by streams abounding in fish. His second — and most important — object was to find and trace the course of the Buenaventura River, which was believed to rise somewhere on the western shoulder of the Rockies and, flowing through a gap in the Sierra, empty into the Pacific.

On this quest, Frémont and his party left their Oregon camp in late November of 1843. During the next two months they worked their way southward, visiting Klamath Lake and proceeding down the east flank of the Sierra to a point a few miles north of Mono Lake. In order to permit greater freedom of movement on this long trek, Frémont left behind in Oregon one of his two-wheeled vehicles: the cart in which the expedition's scientific instruments had been carried. However, he tenaciously held on to his howitzer, which was laboriously trundled through mountain defiles and over passes, carried across streams and drawn over the sandy wastes on the east side of the Sierra.

His failure to come upon either Mary's Lake or the Buenaventura River — for the very good reason that neither existed — plus the barren nature of the semidesert country through which his party had been traveling for weeks, presently forced on him yet another change of plans. This was a decision, reached in late January of 1844, to attempt a winter crossing of the Sierra and, at the Mexican settlements beyond, secure food and animals urgently needed for the journey home. It was only then, as he and his companions contemplated the precipitous canyons and snow-covered crests before them, that he reached the conclusion that he must leave behind his cherished cannon. The decision was a difficult one, for during the previous seven months the little weapon had been dragged and pushed and carried over some 3000 miles of rugged, roadless territory.

It was abandoned January 29 on an eastward flank of the Sierra, at a point about midway between Tahoe and Mono Lake and a few miles to the west of the present California-Nevada state line. "We left it," wrote Frémont in his journal, "to the great sorrow of the whole party, who were grieved to part with a companion which had made the whole distance from St. Louis, and commanded respect from us on some critical occasions, and which might be needed for the same purpose again."

Their progress no longer impeded by this piece of armament, the company pressed forward, following the course of the Carson River up toward its source. On February 14 they

reached the summit, from which point Frémont, looking off
to the northeast, discerned a large mountain lake, its shores
fringed with high, forest-covered mountains. On this impressive body of water he conferred the name Bonpland, in
honor of Amie Bonpland, the botanist who had accompanied Baron von Humboldt on his memorable expeditions
to South and Central America some half a century earlier.
This name, however, failed to stick; the lake — the largest
in the range and one of the most beautiful of all mountain
waters — eventually received the Indian name by which it
is known today: Tahoe.

The Frémont party's midwinter passage over the Sierra
was one that called forth all the fortitude and stamina its
members possessed. On their way to the crest, the pack animals had much difficulty making their way through the deep
snowdrifts and up the precipitous canyons, and every pound
of supplies and equipment save what was urgently needed
was abandoned. To make matters worse, the Indian guide
whom Frémont had engaged to show them the way up to
the pass deserted, and returned to the lowlands. The leader
and his followers nevertheless pushed on, and by mid-February had reached an elevated point from which they could
look over a long succession of snow-covered ridges to the
invitingly green plains of the Sacramento.

They were, however, by no means out of their difficulties.
In his journal Frémont wrote that "between us and the
plains extended miles of snowy fields and broken ridges of
pine-covered mountains." With their food running low and
the animals miring deep in the snow, they pressed onward
at all possible speed. In the same journal entry, Frémont
wrote: "After a day's march of 20 miles, we struggled into
camp, at nightfall; the greater number excessively fatigued."

Four days later, while camped on an exposed ridge at an
elevation of close to 9000 feet, they were beset by a new
peril. "During the night," the leader wrote, "the weather
changed, the wind rising to a gale, and commencing to snow
before daylight; before morning the trail was covered. . . .
We suffer much for want of salt; and all the men are becoming weak from insufficient food." Some days thereafter, Frémont and several companions having gone on ahead of the
main party in search of a feasible route downward, drastic
measures had to be taken by this advance group to ward off
starvation. "I gave Godley leave to kill our little dog (Tla-
math)," Frémont recorded, "which he prepared in Indian
fashion; scorching off the hair, and washing the skin with
soap and snow, then cutting it up into pieces, which were
laid on the snow." When the storm presently passed and
was succeeded by brilliant sunshine, the hard-pressed party
faced new trials: "The glare of the sun, combined with great
fatigue, rendered many of the people nearly blind; but we
were fortunate in having some black silk handkerchiefs,
which, worn as veils, very much relieved the eye."

But despite the perils and manifold discomforts of their
plight, Frémont was not unaware of the scenic grandeur of
the country through which they were struggling. "The night
has been extremely cold," he wrote in mid-February, "but
perfectly still, and beautifully clear. Before the sun appeared
this morning, the thermometer was 3° below zero; 1° higher
when his rays struck the lofty peaks, and 0° when we reached
our camp . . . the purity and deep-blue color of the sky are
singularly beautiful; the days are sunny and bright, and even
warm in the noon hours; and if we could be free from the
many anxieties that oppress us, even now we would be
delighted here. . . . "

Not until February 20, nearly three weeks after leaving the lowlands, did the whole party assemble at camp in a cleft of the summit ridge, which has ever since been known as Carson Pass in honor of Kit Carson, Frémont's chief guide on this and other Western expeditions. Both Carson and his chief were well aware that the balance of the crossing would be no easy one. "Still deep fields of snow lay between," Frémont recalled, "and there was a large intervening space of rough-looking mountains, through which we had yet to wind our way. Carson aroused me this morning with an early fire, and we were all up long before day, in order to pass the snow fields before the sun should render the crust soft. . . . Ascending a height, we traced out the best line we could discover for the next day's march, and had at least the consolation to see that the mountain descended rapidly . . ."

Making their way slowly and painfully downward, and, reported their leader, "obliged to take to the mountainsides, where occasionally, rocks and a southern exposure afforded us a chance to scramble along," they at length gained the South Fork of the American River. Thereafter, the going was easier, with a snow less deep and with occasional patches of grass providing grazing for their famished animals. Convinced that the worst was past, Frémont, Carson, and six others pushed on ahead, following well-defined Indian trails down into the foothills and thence out on the floor of the valley. On the way they came on an Indian village, the inhabitants of which — quite naturally, it would seem — appeared, in Frémont's words, to be "entirely astonished at seeing us." There they partook of a welcome noontime feast of acorn meal, then hurried on to Sutter's Fort, where they arrived on March 8, having been five weeks en route from the far side of the mountains.

After a brief period of rest for men and animals, and after replenishing his stock of the latter — more than half having died during the crossing, or been killed for food — Frémont and his party set off again, heading for home. Being disinclined to tackle for a second time the snowy heights before them, they now swung far to the south, skirting the western flank of the range. On April 14 they crossed Tehachapi Pass at the lower end of the San Joaquin Valley and, rounding the southern extremity of the Sierra, proceeded northeast to Great Salt Lake, from which point Frémont hurried back to headquarters at Washington, D.C.

And what of the small brass cannon he had abandoned on the snowy eastern flank of the range? With the publication in 1845 of Frémont's report of the expedition, its story became widely known, and thereafter, for well over a century, the little mountain howitzer has made periodical reappearances in the news. One of the first of these to attract widespread attention was the finding in the early 1860's of a small howitzer-type fieldpiece in the vicinity of the Walker River, in the same general location where Frémont had reported having abandoned his weapon some fifteen years earlier.

Whether or not this was the authentic Frémont fieldpiece has long been a matter of debate, for cannon of that type were not infrequently carried along by emigrant parties during the gold rush. However, it was widely accepted as such, at the time of its discovery; and the little weapon became a prized possession of a volunteer fire company at Virginia City where, during the middle and late 1860's, it occupied a place of honor in the company's stationhouse and was brought forth and fired on July 4 and other gala occasions. With the decline of the Comstock in the late 1880's, the little cannon again dropped from sight — but not perma-

nently. Something more than a decade later it — or one of
the same general type — reappeared, this time at Glenbrook,
a resort on the eastern shore of Lake Tahoe. Later still, in
the year 1900, it was moved across the lake to Tahoe City,
where it was again put into use to lend a properly martial
note to partiotic celebrations.

Not long thereafter it again vanished, the reason being —
according to one version of its story — that Tahoe City
residents had hidden it in order to thwart the plots of certain
groups on both sides of the Sierra to make off with the venerable relic and install it in their home towns. Not until the
mid-1940's did the peripatetic little weapon — which may or
may not be the one Frémont toted across half the continent
— find a permanent home, this time in the Nevada State
Museum at Carson City.

A Sierra Crusoe

The first group of emigrants to bring their wagons over
the lofty summit of the range was that known as the Stevens-
Murphy-Townsend party, which made the crossing in the
fall of 1844. The group was a considerable one, consisting
in the beginning of some fifty persons, of which twenty-six
were men, eight were women, and the rest children. Members of the train, their belongings stowed in ten of the traditional ox-drawn wagons of the pioneers, set off from Coun-
cil Bluffs on the Missouri River in mid-May. From there
they proceeded, without encountering any unusual hardships, to the eastern base of the Sierra, arriving at the
Truckee River on or about October 9.

From there on, however, their difficulties multiplied.

Then commenced the ever-to-be-remembered journey up the Truckee to the summit of the Sierras [wrote one member of the group many years later]. At first it was not discouraging. There was plenty of wood, water, grass, and game, and the weather was pleasant. The oxen were well rested, and for a few days good progress was made. Then the hills began to grow closer together, and the country was so rough and broken that they frequently had to travel in the bed of the stream. The river was so crooked that one day they had to cross it ten times in the course of a mile. This almost constant traveling in the water softened the hoofs of the oxen, while the rough stones on the bed of the river wore them down, until the cattle's feet were so sore that it became a torture for them to travel.

Despite the fact that this onerous passage up the Truckee had brought both men and beasts close to exhaustion, there was no choice but to press on. For the season was already late and each day increased the likelihood of winter closing in, in which case the entire party might be marooned on the heights above. In fact, a day or two later came a foot-deep fall of snow, "burying the grass from the reach of the cattle, and threatening them with starvation."

At a point near the present town of Truckee part of the group — three men and three women — mounted on horseback and with provisions carried on two pack animals, left the main party and followed the Truckee to Lake Tahoe. From there they made their way upward to the summit and pressed on, following the course of the American River and, having gained the valley, headed for Sutter's Fort, which they reached on December 10.

The main group, with their wagons, made their laborious way up the canyon of the Truckee and presently reached the body of water later known as Donner Lake. There they camped for several days while the steep escarpment ahead was explored in search of a practicable route to the top. At that point some of the members, convinced that their weary, half-starved oxen could not make the ascent, decided to abandon their wagons. The owners of five of the cumbersome vehicles, however, were determined to make the attempt.

Keeping their course on the north side of the lake until they had reached its head [continues the account quoted above], they started up the mountain. All the wagons were unloaded and the contents carried up the hill. Then the teams were doubled and the empty wagons were hauled up. When about halfway up the mountain they came to a vertical rock about ten feet high. It seemed now that everything would have to be abandoned except what the men could carry on their backs. After a tedious search they found a rift in the rock, just about wide enough to allow one ox to pass at a time. Removing the yokes from the cattle, they managed to get them one by one through this chasm to the top of the rock. There the yokes were replaced, chains were fastened to the tongues of the wagons, and carried to the top of the rock, where the cattle were hitched to them. Then the men lifted at the wagons, while the cattle pulled at the chains, and by this ingenious device the vehicles were all, one by one, got across the barrier.

Having gained the crest — the present Donner Summit — the party continued down a ridge paralleling the course of the Yuba River for a distance of some twenty miles. From there most of the able-bodied men, driving what remained of their cattle, pushed on to the valley below. Those who remained behind, including the women and children, made camp high in the mountains for the balance of the winter, some using the wagons for shelter, others putting up rude cabins to ward off the snows and fierce winds. These eventually reached Sutter's Fort in the spring of 1845, being the first to bring wagons across the range.

One phase of the saga of the Stevens-Murphy-Townsend party's crossing remains to be told. When, in late November of 1844, the decision was reached to leave some of the wagons at Donner Lake rather than try to hoist them up to the summit, three of the company agreed to remain behind and keep watch over them and their contents until members of the advance party returned with fresh animals to help them over the hump.

One of the trio who chose to stay behind was a seventeen-year-old youth named Moses Schallenberger, an orphan who was making the trip in company with his sister and brother-in-law, Dr. and Mrs. John Townsend. Some forty years later Schallenberger put on paper an account of the journey, which has ever since been the chief source of information concerning it. Although the original of his narrative has unfortunately dropped from sight, several later writers had access to it and thus much of its contents has been preserved, including the story of his experiences during the long winter weeks spent beside the lake. That portion of his reminiscence begins by stating that he and his two comrades felt no hesitation about remaining behind while the rest of the company went on:

> Game seemed to be abundant. We had seen a number of deer, and one of our party had killed a bear, so I had no fears of starvation. The Indians in that vicinity were poorly clad, and I therefore felt no anxiety in regard to them, as they probably would stay further south as long as the cold weather lasted. Knowing that we were not far from California, and being unacquainted, except in a general way,

with the climate, I did not suppose that the snow would at any time be more than two feet deep, or that it would be on the ground continually.

After the others had left, the three occupied themselves building a cabin, they having, in Schallenberger's words, "determined to make ourselves as comfortable as possible, even if it was for a short time."

But on the evening of the day they finished their shelter, the Sierra winter closed down in earnest — snow to a depth of three feet falling that night. At first they were not alarmed, believing that this snow would presently melt. Instead, a succession of other storms followed, one after the other, with the result that by the end of November their little cabin was all but buried. Moreover, the once-abundant game grew scarcer day by day, and they presently began to realize their true situation. Two cows that had been left behind as too weak to travel with the other livestock were thereupon slaughtered and the marooned trio ate sparingly of these, well knowing that the supply could not last them through the winter.

> We now began to feel very blue [he continued] for there seemed no possible hope for us. We had already eaten about half our meat, and with the snow on the ground getting deeper day by day, there was no chance for game. . . . At last, after due consideration, we determined to start for California on foot. Accordingly, we dried some of our beef, and each of us carrying ten pounds of meat, a pair of blankets, a rifle and ammunition, we set out. . . .

Wearing cumbersome snowshoes fashioned out of such materials as were on hand, the group managed to reach the summit after a day-long struggle. Young Schallenberger, however, was so exhausted by his exertions that he was hardly able to gain the crest. After spending a cold, sleepless night on the snow-clogged pass, they, in his words, "ate our jerky while we deliberated as to what we should do next." Being, as he stated, "so stiff I could hardly move," it was clear to all that he was in no condition to make the long trek down to the valley. Moreover, it was realized that should he drop from exhaustion along the trail, his companions would have no option but to leave him to his fate.

> I fully realized the situation [his narrative goes on], and told them that I would return to the cabin and live as long as possible on the quarter of beef that was still there, and when it was all gone I would start out again alone for California. They reluctantly assented to my plan, and promised that if they ever got to California and it was possible to get back, they would return. . . .

After an exchange of handclasps the trio parted, the two men setting off toward the west and Schallenberger making his way back to the cabin, where he arrived at nightfall so weak that, as he reported, he had difficulty lifting his feet high enough to pass over the doorsill.

Then the youth began the lonely, Crusoelike existence that constitutes one of the most extraordinary true-adventure stories of the Old West. The direct, unpretentious narrative he wrote four decades later relates that early the next morning he put on his clumsy snowshoes and, with his rifle, explored the wooded area surrounding the cabin, seeing — as on previous occasions — numerous tracks on the snow made by foxes but no trace of the animals themselves.

On returning to the cabin, his eye fell on a number of traps belonging to one of the leaders of the expedition. For the remainder of the day he busied himself setting out the traps, using some of his meager supply of beef as bait. On visiting them the next morning he was delighted to find in one of them — not a fox, to be sure — but a coyote, a smaller member of the wolf family then common throughout the area. "I soon had his hide off and his flesh roasted in a Dutch oven," he wrote. "I ate this meat, but it was horrible. I next tried boiling him, but it did not improve the flavor. I cooked him in every possible manner my imagination, spurred by hunger, could suggest, but could not get him into a condition where he could be eaten without revolting my stomach."

Two nights later, however, his traps yielded more appetizing fare: two foxes. Upon roasting these he found them so delicious that he could, he stated, have devoured one in two meals; instead, he forced himself to eat sparingly, thereby making his windfall last four full days. During the days and weeks that followed, his traps continued to capture an occasional wolf or coyote — the average was one every two days — and he was thus able to sustain life, but always on a precarious footing. "I never really suffered for something to eat," he recalled, "but was in almost continual anxiety for fear the supply would give out. . . . As soon as one meal was finished I began to be distressed for fear I could not get another one. My only hope was that the supply of foxes would not become exhausted."

Indicative of the grimness of the youth's battle to ward off starvation is the following incident:

One morning two of my traps contained foxes. Having killed one, I started for the other, but, before I could reach it, the fox had left his foot in the trap and started to run. I went as fast as I could to the cabin for my gun, and then

followed him. He made for a creek about a hundred yards
from the house, into which he plunged and swam across.
He was scrambling up the opposite bank when I reached
the creek. In my anxiety at the prospect of losing my breakfast, I had forgotten to remove a greasy wad that I usually
kept in the muzzle of my gun to prevent it from rusting, and
when I fired, the ball struck the snow about a foot above
reynard's back. I reloaded as rapidly as possible, and as my
gun was one of the old-fashioned flint-locks that primed
itself, it did not require much time. But, short as the time
was, the fox had gone about forty yards when I shot him.
Now the problem was to get him to camp. The water in the
stream was about two and a half feet deep and icy cold.
But I plunged in, and, on reaching the other side, waded for
forty yards through the snow, into which I sank to my arms,
secured my game, and returned the way I came. . . .

How did this seventeen-year-old youth occupy himself during the weeks he spent in the lonely, snowbound cabin? He
himself makes it clear that the hours dragged slowly. "What
I wanted most," wrote he, "was enough to eat, and the next
thing I tried hardest to do was to kill time. I thought the
snow would never leave the ground, and the few months I
had been living there seemed years." He made it clear, too,
that his thoughts were much occupied with wondering what
had befallen those who had gone on ahead, not only the
main party but the two from whom he had parted on the
summit pass above. As for himself, he was still determined,
should the supply of foxes fail, to set off across the mountains. With this in mind, he kept untouched the frozen quarter of beef, intending to use it to sustain him on the journey.

Fortunately, one means of easing the loneliness of his lot
and of whiling away the slow-moving hours was at hand.
For among the belongings his brother-in-law, Dr. Townsend,
had brought West was a modest supply of books, including

Chesterfield's *Letters to My Son* and a volume of Byron's poems. "I often used to read aloud," stated Schallenberger, "for I longed for some sound to break the oppressive stillness. For the same reason I would talk aloud to myself. At night I built large fires and read by the light of the pine knots as late as possible, in order that I might sleep late the next morning. . . ."

Thus, in complete solitude, shut off from every contact with the outer world, the youth passed the weeks and months until at last, near the end of February, 1845, came deliverance.

One evening, while walking a little distance from the cabin, he was startled to observe a long-unfamiliar sight: a man approaching over the snowdrifts. At first he mistook the newcomer for an Indian, but when the other drew nearer he recognized him as Dennis Martin, one of the young men who had gone forward with the wagons some three months earlier. From him, Schallenberger learned that Martin and a number of his companions had got safely through to Sutter's Fort; that Martin had recently returned to the party's main camp on the Yuba River and from there, on the urging of Mrs. Townsend, had pushed on across the summit to learn what had befallen her brother.

On the morning following Martin's arrival, the pair headed westward to rejoin the others at the Yuba camp. Although the trip over the snowy ridge proved an ordeal to young Schallenberger, weakened as he was by his limited diet and lack of exercise, it was successfully accomplished. A few days later, the reunited party made their way, together with their wagons, down to safety on the plains below.

"Ordeal by Hunger"

Only a year after Schallenberger's long vigil on the shores
of this mountain lake, another, and far less happy, drama
was enacted on the same spot. This was, of course, the ordeal
of the Donner Party, perhaps the most widely known episode in the entire annals of the Sierra.

The tragic saga of the Donners has been so frequently
told that its outlines are familiar to all who have even a
casual knowledge of the pioneer West. It is easy to under-
stand why this is so, for the tribulations through which
members of this ill-starred party passed have all the ele-
ments of a tragic drama; namely, man's struggle for survival against the inimical forces of nature; suffering and privations borne with courage and fortitude by some and with
cowardice by others; occasions when the desperation of their
plight was relieved by flashes of grim humor.

The story of the trials and misadventures of this unfor-
tunate group can be briefly told. In the spring of 1846 a
party of Illinois farmers, under the leadership of George
and Jacob Donner and James F. Reed, lured by accounts of
the attractions of California then circulating throughout the
Western frontier, set off on the long journey to the promised land. By then, migration to the far coast was just beginning to get under way; and when, at the beginning of
May, the Donner group reached Independence, Missouri —
their jumping-off point — they found from two to three
hundred wagons assembled there, their owners waiting only
for the grass of the prairies to grow high enough to sustain
their animals before setting forth.

After an uneventful passage over the by then well-marked

trails, the party, having crossed the Continental Divide, reached Little Sandy Creek, in present-day Wyoming, in mid-July. There a decision was reached that was to have a dire effect on the destiny of the Donner group. For at that point they were met by the agents of one Lansford W. Hastings, who had earlier published a book on California and Oregon and on the trails leading to them. These urged the California-bound emigrants to turn off there and follow the Hastings Cut-Off which, swinging to the south, was represented as a far shorter and easier route. While a majority of the travelers turned a deaf ear to these arguments and continued over the well-defined northern trail, others — including the Donner-Reed party — allowed themselves to be persuaded. Accordingly on July 20 a train, numbering some twenty ox-drawn wagons, swung off to the south on what they believed would be an easy, timesaving short cut.

They were speedily disillusioned. For the route proved to be far more difficult than the one they had abandoned, passing as it did through many miles of completely arid country and over a succession of mountains. Far more important than the hardships encountered, however, was the fact that much precious time was lost. For it was not until the end of October that the travel-weary party reached the eastern base of the Sierra — dangerously late in the season to attempt a crossing. Nevertheless, although the first heavy snowfalls had already covered the upper ridges, an attempt was made in early November to snake their wagons up to the pass from their camping place beside the lake.

Because a recent snowstorm had obliterated the trail, this first group was forced to abandon the attempt and return to camp. The next morning all but a few of the party, alarmed at increasing evidences that the Sierra winter had begun in earnest, made a new attempt to scale the barrier ahead. This time they left their wagons behind and carried on the backs of the oxen only such supplies as were considered necessary to sustain them on their race over the mountains to safety in the valley beyond. Two of the party, constituting themselves advance scouts, struggled through the new-fallen snow — which by then had reached a depth of three feet — located the trail, and succeeded in reaching the summit.

However, when they returned to guide the others, the day had far advanced and it was accordingly decided to put off making the ascent until the next morning. That decision, as subsequent events were to prove, had tragic consequences. For it snowed steadily all that night; and the next morning the party, after having assembled their wagons at the base of the precipitous barrier, abandoned all hope of making the ascent and straggled back through the deep drifts to their former camp beside the lake. There, the emigrants busied themselves putting up shelters for protection against the by then almost continuous storms. Most of the party established winter quarters on the lake's shore, some moving into the cabin young Schallenberger had occupied the previous winter. However, George and Jacob Donner, with their families, set up their camp at Alder Creek, some six miles to the east of the lake.

At first, the situation of the marooned group seemed more uncomfortable than dangerous, for deer, bears, and foxes were still to be seen in the snow-mantled mountain valley, and, should that source of food fail, their own oxen could be slaughtered to ward off hunger. Moreover, it was not their plan to spend the entire winter encamped in the wilderness, but rather to push on across the mountains as soon

as a break in the succession of storms offered a favorable
opportunity. However, when in mid- and late November
two separate groups essayed the crossing and both were
forced back by the tremendous snowdrifts encountered on
the upper ridges, the true nature of their plight began to
grow clear to them.

Several weeks later, toward the middle of December, a
group of young adults, ten men and five women, mounted
on crude, homemade snowshoes, set off on a desperate attempt to break through to the valley beyond and summon
help for their marooned fellows. After much suffering during their thirty-two-day crossing of the range, the remnants
of this party — which became known as the "Forlorn Hope"
— reached the lowlands and safety. However, only five of
the fifteen who had started, three women and two men, had
survived that long ordeal.

Meanwhile, those who had remained behind were faring
but little better. Confined in their cabins and rude shacks,
which by then were almost completely buried beneath the
snow, and with their never-large supply of food daily growing more scanty, they were presently reduced to subsisting
on broth made by boiling the bones and hides of their long-
since slaughtered oxen and on the flesh of their half-starved
dogs. This meager diet, combined with inadequate shelter
against the subzero cold and a complete lack of drugs or
medical care, soon had its effect. As the winter advanced,
there were almost daily deaths, particularly among the more
elderly members of the party and the children. Of the
eighty-odd persons who spent the winter at the Donner Lake
and Alder Creek camps, close to forty perished.

With the arrival in the Sacramento Valley of the five sur-

vivors of the "Forlorn Hope" party, the plight of the snowbound group at the lake became known throughout California. In early February, a party numbering fourteen, all
experienced mountaineers, set out to their relief. Arriving
at the snow-covered cabins at sunset on February 18, these
found the survivors in a deplorable state, their gaunt faces
and emaciated bodies clearly showing the effects of the long
weeks of strain and privation they had endured. Gathering
together a number of members of both camps, they began
the journey back over the mountains on the morning of the
twenty-second. It proved a difficult and hazardous trip for
the weakened emigrants. Several were forced to turn back,
and others died before reaching the first settlements on the
western flank of the range.

Nor was the lot of those who had chosen to remain behind
more fortunate. When a second rescue party reached the
lake on March 1, they learned that still others had died
of starvation — and that some of the survivors had resorted
to cannibalism in order to sustain life. Rounding up those
who were able to travel, this party, too, headed back over
the mountains. While they were en route, a particularly
severe storm closed down.

The trapped group huddled for three days about a fire
near the summit — without food, and suffering intensely
from the cold — while three of the rescuers pushed on to an
advance camp that had been set up high on the west side of
the range. There another rescue group was formed and set
off toward the isolated party on the summit. On arriving,
they found that three of the party had died and that their
bodies had been partly eaten by the others.

After seeing the survivors started on their way west, part

of this rescue crew continued on to the lake. There they
learned that yet others had succumbed, and that virtually
all who remained here had been reduced to cannibalism.
And of these, only six — three adults and three children —
were able to set off with the rescuers on the long trek over
the range. On their departure, but five members of the once-
numerous band were left in the mountains, all too old or
too feeble to attempt the journey.

More than a month later, in mid-April, a new group of
Californians set out for the lake, on the remote chance that
some of the abandoned five might have survived. Upon
reaching the cluster of cabins by the lake, no sign of life
greeted them — only the belongings of the emigrants scattered about in disordered heaps on the melting snow, and
among them the mutilated bodies of the dead. By then
spring had well advanced, revealing to the full the grisly
details of the months-long ordeal through which the party
had passed. Finding no one in the littered cabins there, the
rescue group pushed on to the Donners' camp, on Alder
Creek. This, too, was deserted, with the property of the former inhabitants strewn about. Inside one of the hovels, however, they came on the mutilated body of George Donner,
and, in a large iron pot outside, pieces of his flesh. Moreover, there were freshly made footprints on the snow which
indicated that someone had headed back toward the camp
by the lake.

After camping overnight in the vicinity of these grisly
relics, the rescuers returned the next morning to the main
camp. There, in one of the cabins, they came on the sole
survivor: Lewis Keseberg. Keseberg, who had beside him a
pan containing human flesh, readily admitted having vis-

ited the Donners' camp site the previous day. On being asked what had become of a considerable sum of money which George Donner was known to have carried with him — and for which members of the rescue group had been searching — he denied having any knowledge of it. The others, whose purpose was to recover the coin for the surviving Donner children who had been carried to safety, then threatened Keseberg with hanging unless he revealed its location. Not until a rope had been procured and its noose tightened about his neck did he lead them to the spot where he had secreted part of the loot: something less than five hundred dollars. The rest was never found. The next day the rescue party, taking Keseberg with them, set off across the mountains. They reached the lowlands on April 25, thereby bringing the grisly saga to a close.

This tragic episode, involving as it did the extremes of privation and suffering, and characterized by fortitude and courage on the one hand and greed and intrigue on the other, has been touched upon by numerous historians of the West from the late 1840's down to date. Mainly responsible for the persisting interest in the subject is the fact that members of the starving, snowbound party resorted to cannibalism in order to survive. Over the years, this phase of the tragedy has been a topic of endless discussion and debate; it bids fair to keep the fate of the Donners fresh in mind long after countless other events of at least equal importance in the annals of the West have faded from memory.

Wagons West

The dire straits in which members of the Donner party found themselves were, of course, primarily due not to the difficulties of crossing the range, severe as these were, but to their having made the attempt so late in the season. For, by the close of 1846, transmountain travel was no longer a novelty. California had by then been wrested from the control of Mexico, and from other parts of the United States the migration of settlers to the new West Coast possession was already getting under way.

As a matter of fact, the movement toward California had had its beginnings well before the territory's annexation to the United States. One of the first to make the journey was a party of Ohio farmers who, under the leadership of William B. Ide, crossed the plains in the summer of 1845. These, mounted on horseback and with their belongings stowed in ox-drawn wagons, reached the eastern base of the Sierra by following the course of the Humboldt River across present-day Nevada and then making their way up the winding canyon of the Truckee to Donner Lake. There, confronted by the rocky wall that rises from the floor of the valley — the same steep barrier faced by later parties — they were informed by their guide, a grizzled frontiersman named Caleb Greenwood, that the only way to get their wagons up its precipitous face was to "take them to pieces and haul them up with ropes."

Ide, however, having first made his way on foot up to the crest, carefully examining the intervening terrain, decided to ignore this advice. He had, he stated later, observed "on the line of ascent several abrupt pitches, between which there were comparatively level spaces for several rods distance, where the teams might stand to draw up at least an empty wagon." Accordingly, the men of the party set to work "removing rocks, trees, etc., and grading a path 6 or 7

feet wide, up the several steep pitches and levels to the summit."

The next task was to get the draft animals up to the first
shelf. This one may well believe proved, as Ide said, "a
tedious process." One by one, the oxen, drawn by ropes
above and pushed from behind, were hoisted upward. When
from ten to a dozen animals had been assembled on the
upper level space, ropes and chains were attached to the
empty wagons and they in turn were drawn up, whereupon
the whole proceeding was repeated to gain the next shelf.
Ide, recalling the exploit, states that it had involved "the
two hardest days labor" the men of the party had encountered during the entire course of their journey.

His eighteen-year-old daughter later described their experience in these words:

> It took us a long time to go about 2 miles over our rough,
> new-made road up the mountains, over the rough rocks, in
> some places, and so smooth in others, that the oxen would
> slip and fall on their knees; the blood from their feet and
> knees staining the rocks they passed over. Mother and I
> walked (we were so sorry for the poor, faithful oxen), all
> those two miles — our clothing being packed on the horses'
> backs. It was a trying time — the men swearing at their
> teams, and beating them most cruelly, all along the rugged
> way.

Having gained the summit, all the pioneer parties faced
the hardly less difficult task of getting their cumbersome
wagons down the long western slope of the range. The descents too were hard; in the words of William A. Trubody,
member of an emigrant train that crossed that way in the
summer of 1847, "the road was so steep [that] only one yoke
of oxen was used, so as to hold up the wagon tongue and

keep the wagon in the track." He added that as a further means of easing the wagons down such inclines, their wheels were locked and a long rope was attached to the rear axle, wrapped about the trunk of a tree above, and played out slowly as the vehicle inched downward. Others used yet another means of holding back their wagons during such descents: a sizable tree with numerous widespread branches was cut down and tied on behind, thus forming an effectual brake.

Lassen's "Cape Horn" Route

Not all those who crossed the range during that early period traveled from east to west. One of those who made the passage in the opposite direction was James Clyman, who in the spring of 1846 set off with several companions from the Sacramento Valley, followed the course of the Yuba River during the first part of their ascent and crossed the summit at or near the present Donner Pass. Clyman's diary tells something of the character of the country through which his group made their way, and of the hardships encountered in the deep snow of the upper ridges.

Under date of April 27, while encamped in a mountain meadow waiting the arrival of the rest of his party, he wrote:

> Walked out to the N.E. of the vally on the point of a Ledge of rock . . . the first thing that attracts your notice is a high rough ridge of snow cap^d mountains proceede a little further the ridge descends in front into an impassable cliff of Black rocks divested of any Kind of covering still further and you behold a river dashing through an awfull chasm of rocks several thousand feet below you your head becomes

dizzy and you may change the [view] to [the] right here at
the distance you have ridges of snow and ridges of pine
timber to the Left you have a distant view of the eternal
cliffs of black volcanic rocks that bound the river Eubor
[Yuba].

Three days later, on the thirtieth, Clyman thus described
the group's passage through the area just to the west of the
summit:

Early under way in hope that the snow would bear us to
travel over the crust but as it did not [freeze] much during
the night we found our progress but slow all the ravines
running full of water under the snow our pack horses ware
continually stuck fast and Floundering in the snow to avoid
this we assended a steep rocky mountain to the north of our
rout but on ariving near the top we found the snow much
deeper and as it had not been much thawed during the day
privious it would not carry us atall however after an hours
plunging and several times repacking we at length descended
again to an open Prarie vally that [lies] at the immediate
head of Euba and about noon came to an Entire halt for
the rest of the day haveing made 3 miles.

Although during these first years the bulk of the trans-
Sierran traffic passed over the range by way of the Donner
or Carson Pass — both in the vicinity of Lake Tahoe — it
was not long before yet other routes came into use. One of
the first of these was the Lassen Trail, far to the north, over
which thousands of emigrants traveled during 1849 and
later. This circuitous and by no means easy trail was named
for Peter Lassen, native of Denmark, who, having come
west to Oregon in 1839, reached California the following
year. There he joined John A. Sutter's Sacramento Valley
empire of New Helvetia, and, having taken out naturaliza-

tion papers as a Mexican citizen, obtained from Governor Micheltorena a grant of five square miles of land at the northern end of the valley. There he established a settlement on one of the tributaries of the Sacramento, naming it Benton City in honor of Missouri's Senator Thomas Hart Benton. There he built an adobe house — where in the spring of 1846 he hospitably entertained Benton's distinguished son-in-law, Captain Frémont — and became a prominent figure in the affairs of the province both before and during the American conquest.

In 1847 Lassen journeyed overland to Missouri, his purpose to recruit a party of emigrants to settle on his lands. In this he was successful, assembling a considerable group that set out the following spring in a train consisting of twelve wagons. Taking the regular Oregon Trail as far as Fort Hall, they then swung to the southwest toward the valley of the Humboldt. Since, however, Lassen's destination and that of his followers lay near the upper end of the Sacramento Valley, they followed this trail for only a few days before again turning toward the northwest, making their way across the wide, semiarid region that now constitutes northwestern Nevada. Then, skirting the lower edge of Goose Lake on the present California-Nevada border and following the winding course of the Pit River through the Cascade Range, the group eventually reached their destination, but only after weeks of struggle through a rugged, uncharted wilderness.

Although this swing to the northward added some three hundred miles to the distance from the Missouri River to California, the route was, as stated, heavily traveled during the first several years of the gold rush. Many chose to follow it because they thereby avoided a forty-mile stretch of waterless desert that lay beyond the Humboldt and Carson sinks, the crossing of which had caused much hardship to the men and animals of numerous early parties. Followers of the Lassen Trail, however, frequently had cause to regret their choice, for over long stretches of this route, too, both water and grass were scarce. Thus by turning off the main-traveled central route the wayfarers had, in the words of Asa Merrill Fairfield, who had himself passed that way, "jumped from the frying pan into the fire, and their troubles had only begun. . . . Their teams gave out or died . . . and they had to leave their wagons and go on as best they could. Some cut their wagons in two, and made carts out of parts of them; and on these they hauled their families and what little else they could."

Some parties, having reached the gold fields by this extremely roundabout course, ironically dubbed the trail "Lassen's Cape Horn Route." Others, striving to account for its seemingly erratic course, asserted that after reaching Goose Lake Lassen had led his party through the mountains by heading first toward one and then the other of the two most prominent landmarks in the region, namely Mount Shasta and Mount Saint Joseph — the last-named of which was later rechristened in his honor, becoming Lassen Peak.

During 1849 and 1850, when travel that way was at its heaviest, Lassen himself made several trips over the trail to guide parties that had got into difficulties along the way, either from the heavy snow in the mountains or from raids by the larcenous Pit Indians who, unless a vigilant watch was made, would drive off livestock and pilfer whatever they could lay their hands on.

After 1852, traffic over Lassen's Trail declined sharply, a new and much shorter route, the Noble Pass Road, having been opened that year. By it, emigrants heading for the northern end of the state crossed the Sierra at a point just to the south of Lassen Peak. However, evidences are not lacking of the heavy traffic that the more northerly trail once bore. Even today, more than a hundred years later, those who pass that way sometimes come on mementoes of the past in the form of broken wagon wheels, rusted tires and chains, and other objects discarded by the forty-niners on their passage over its high ridges and deep canyons toward the promised land.

Lassen's own end was a tragic one. In 1850 he sold his large holdings in the valley and, moving to the Honey Lake area on the east side of the range, staked out a square mile of fertile farming land. By 1855, a considerable number of others having settled in the district, the group severed all relations with California and set up the short-lived Territory of Nataqua — the story of which is told elsewhere in this work. Lassen took a leading part in that movement, presiding over the meeting where a constitution was drafted and laws drawn up and adopted.

Throughout his stay in the West, he had remained on friendly terms with the Indians and so had enjoyed their confidence and respect. Consequently, when in 1859 he and a party of other Honey Lakers set off on a prospecting trip into the desert region in the extreme northwest corner of Nevada Territory, no misgivings were felt for their safety, since he and Winnemucca — the chief of the tribe of that area — were on friendly terms. It was therefore a shock to residents of the Honey Lake Valley to learn that, in late April, Lassen and two companions had been set on in the early morning hours while they were asleep in their camp, their assailants firing rifles from the top of a nearby cliff.

Two of the trio — Lassen and Edward Clapper — were killed, and only the third, Lem Wyatt, managed to escape.

Although it was widely believed by the settlers that Winnemucca's Indians were the slayers, there was no proof that such was the case, for Wyatt, the sole survivor of the onslaught, had not caught sight of the attackers. Thus Lassen's death remains to this day one of the many unsolved mysteries of Western lore.

III

A Valley Called Ahwahnee

Chief Tenaya and His Braves

THE DISCOVERY of the Yosemite Valley, one of the most noted of the Sierra's scenic attractions, was curiously delayed. During the three quarters of a century the Spaniards and Mexicans occupied the coastal area, the great range to the east was in the main a *terra incognita*, its lofty peaks and deep canyons unexplored save for occasional forays by squads of soldiers pursuing Indian horse thieves for a little distance into the foothills.

So far as is known, the first white men to look into the mighty gorge of the Yosemite were members of the party described in Chapter II — that led by Joseph Reddeford Walker, who in 1833 had crossed the Sierra over a route through the heart of what is now the Yosemite National Park. In his account of that part of their long trek, Zenas Leonard, the clerk of the expedition, wrote of their having viewed "mile-high precipices" and seen mountain streams that, having plunged downward from the top, "precipitated themselves from one lofty precipice to another." From these and like phrases, it has long been assumed that during their crossing the Walker party looked down into the chasm of the Yosemite — although the possibility remains that Leonard might have been referring to the hardly less spectacular Hetch Hetchy Valley, which lies some fifteen miles to the north.

At any rate it is certain that if Leonard and his companions were the discoverers of Yosemite, they viewed it from afar, looking down on its floor from some point on its upper rim. It was not until nearly two decades later, in the spring of 1851, that the first party of whites made their way into the gorge itself. This came about as a result of the same set of circumstances that had earlier drawn groups of Spanish or Mexican soldiers into the mountains; namely, the pursuit of a band of obstreperous Indians.

The influx of gold hunters into the southern mines in 1849 and 1850 having resulted in the establishment of many camps on the lower reaches of the Tuolumne, Merced, and adjacent streams, the warlike Indians of the area from time to time descended in force on one or another of the outpost settlements, burning and pillaging, and retiring with their loot to their mountain hideaways. Matters were brought to a climax in December of 1850, when two such raids, one on a trading post on the Fresno River and the other on Mariposa Creek — both owned by a trader named James D. Savage — resulted in the burning of the buildings and in the slaying of the men in charge, five in all.

Following this butchery, residents of the district banded together and sent an urgent appeal to Governor McDougal for help in running down and punishing the raiders. The result was the formation of three companies of militia numbering some two hundred men. These, under the command of Savage, presently started mountainward on their mission. Taking a route that closely followed the present Wawona road into the Yosemite, they, on reaching the South Fork of the Merced, came on an advance camp of the offending tribe. Having surrounded it, they launched a surprise attack and succeeded in capturing all the warriors stationed at that outpost.

The prisoners assured Savage that those comprising the main body of the tribe would give themselves up, and an Indian courier was accordingly dispatched higher into the mountains to bring them in. Although their leader, Chief Tenaya, appeared promptly in response to this summons, the others were so slow in arriving that Savage lost patience and with a major part of his battalion set off to round them up. After they had advanced a considerable distance, they encountered the Indians, some eighty in all, trooping down the snowy canyon trail. Savage, after taking them prisoner and sending them back under escort to the base camp, continued on, wishing to assure himself that no members of the tribe had remained behind in their mountain hideaway.

Thus on March 25, 1851, the troop came out on the floor of the valley, becoming the first white men to have a near view of its peaceful meadows walled in by stupendous cliffs over which mountain streams plunged in long, graceful cascades. The party made camp that night near the base of Bridal Veil Falls, and the next day conducted a thorough search of the valley, finding but a single Indian there, an ancient squaw who had been too feeble to accompany the others.

Before leaving the valley the company, assertedly at the suggestion of one of its members, a young man named Lafayette H. Bunnell, christened it Yosemite, that being the name of the tribe they had come to round up. Thus the valley got its present name; thus the name that the Indians themselves had applied to it — Ahwahnee — was forgotten until the building of the Ahwahnee Hotel there some seventy years later. Incidentally, Savage's expedition against the aboriginals failed in its primary purpose of punishing them, for while they were being driven to a prison camp in the lowlands the entire tribe managed to elude their captors and make their way back into the mountains.

Some two months later, a second company, this one under the command of Captain John Boling, was sent out charged with once more rounding up the Indians who had escaped. This time, only a few stragglers were found on the valley's floor, the main body having prudently withdrawn into the high country to the north. However, one detachment of Boling's force, coming on the footprints of the fleeing warriors, followed their trail through the snow and, on the shores of Tenaya Lake, managed to surround and capture them. This time the elusive band was successfully driven down out of the hills and lodged in a reservation in the San Joaquin Valley. However, life in the lowlands proved so uncongenial to the Yosemites' Chief Tenaya that the agent in charge of the reservation presently permitted him and his family to return to the mountains, after first extracting his promise to commit no further breaches of the white man's laws. After Tenaya's departure, his subjects managed one by one to slip away until soon the entire tribe was once more ensconced in the Yosemite, their ancestral hunting ground.

No immediate attempt was made to recapture the fugitives and through the remainder of 1851 their chief seems to have kept his promise to cause no further trouble. In the spring of the following year, however, a group of eight prospectors, having left the Mariposa diggings and followed Indian trails to a point on the south rim of the valley, decided to make their way down to its floor. Having accomplished this and camped there overnight, all but two of the party set off the next morning, some to prospect along the stream that flowed through the valley and the others to hunt for game.

Not long after the others had left, the pair who remained behind heard the sound of firearms, accompanied by shouts and screams. Shortly thereafter one of their party, bearing arrow wounds in his arm and neck, stumbled into camp and announced that he and his companions had been set on by a large band of savages. Two others of the six who had been ambushed presently succeeded in joining them, and the party, by then reduced to five — two of whom were wounded — strove to fight their way through the circle of Indians and make their way out of the valley over the same trail by which they had entered.

Their progress upward to safety proved both difficult and perilous. For, as they scrambled up the steep, narrow trail, the Indians spread out until they were both above and below them and from their places of concealment in the thick underbrush released showers of arrows whenever a target presented itself. At one point where the hard-pressed group sought safety from this fusillade by huddling close to the wall of the cliff, the wily Indians dislodged them by rolling rocks down upon them from above.

Eventually one of the whites, an expert marksman, having spied a leader who was directing the attack from the valley's floor, took careful aim and fired. The ball went true to its mark, for, as one of the party later recalled, the "redskin" below "suddenly threw up his hands and with a terrible yell fell over backwards with a bullet through his body." "Immediately" — his account continues —

. . . the firing of arrows ceased and the savages were thrown into confusion, while notes of alarm were sounded and answered far up the Valley and from the high bluffs above us. They began to withdraw and we could hear the twigs crackle as they crept away.

The survivors, without supplies and with only such clothing as they had on their backs, succeeded in making their way down to the foothill settlements, having had the good fortune to kill a deer which provided them with food during the five-day journey. The news that the Yosemites were again on the warpath and had slain two of the prospectors — the third eventually reappeared, having made his way back to the camps, traveling by a circuitous route — aroused widespread alarm and a demand for their summary punishment. This time regular army troops, a detachment of the Second Infantry, then stationed at Fort Miller, was dispatched to the valley. There five members of the tribe, all of whom were wearing articles of clothing taken from the dead prospectors, were rounded up and executed before a firing squad. This object lesson appears to have had its desired effect on the Yosemites, for there exists no record of their having caused further trouble.

After the attack on the prospecting party in the spring of 1852, Chief Tenaya and a number of his braves fled across the mountains and remained until the following year, they having been taken in by the Mono tribe which occupied that area. The Yosemites, however, true to their larcenous nature, presently repaid the hospitality of their hosts by appropriating a number of the others' horses and on them fleeing back to their old hunting grounds on the west side of the range. This, as events were to prove, was bad judgment on their part, for the Monos, outraged by such ingratitude, pursued

the thieves over the mountains, descended on them as they
were enjoying a horse-meat banquet, and killed all but a
few of their number. Among the slain was crafty old Chief
Tenaya, who had his ancient skull crushed by a rock hurled
by one of his erstwhile hosts.

Thereafter the Yosemites, bereft of their leader and much
reduced in numbers, passed from public notice, although
a few remnants of the tribe continued to dwell in the valley
for several decades longer.

Mine Host Hutchings

For a considerable period after the valley was discovered
and its attractions made known to the world, visitors to the
spot were few and far between. One reason for this was that
the average Californian of the day had no overwhelming
interest in mountain scenery, he having seen quite enough
of it on his passage over the Sierra on his journey west, or
— if he had come out by sea — during his laborious (and
usually unremunerative) stay at the diggings. Yet another
reason why there was no immediate rush of sightseers to
view the Yosemite's wonders was that to do so involved a
journey far too long and tedious to be undertaken lightly.
For to reach it required days of travel across steep mountain
ridges and through narrow river canyons over ill-defined
Indian trails that even experienced woodsmen sometimes
had trouble following.

Not until the summer of 1855 did the first tourist party
make its way into the Yosemite Valley, and the distinction
of having organized and led this group belongs to J. M.

Hutchings. Hutchings — a San Franciscan who was preparing to launch a new monthly periodical, *Hutchings' California Magazine* — having heard tales of the spectacular
scenery of the area, including waterfalls said to be thousands
of feet high, had decided to investigate. With three companions — one of whom was the pioneer California landscape artist, Thomas Ayers — he proceeded to the foothill
town of Mariposa and from there, picking up two Indian
guides, pushed on into the mountains. After an arduous
journey the party reached the valley's floor — where, in the
leader's words, they spent "five glorious days in luxurious
scenic banqueting" before returning to the lowlands. The
publication a few weeks later of his description of the natural grandeur of the spot, together with the sketches Ayers
had made, did much to spread abroad knowledge of the
Yosemite's attractions and helped set in motion a stream of
visitors that has continued, in steadily growing volume, ever
since.

Improvement in the trails over which early visitors
reached the valley — and facilities for their accommodation
after they arrived — followed apace. Later in the same summer of 1855 two brothers, Milton and Houston Mann, owners of a livery stable at Mariposa, began the construction of
a pack trail from that town into the Yosemite, which wound
up at the South Fork of the Merced and crossed the intervening ridge near Wawona. On its completion the following
year its owners did a brisk business not only by renting
pack animals to tourist parties but by charging substantial
tolls for the privilege of passing over their trail. In 1858,
however, the brothers' monopoly was broken by the opening
of a second and more direct trail, this one beginning at
Coulterville; and when most of the visitors started taking

that route the Manns sold their trail to Mariposa County, and it became toll-free.

Meantime food and shelter — of a sort — had been provided in the valley itself. The first house was put up in the winter of 1856–1857, and added to during the next year; and soon, under a succession of owners and lessees, it was offering meals, drinks, and sleeping quarters to early-day tourists, thus becoming the forerunner of the complex assortment of hotels, cabins, and tent cities that today cover many acres of the valley's floor.

This pioneer hostelry, which one of its early patrons described as "a slightly oversized log-cabin," was nonetheless welcomed with joy by the travel-weary parties who partook of its accommodations. When Clarence King made his first visit to the valley in the early 1860's, the place was presided over by one Longhurst, whom King described as "a weather-beaten around-the-worlder, whose function . . . was to tell yarns, sing songs, and feed the inner man." Evidently it was in this last department that he excelled — or it may have been that, after several days of eating the food the travelers themselves had prepared en route, any regularly prepared meal would have tasted like ambrosia. At any rate, King waxed lyrical over the first breakfast — pancakes — served him by Longhurst, stating that it was "like dining in sacrilege on works of art."

In 1864 Hutchings himself took up permanent residence in the valley and for the next dozen years he was its leading — and for much of that time its only — innkeeper. At his establishment, built of rough, handhewn logs and known to early-day visitors as the Hutchings House, the genial host entertained his guests by lectures on the geology of the region and by conducting them on tours of its points of interest, all the while discoursing learnedly on its flora, fauna, Indian lore, and kindred topics. Unfortunately, however, his accommodations were not on a par with his discourses on the natural wonders of the valley, a circumstance that led one disgruntled early visitor to remark that guests would be better served if the proprietor paid less attention to describing the beauties of the valley and more to providing comfortable beds and properly prepared meals.

The Hutchings House's informal accommodations and services presently gave rise to a standing joke which returning visitors delighted to play on those making their first visit to the valley. At meetings along the trails the newcomer would be gravely warned to lock the doors of his hotel room, for thieves had recently been active in the valley and many valuable articles had been pilfered. The payoff was when the forewarned tourist reached the Hutchings House and discovered to his consternation that "his door was a sheet, and his partition from the adjoining sleeping-chamber was also a cotton cloth."

Charles Loring Brace, who stopped there in 1867, commented that "bedroom conversations conducted under these circumstances, it may be judged, are discreet."

Brace, however, added that the house was clean, the meals good, "and Hutchings himself enough of a character to make up for innumerable deficiencies."

That such deficiencies were numerous this writer made clear in his account of his stay. At one point he wrote:

> Thus we came down, very hungry, to a delicious breakfast of fresh trout, venison, and great pans of garden strawberries; but, unfortunately, there were no knives or forks. A romantic young lady asks, in an unlucky moment, about the best point of view for the Nevada Fall. "Madam, there is

but one; you must get close to the Upper Fall, just above the mist of the lower, and there you will see a horizontal rainbow beneath your feet, and the most exquisite — "

Here a strong-minded lady, whose politeness is at an end, breaks in: "But here, Hutchings, we have no knives or forks!" "Oh, I beg a thousand pardons, madam!" and he rushes off; but meeting his wife on the way, she gives him coffee for the English party, and he forgets us entirely, and we get up good-naturedly and search out the implements ourselves. Again, from an amiable lady, *"Please,* Mr. Hutchings, another cup of coffee!" "Certainly, madam!" When the English lady from Calcutta asks him about some wild flowers, he goes off in a botanical and poetical disquisition, and in his abstraction brings the other lady, with great eagerness, a glass of water. Sometimes sugar is handed you instead of salt for the trout, or cold water is poured into your coffee; but none of the ladies mind, for our landlord is as handsome as he is obliging, and really full of information.

The "Sneezeless Sierra"

In the summer of 1870, Professor Joseph Le Conte accompanied a group of University of California students on an outing in the Sierra, and after a long, hot ride across the San Joaquin Valley and over the mountains, arrived at Yosemite. There he one day encountered a man whose knowledge of the natural wonders of the area exceeded even that of the well-posted Hutchings. This other was a spare, blue-eyed young Scot who was then living and working at a sawmill owned by Hutchings. Of this stranger — whose name was John Muir — Le Conte wrote:

... A gentleman of rare intelligence, of much knowledge of science, particularly of botany, which he has made a specialty. He has lived several years in the valley, and is thoroughly acquainted with the mountains in the vicinity. A man of so much intelligence tending a sawmill! — not for himself, but for Mr. Hutchings. This is California!

Muir, who was in his early thirties, was then at the beginning of a career that was to make him the foremost authority on geology, flora, and numerous other features of the Sierra, and had been making his headquarters in the valley for two years. Born in Scotland and brought to this country when he was eleven, he had spent his youth on a midwest farm, and worked his way through the University of Wisconsin. Having developed a consuming interest in botany and a liking for solitary rambles through unspoiled regions far from human habitation, he had seized every opportunity to set off on prolonged field trips: into neighboring states, into Canada, and, soon after the close of the Civil War, on a thousand-mile tramp through the south to Florida.

When, at the end of that long trek, a spell of sickness caused him to abandon his plan of continuing on to South America, he had turned westward instead, taking passage on a sailing ship bound for California and landing at San Francisco early in 1868. It was altogether characteristic of the man that immediately on his arrival he shouldered his knapsack and set off on foot for the distant Sierra, his destination the Yosemite Valley, descriptions of which had stirred his interest. His long tramp over the Coast Ranges and across the central valley filled him with delight, for the spring was then at its height.

It was [he wrote] one sea of golden and purple bloom, so deep and dense that in walking through it you would press more than a hundred blooms at every step. In this flowerbed five hundred miles long, I used to camp by just lying down wherever night overtook me . . . and in the morning I sometimes found plants that were new, looking me in the face, so that my botanical studies would begin before I was up.

Thereafter for close to half a century not only was Muir tireless in his exploration of the range but, through his voluminous writings, more than anyone else he made its scenic attractions known to the world. During the first five years, from 1868 to 1873, his headquarters were at Yosemite, and he earned enough for his simple wants by turning his hand to whatever tasks presented themselves: as sheep-herder, mill hand, guide, and the like. Later, his writings having found an ever-widening circle of readers, he became a literary figure of standing and a recognized authority on all things connected with what he termed "the Range of Light."

Although in his later years he came to be looked on as the foremost spokesman for the Sierra and, as such, was usually on hand to welcome distinguished visitors to the region, this was, of course, not true during the days of his obscurity, as when Ralph Waldo Emerson, then at the height of his fame, paid a visit to California in 1871.

Crossing the continent with a group in a private car belonging to their host, the railroad magnate John Murray Forbes, Emerson's party promptly set off for the Yosemite, where they put up at Leidig's Tavern, then the most popular resort in the valley, and spent the next several days admiring the scenic wonders of the area. The presence among them of so eminent a literary personage was highly gratifying to residents of the valley — and in particular to Muir, who was then operating the little sawmill for Hutchings.

The Scot was on hand the day Emerson arrived, but so great was his awe of the sixty-nine-year-old philosopher that, as he later reported, he hovered on the edge of the crowd, not daring to step forward and introduce himself. At length, however, upon learning that Emerson and his party were soon to leave, Muir wrote the other a letter urging that he spend more time acquainting himself with the surpassing beauties of the valley and the surrounding district.

The result was that the following day Emerson, accompanied by another member of his party, sought out the letter writer. Muir, who was alone at the mill at the time, welcomed his callers and invited them to come up to his living quarters — a small room he had built beneath the gable of the mill — to view his collection of botanical specimens and sketches of mountain scenery. To reach this lofty perch involved some difficulty on the part of the elderly New Englander, for, as Muir later recalled, the stairway consisted of "a series of sloping planks roughened by slats like a hen-ladder." Nonetheless, the visit proved so pleasant to Emerson that during the next several days he, in Muir's words, returned "again and again."

When, on the morning of May 11, the party set off on horseback to see the big trees at the Mariposa Grove, Muir went along, he having obtained Emerson's promise that the two would camp out overnight among the sequoias. To Muir's great disappointment, however, when the cavalcade reached Clark's Station, at the edge of the grove, the party dismounted in front of the tavern and prepared to go inside.

> When I asked if we were not going into the grove to camp [stated Muir], they said: "No, it would never do to lie out in the night air. Mr. Emerson might take cold; and you know, Mr. Muir, that would be a dreadful thing." In vain

I urged that only in homes and hotels were colds caught, that nobody was ever known to take cold camping in the woods, that there was not a single cough or sneeze in all the Sierra . . . But the house habit was not to be overcome, nor the strange dread of pure night air, though it is only cooled day air with a little dew in it. So the carpet dust and unknowable reeks were preferred . . .

Rather than part company from his admired friend, Muir, too, spent the night at the resort, and the next morning the party — seemingly none the worse for having slept beneath a roof — rode out to the grove. There an hour or two were spent in what Muir scornfully termed "ordinary tourist fashion — looking at the biggest giants, measuring them with a tape line, riding through prostrate fire-bored trunks, etc." Then after Emerson had been asked to select one of the huge sequoias and confer a name on it, and the party was about to leave, Muir made a final effort to persuade him to tarry longer.

"You yourself are a sequoia," he stated. "Stop and get acquainted with your big brethren."

But it was of no avail: the party was traveling on a rigid schedule that brooked no delays. So they set off; and Muir, having exchanged a final wave of the hand with Emerson as the other disappeared around a bend in the trail, reflected that "he was past his prime, and was now as a child in the hands of his affectionate but sadly civilized friends."

Muir's account of this, his first and last meeting with the great New Englander, ends with these words:

I felt lonely, so sure had I been that Emerson of all men would be the quickest to see the mountains and sing them. Gazing for a while on the spot where he vanished, I sauntered back to the heart of the grove, made a bed of sequoia

plumes and ferns by the side of the stream, gathered a store
of firewood, and then walked about until sundown. The
birds, robins, thrushes, warblers, etc., that had kept out of
sight, came about me, now that all was quiet, and made
cheer. After sundown I built a great fire, and as usual had
it all to myself. And though lonesome for the first time in
these forests, I quickly took heart again — the trees had not
gone to Boston, nor the birds; and as I sat by the fire, Emerson was still with me in spirit.

When, however, nearly a quarter-century later, another
and yet more eminent American visited the Yosemite, Muir
had better luck. In the early 1900's Theodore Roosevelt,
recently elevated to the presidency and about to set off on a
tour of the country, dispatched a letter to Muir stating that
he planned to spend a few days in the Yosemite and wished
to see it under his guidance. On receiving this news Muir
— who habitually wore the rough garb of the mountaineer
— felt impelled to tog himself out in a costume befitting
the importance of the occasion.

Years later a mutual acquaintance recalled the naturalist's
visit to the San Francisco studio of his close friend and fellow Scot, the landscape painter, William Keith, a few days
before the Roosevelt party was due to arrive. Muir had come
around to show off his new garb and to get Keith's opinion
as to its appropriateness. The effect, reported this observer,
was highly picturesque, for the tall, lanky Muir had fitted
himself out in a ready-made suit, bright yellow in color —
the trouser legs ending some distance above his thin shanks,
the sleeves of the coat correspondingly short. Keith, having
looked him over carefully, hazarded the guess that Muir
must have picked up his fancy raiment at a fire sale.

Roosevelt arrived at the valley togged out in a costume

reminiscent of his role as Rough Rider in the recent war: broad-brimmed campaign hat, a scarf tied loosely about his neck, khaki pants, and with his ample calves encased in leather leggings. However, the oddly matched pair managed to see the wonders of the park together, unimpeded by the horde of hangers-on who had accompanied the President into the mountains. This took a bit of doing, for those in charge of the arrangements were determined to make T.R.'s stay at the park a social event of the first magnitude. Accordingly, elaborate preparations had been made. A renowned chef was sent up from San Francisco to prepare the banquet planned for the night of Roosevelt's arrival; also a corps of waiters, together with suitable dishes, cutlery, and table linen, were dispatched to the park, and colored searchlights were rigged up to play on the waterfalls and thus add further brilliance to the scene.

T.R., however, had other ideas as to how his time in the valley was to be spent; he had been planning for days to view its sights under the guidance of the venerable Muir, and he did not intend to be deprived of that pleasure. Accordingly, he showed up only briefly at the banquet, went to bed early, and at the crack of dawn the next morning — hours before the others of his party were awake — got up, mounted a horse, and rode off to meet the naturalist at a previously designated spot. The two thereupon toured the valley, then took an unfrequented trail into the back country, and there spent a night at a simple camp Muir had prepared. It was not until late the following afternoon that the truant pair rejoined the main party. Roosevelt later declared that this brief escape into Arcadia, and in particular the long evening the two had spent beside their campfire, had been the high point of his entire Western tour.

John Muir vs. *Josiah Whitney*

From the moment he first laid eyes on the valley Muir had — like many others before him and since — speculated on by what forces of nature the mighty chasm had been formed. At that period the most widely accepted theory was one first advanced by the distinguished scientist, Josiah Dwight Whitney, who since 1860 had been the California State Geologist. Whitney maintained that the stupendous gorge could have been created only by a major natural cataclysm, during which the area forming its present floor had literally, as he expressed it, "dropped down," thereby exposing the walls of lofty cliffs on both sides.

From the beginning Muir seems to have questioned the validity of Whitney's hypothesis, and the more he pondered the matter the stronger his doubts grew. For during his frequent rambles through the mountains of the region he had been struck by the evidences of glacial action everywhere visible: in the rounded, domelike contours of some of the peaks, their upper surfaces swept bare of all protuberances; in the "glacier-polished pavements" of certain of the canyons, the granite sides and floors of which had been "scored and striated in a rigidly parallel way"; and, on the lower levels, by the vast deposits of boulders and rubble that marked the glaciers' terminal moraines.

Muir presently reached his own conclusion as to the Yosemite's origin, and in the fall of 1871 he wrote a friend that in his opinion "the great Valley itself, together with all its various domes and sculptured walls, were produced and fashioned by the united labors of a grand combination of glaciers which flowed over and through it, their forces having been rigidly governed and directed by the peculiar physical structure of the granite of which the region is made, and, moreover, that all the rocks and lakes and meadows of the whole upper Merced basin owe their specific forms and carving to this same glacial agency."

His belief that the valley had been thus carved out Muir imparted to all who would listen, and in particular to geologists who visited the spot. Moreover, it was not long before his theory had gained adherents among some of the most eminent scientists in that field. Professor Joseph Le Conte, in a paper on *Some Ancient Glaciers of the Sierra,* gave Muir credit for valuable pioneer work in that field, and Louis Agassiz, then at the height of his fame, wrote that "here is the first man who has any adequate conception of glacial action . . . [He] is studying to greater purpose and with greater results than anyone else has done."

It was not long until these and other plaudits reached the ears of State Geologist Whitney. To have his own widely accepted theory as to the valley's origin thus challenged — and by an amateur who had had no formal training in geology — was naturally galling to the scientist. He promptly responded with this vigorous counterblast:

> A more absurd theory was never advanced than that by which it was sought to ascribe to glaciers the sawing out of these vertical walls and the rounding of the domes. Nothing more unlike the real work of ice, as exhibited in the Alps, could be found. Besides, there is no reason to suppose, or at least no proof, that glaciers have ever occupied the valley, or any portion of it . . . so that this theory, based on entire ignorance of the whole subject, may be dropped without wasting any more time on it.

Later he heaped further ridicule on the obscure amateur

who had presumed to challenge his findings, referring to him as a "sheepherder" and "guide."

Muir, on his part, was by no means loath to defend his position and to poke fun at what he termed the other's "bottom-dropped-out" theory. In one of a series of papers under the general heading of *Studies in the Sierra,* which appeared in the *Overland Monthly* in 1874 and 1875, he wrote:

> The argument advanced to support this [that is, Whitney's] view is substantially as follows: It is too wide for a water-eroded valley, too irregular for a fissure valley, and too angular and local for a primary valley originating in a fold of the mountain surface during the process of upheaval; therefore, a portion of the mountain bottom must have suddenly fallen out, letting the super-incumbent domes and peaks fall rumbling into the abyss, like coal into the bunker of a ship. This violent hypothesis, which furnishes a kind of Tophet for the reception of bad mountains, commends itself briefly to the favor of many, by seeming to account for the remarkable sheerness and angularity of the walls, and by its marvelousness and obscurity, calling for no investigation, but rather discouraging it.

Although for some time longer Whitney's theory continued to be upheld, both by himself and his disciples, in the end Muir's more logical explanation came to be quite generally accepted. Today geologists are virtually unanimous in maintaining that it was primarily due to the tremendous forces exerted in past ages by great flowing masses of ice that the Yosemite, along with numerous other Sierra canyons, came into being. Thus the once unknown Scotch millwright, sheepherder, and general handyman was trium-

phantly vindicated, and so laid the foundations of what was
to prove a lasting fame.

Although Muir's scientific interests later drew him far
afield, to South and Central America, Alaska, and elsewhere,
the Sierra always held first place in his affections. Even in
his last years — he died in 1914 at the age of seventy-six —
he frequently left his home at Martinez, on the shores of
upper San Francisco Bay, and spent a few weeks at Yosemite, at the Sequoia National Park, or at other favorite spots.

The story is told that one summer in the early 1900's,
upon arriving at a hotel in the Giant Forest, he signed his
name on the register and in the space for his address wrote
the words "The World." The next guest to register chanced
to be a Los Angeles judge who, having observed Muir's
place of residence, wrote beneath it "The Universe." On
learning of this, the old scientist recognized in the new arrival a kindred spirit; he hunted up the other in the dining-
room, made himself known and insisted that the stranger
take a place at his table. The talk during the meal, and on
the tour of the park under Muir's guidance that followed,
was later pronounced by the jurist to be among the most
enjoyable experiences that had ever befallen him.

The People's Playground

Once the Yosemite's manifold attractions as a beauty spot
and recreation center came to be recognized, a movement
got under way in California to have the valley declared public property and so prevent its falling into private hands.
Accordingly, in 1864, a bill was introduced in Congress
granting "the Cleft, or Gorge . . . in the Sierra Nevada

Mountains . . . known as the Yosemite Valley" to the state, to be held in perpetuity for the use of the public. The bill was duly passed and signed by President Lincoln, and for the next forty-two years the valley remained a California state park.

Long before that period ended, however, dissatisfaction arose in many quarters over the manner in which the park was being administered, with the result that persistent efforts were made to have its ownership transferred back to the Federal government. Those who advocated that move found their position much strengthened by the fact that in 1890, largely as a result of a campaign waged jointly by John Muir and Robert Underwood Johnson, an editor of the *Century Magazine,* a huge section of the high Sierra — the boundaries of which enclosed the Yosemite Valley on all four sides — was withdrawn from settlement and incorporated in the National Park system. The consequence was that one park — the valley itself — was state-owned and state-controlled, whereas the territory for many miles about was under the jurisdiction of the Secretary of the Interior and administered from Washington. Conflicts inevitably arose and, as the century ended, bills were regularly introduced into the legislature at Sacramento providing for the return of the valley to the national government.

These Recession Bills, as they came to be called, stirred up much controversy, and no little bitterness. Those who supported them claimed that the professionally trained personnel of the Federal service were better qualified to manage the park than the political appointees then in charge. On the other hand, the opposition — which included many of the state's most influential newspapers — protested that the measures were no more than brazen attempts to "rob"

California of one of its most cherished beauty spots. "One would have thought," remarked a visitor to Sacramento during one of the hearings on the measure, "that once the bill was passed the Yosemite would be moved bodily to the banks of the Potomac."

Muir, who was all for making the transfer, did yeoman service in support of the bills, making frequent trips to Sacramento and presenting his arguments to whatever lawmakers could be persuaded to listen. Moreover, although he was quite generally looked on as a naïve and simple child of nature, unversed in the ways of the world, when the occasion arose he proved himself able to play the role of politician with the best of them.

Thus when the Recession Bill once more came up for consideration in 1905, a poll of the members of the lower house made it clear that a majority were opposed to its passage. Learning that the Southern Pacific Railroad, which for nearly half a century had been a potent factor in California politics, still wielded influence over some members of the Assembly, Muir proceeded to get in touch with the company's president, E. H. Harriman, urging that he use his good offices to help assure the passage of the bill. Muir was, it developed, on excellent terms with the railroad magnate, having been a member of Harriman's scientific expedition to Alaska some years earlier. The other proved quite willing to do this small favor for his friend; accordingly, word was quietly passed among those legislators who were beholden to the railroad, and when the bill came to a vote it carried by a narrow margin. Then, having seen it through the upper house, where it encountered no serious opposition, Muir returned to his nature writings and botanical studies, well

satisfied with the outcome of his brief foray into the field of practical politics.

In the fifty years that have passed since control of the Yosemite reverted to the Federal government, numerous changes have, of course, taken place there, changes that, in the opinion of many, have not all been for the better. For whereas during the earlier period the park — situated deep in the Sierra range and removed by long distances from the densely populated urban centers on the coast — was so remote that the number of visitors who annually made their way there rarely exceeded 10,000, nowadays it is by no means unusual for crowds averaging that number, or more, to pour into the valley during the course of a single week end.

To accommodate these hordes a steadily growing area of the park has had to be given over to facilities for lodging, feeding, and entertaining them. Campsites many acres in extent cover the wooded meadows; at numerous points hotels, tent cities, and extensive clusters of housekeeping cabins spread over the valley floor from wall to wall, and restaurants, shops of various sorts, and other features of city life are available at many points.

That these establishments, necessary as many of them are, defeat the primary purpose of the park has long been the contention of the nature lovers. These claim that the true function of a park of the type of Yosemite is to afford visitors an opportunity to admire the grandeur of its setting, and that to convert it into a vast amusement center defeats that purpose. To be sure, as those who hold a contrary view frequently point out, the hotels, cabins, stores, and campgrounds that crowd much of the valley floor in no serious way mar the beauty of its surroundings: the stupendous domes, cliffs, and waterfalls that rim it on three sides. These argue, too, that since the far-famed attractions of the spot draw such great numbers of visitors, adequate provision must be made for their accommodation after they arrive, and that, for those who prefer to commune with nature in a less crowded environment, there remain vast areas of the back-country where the solitude that they crave can be found.

Thus for a generation or longer the argument has gone on, with those who deplore what they term the "spoliation" of the park arguing that automobiles be banned from the valley, and the opposing faction maintaining that, since the park belongs to the people, to place such restrictions on their comings and goings would be a clear violation of their vested rights. In the end this last-named view has prevailed, and as a consequence Yosemite's development as an ever-expanding tourist center has continued apace, while in increasing numbers the dyed-in-the-wool mountaineers have tended to give it a wide berth.

IV

Over the Hump

The Dutch Flat Swindle

THE EARLIEST routes of travel across the Sierra range were, as the narratives of those who passed over them make abundantly clear, a far cry from the wide, gently curving highways known to present-day motorists. When, following close on Jim Marshall's discovery of 1848, the great westward push began, such trans-Sierran roads as existed were little more than ill-defined trails, their surfaces strewn with boulders and the trunks of fallen trees, and in places so steep that, as stated earlier, wagons passing over them had to be raised or lowered by ropes.

As the Argonauts poured into California in an ever-broadening stream, overrunning the foothill placers and penetrating higher into the mountains in quest of new and richer diggings, other trails were opened from one end of the range to the other. Thus a complex network of such trails presently led upward from the central valley, over which a heavy volume of traffic passed, the miners for the most part traveling on foot and carrying their supplies and equipment on their backs or on those of pack animals.

This situation held all during the first part of the gold

rush. By the early 1850's, however, the demand for more
adequate roads to certain of the populous mountain communities had become a lively political issue, both at Sacramento and at the seats of government of half a dozen Sierra
counties. Although funds for road building were voted by
various legislative bodies — and in some cases were raised by
voluntary contributions on the part of residents of the isolated towns and camps — progress in general was slow. This
was particularly true in the higher areas, where granite
ridges, deep canyons, and swift-flowing streams made the
task a difficult and costly one. In some localities where attempts to finance such projects by other means had failed,
the work was undertaken by individuals or groups, who
laid out and built the badly needed roads, kept them in
repair, and levied tolls on those making use of them.

The fees such owners charged were, in theory, fixed in
accordance with the length of the roads and the nature of
the country through which they passed. Many operators,
however, fixed the tolls so high that those who had to use
them complained bitterly. In Mono County in the early
1860's one such highway, some fifteen miles in length, had
the following price scale — one more or less similar to others
of approximately the same length: LOADED WAGON AND TEAM,
$1.50; EMPTY WAGON, 75¢; MAN ON HORSEBACK, 50¢; LIVE-
STOCK, 10¢ *per head.*

Throughout the first two decades after 1849, this matter
of roads was a lively one — not only to residents of communities deep in the mountains, but to merchants in the
valley supply towns. For the latter were of course aware that
the volume of business they did depended, in no small degree, on how accessible they were to the populous mining
camps that lay to the east. Hence the three chief trading

centers — Marysville, Sacramento, and Stockton — were active in promoting the building of roads that would bring a major share of the mountain trade to them and away from their rivals.

In the spring of 1863 we find a Stockton newspaper, the *Independent,* energetically supporting a bond issue of four hundred thousand dollars to build a toll-free road over the lofty Sonora Pass, arguing that it would be a means of attracting much of the business of the then booming Nevada silver towns, of which Sacramento, served by two routes — Donner Pass and Carson Pass — was then getting the lion's share. Spurred by such weighty arguments, the voters of San Joaquin, Tuolumne, and Mono Counties duly approved the bonds, and work on the Sonora road got promptly under way. But the region over which it would have to pass was one of the most rugged of the entire range; long before the road reached the ninety-six-hundred-foot crest, the entire four hundred thousand dollars had been expended. Accordingly, a private company was given a franchise to complete it, and the work went on. Although substantial tolls were charged, investors in the project are said to have lost heavily, for deep snows on and near the summit closed the road to through traffic during four or five months each year.

From 1849 onward, Californians had recognized that one of their most urgent needs was an adequate roadway passing entirely over the range, by which the steadily growing number of stages, freight wagons, and vehicles of the emigrants could cross in safety and at reasonable speed. The first wagon road — the old Emigrant Trail — crossed the crest at Donner Pass and, in its roundabout descent to the Sacramento Valley, followed a course to the north of the Bear River. There were a number of branches to this route, one of which turned off at Emigrant Gap and wound down into scenically spectacular Bear Valley. At several points on this Bear Valley road, where it descended in a series of steep inclines to the valley's floor, may still be seen rusty iron spikes projecting from the granite faces of the cliffs, used by early-day travelers to lower their wagons down near-vertical declivities.

Throughout the early and middle 1850's this Donner Pass road, although it afforded the most direct route to and from the populous towns and camps of the northern mines, was too rough and precipitous for wide general use. Consequently, the major part of the transmountain traffic passed over one or another of several alternate routes farther to the south. Proposals for the improvement of the Donner crossing were frequently made, mostly by residents of the prosperous mining communities in the Auburn-Grass Valley area, but the magnitude and expense of the undertaking were such that little was done.

As the decade of the 1850's closed, however, the discovery of rich silver ledges in the hills to the northeast of Lake Tahoe, and the rise of Virginia City and other Comstock towns, pointed up the need for a more adequate northern crossing. Curiously enough, when the improvement of this long-neglected route eventually got under way, the work was undertaken by the same group of Sacramento merchants who controlled the Central Pacific Railroad, organized in the early 1860's to lay rails over the Sierra and on eastward until they joined those of the Union Pacific. For soon after they had been awarded the coveted contract to build the western half of the long-projected transcontinental line — plus liberal subsidies from Federal, state, and county governments — the group had organized the Dutch Flat and Donner Lake Wagon Road Company.

This shrewd move was designed to serve two purposes: first, to provide a convenient means of hauling supplies and equipment to advance construction camps along the route of the railroad and, second, to attract a major share of the heavy freight and passenger traffic then flowing over the Sierra to and from the Comstock. Both these objectives were handsomely realized. As rails were laid across the valley floor and through the foothills, then upward into the mountains, straddling the divide between the Bear River and the North Fork of the American, goods and passengers destined for the Comstock were carried by train to the end-o'-track and there transferred to stages or freight wagons for the balance of the journey over the company's wagon road.

This business proved so lucrative that, throughout the early and middle 1860's, numerous Californians came to believe that the Central Pacific's owners planned to lay their rails only high enough into the mountains to permit them to corner the Comstock traffic, and that the long-hoped-for through railroad would never materialize. During those years the California newspapers that opposed the methods of the men in control of the Central Pacific made much of this, terming it the "Dutch Flat Swindle" — that town being the western terminus of the wagon road. As time passed, however, such criticism grew less frequent, for the railroad's construction gangs pushed ever higher into the mountains, and it presently grew clear that the owners planned to build entirely across the range. When, in late 1868, that mighty task was accomplished, and the Iron Horse took over from the stages and freight wagons the job of transporting men and goods over the lofty summit, nothing further was heard of the so-called "Dutch Flat Swindle."

A Symphony of Turning Wheels

Next to the south of Donner Pass road, and long its chief rival for the transmountain traffic, was one that wound upward from the California foothills, following the South Fork of the American River, gained the crest at Carson Pass, and slanted steeply downward to the plains below. This trail, originally broken by Frémont in 1844, became known to later travelers as the Carson Emigrant Road. The first wagon to pass that way is said to have been Jefferson Hunt's when he made his east-to-west crossing in the spring of 1849. That summer and during the next several years a heavy traffic followed in his wake, for the route, while somewhat longer than the more northerly one, and considerably higher — Carson Pass being 9000 feet as compared to 7135 at Donner Summit — still was less rugged and had fewer steep inclines where vehicles had to be eased downward by mechanical means.

Of the trials and rewards of the Sierra crossing over this Carson Pass route, the journalist J. Ross Browne, who made the trip by stage in the fall of 1860, wrote with engaging realism.

Having decided to pay a visit to Nevada's new silver towns, he took an overnight passage on a river steamer from San Francisco to Sacramento. There, after partaking of "a hasty breakfast of water bewitched and coffee begrudged, leathery beefsteak and saleratus slightly corrected by flour," he boarded a diminutive train of the Sacramento Valley Railroad for the twenty-one-mile ride to Folsom.

At that foothill town, every second building of which

seemed to him to be "a house of entertainment, in which
the public are feasted on billiards and whisky," he ran the
gamut of dozens of touts noisily shouting the praises of competing stagelines. After Browne had made his choice and
climbed aboard, the driver cracked his whip and the heavily
laden vehicle swung out of its place in line and in a cloud
of dust headed for the distant mountains.

It is always a pleasure [Browne commented] to make a
start; yet if anybody can say the road from Folsom to
Placerville is an agreeable road to travel in the early part of
October, before the autumn showers have commenced, he
must be fond of dust and ruts and hills.

So dusty was this first part of the journey — in the course
of which the road passed through scores of once-rich placer
diggings — that on reaching Placerville Browne hazarded
the guess that if the passengers were "put through the hydraulic process" their washings would yield around fourteen
dollars per ounce.

At that point, the ascent into the mountains began.
Browne, having had the good fortune to get the seat of honor
— "by the side of that exalted dignitary the driver" — was
duly appreciative of that distinction, especially in view of
the fact that the road ahead was, as he stated, "supposed to
be a little undulating even by its best friends." Swaying and
rumbling through the dust clouds and growing darkness,
which permitted him only occasional glimpses into deep
canyons and sheer roadside precipices, he presently fell into
conversation with the driver.

Asked if serious accidents were frequent on that route,
the man at the reins replied that they were virtually unknown. "Last summer a few stages went over the grade," he

admitted, "but nobody was hurt bad — only a few legs'n arms broken." Such mishaps, he added, usually happened to stages operated by competing companies; as a general thing those of his own firm made a practice of staying on the road. When the ascending roadway presently entered a forest of pine trees and they clattered on at unslackened speed in total darkness, the journalist was curious to know how the driver knew where he was. He learned then that the other had passed that way so many times that he was able to determine his precise location by the sound of the stage wheels as they rumbled over alternate stretches of gravel, flinty rock, and deep sand.

Coming out at length on a promontory high above the American River, with a rising moon illuminating the canyon below, Browne waxed poetic over the beauties of the scene.

> How calm and still the night was! how exquisitely balmy the air! how sublime the repose of these grand old mountains! There is something in the mystic lights and shades, and the profound solemnity of the night, which lends an awful sublimity to these wild regions. The gigantic forest trees standing in bold outline on the opposite sides of the mountains, seem to pierce the sky; and the moonbeams, pouring down into the mysterious abyss through which the river dashes, fringe the tops of the pines, as far down as the eye can reach, with a frost-like drapery.

By the time Browne passed over it, this road no longer traversed an unspoiled wilderness. Indeed, the works of man were everywhere visible. "There is," wrote he, "probably not an acre of ground, possessing a water privilege, on the entire route between Placerville and Virginia City which has not been taken up and settled upon by some enterprising squatter" engaged in serving the wants of the thousands bound for the Nevada silver towns. During the first months of this rush, in 1859 and 1860, most of these roadside resorts had been housed in tents or hastily-thrown-up shanties. There water was provided for the thirsty animals — and stronger beverages for the humans — and, for those desiring overnight lodgings, some of the more pretentious establishments offered straw-filled mattresses laid out on the floors of common sleeping chambers.

However, when Browne made the crossing five years later all that had changed:

> Good and substantial taverns, well supplied with provisions, beds, fleas, bugs, etc., to say nothing of the essential article of whisky, are to be met with at intervals of every two or three miles all along the route. Here the stages stop, and here the horses are watered and changed; and here the drivers and passengers get down and stretch their legs, but as a general thing they don't indulge in as much water as the horses.

Many of these early-day stopping places bore names that informed eastbound passengers how far they had traveled since leaving Placerville: Six-Mile House, Ten-Mile House, Thirteen-Mile House, and so on. A few miles beyond the last-named resort the ascending road came out on Observation Point, from which could be had the first clear view of the lofty, snow-capped ridges ahead. From there the roadway — a narrow shelf cut into the canyon's side — slanted down to the American River, crossing and recrossing that stream as it followed its course upward toward its source. Then, many miles farther on and only a short distance from the summit, the highway debouched into Strawberry Flat, an attractive mountain meadow walled in on the north and south by the sheer walls of granite.

There travelers were made welcome at Strawberry House, long one of the most popular stopping places of the entire route. The manner in which this resort got its name is curious. According to the legend, the first to settle on the spot was a man named Berry, who in the late 1850's set up a one-room shack where he dispensed food and drinks to travelers passing that way. A year or two later, the rush to the Comstock having got fully under way, Berry found his business far brisker. He accordingly enlarged his resort, providing meals, drinks, and sleeping quarters of such quality that it soon became a favorite stopping place for the horde of Nevada-bound Californians.

Among the services Berry offered wayfarers was hay for their animals. However, during the first months of the rush his supply of that commodity ran out and he was able to furnish instead only straw, for which — being of a frugal nature — he exacted the same price he had formerly charged for hay. Because of this practice, he became known to teamsters using that route as "Straw Berry" — a name that has ever since been applied to the resort and to the meadow on which it stands. One early patron of "Straw Berry's" tavern described the scene there at mealtime, stating that the hungry customers "pressed in double file against the dining room door awaiting the fourth or fifth charge at the table. At the first tinkle of the bell, the door burst open with a tremendous crash, and no Crimean avalanche . . . could have equalled the terrific onslaught of the gallant troops of Strawberry."

Of the many thousands who used this Placerville-Carson road during the early and middle 1860's — and who left a record of their journey — few failed to comment on the heavy traffic that passed over it. It was no uncommon experience for those traveling by stage to encounter strings of freight wagons a mile or more in length rumbling slowly up the inclines amid swirling clouds of dust, the little sets of bells attached to the leaders of each four- or six-horse team setting up a tinkling accompaniment to their progress.

At sundown, the teamsters and their weary animals stopped at one or another of the way stations, about which were usually clustered a score or more of the big wagons. There, having unhitched the horses, watered and fed them and tied them to the tongues of the vehicles, the drivers repaired to the taverns for their own meals, spent a social hour afterwards in the barroom swapping tales of the road, then spread their blankets on the ground beneath the wagons and slept until dawn, when preparation for the next day's journey began.

One traveler who passed that way in the fall of 1863 stated that by then no less than five thousand wagons were engaged in hauling freight over the range to the Nevada mining towns. Round trips from Sacramento to Virginia City were made in from ten to twenty days, each outfit making an average of no more than eight trips per season — for, of course, heavy snows on the upper levels caused the suspension of all such traffic during the winter months.

Freight charges for this 160-mile haul fluctuated widely. In the spring of 1860, the rate for several weeks reached the fantastic figure of twenty-five cents a pound. Soon, however, so many entered the lucrative trade that charges dropped sharply; by midsummer some were offering to carry goods over the mountains for as little as twenty dollars per ton. Faced by ruinous price-cutting of that type, the freighters

presently got together and fixed a standard tariff of forty
dollars a ton — with the rate somewhat higher on smaller
lots — and this held until the completion of the railroad
some years later put virtually all of them out of business.

Many of the drivers took pride in the appearance of their
teams and vehicles. Charles Everett Shinn, writing in the
mid-1860's, gave this picture of the sight presented by the
big wagons as they entered the Comstock towns at the end
of their journeys:

> These long trains came gaily into Virginia City after cross-
> ing the Sierra and climbing up from Carson Valley. Each
> animal had a row of small bright bells hanging from an iron
> arch over his neck. Great squares of combed and glossy
> bearskin — black, brown or grizzly — covered the collars. All
> the metal of the harness glistened in the sunlight, while the
> leather was clean, flexible and black. . . . Bearded, weather-
> beaten men walked beside the wagons or rode in on the
> mules. . . . Mark them well! No better race was ever bred in
> fruitful America, not merchants these or prospectors or spec-
> ulators but a brave, honest outdoor race whose huge Washoe
> wagons were the forerunners of the railroad.

Knights of the Whip

Throughout the 1850's and 1860's the aristocrats of the
transmountain traffic were, of course, the stages, and many
are the tales told of these sturdy vehicles and of the skill
and daring of their drivers.

In the early period the stages plying between Sacramento,
Stockton, Marysville, and other valley towns and the camps
in the Sierra foothills were a far cry from the handsome vehicles that later came into general use. In the beginning

almost anything that, as one traveler put it, "had four wheels and a makeshift platform above" was pressed into service. J. D. Borstwick, an English journalist who toured the gold fields in 1851, wrote:

> The coaches were of various kinds. Some were light spring-wagons — mere oblong boxes, with four or five seats placed across them; others were of the same build, but better finished, and covered by an awning.

It was not long, however, until more formal equipment became available, some coming by sailing ship round the Horn and others driven over the long overland trails. Among the first to arrive was a type of vehicle that the Argonauts dubbed "mud wagons." These usually carried fourteen passengers, twelve on traverse seats behind and two up front with the driver. Sometimes extra "dickey seats" provided accommodations of a sort for six more, making twenty in all. By all accounts, a ride of any length on one of these mud wagons was an ordeal, for when — as often happened — they were loaded to capacity, passengers and their belongings were so closely packed together that movement of any sort was difficult. Moreover, when the horses came to a hill, or a stretch of mud or deep sand, all but women passengers were obliged to get out and walk.

Soon progressive stageline operators began importing more elegant and comfortable vehicles for use on the main routes, and the mud wagons were relegated to less heavily patronized lines, mostly in the mountains where their lighter weight and lower centers of gravity made them better adapted to the steep grades and hairpin turns.

The favorite stages of the day were the celebrated Concords, manufactured by the Abbott-Downing Company of

Concord, New Hampshire. Their chief feature was that their bodies were suspended on thorough braces made of many thicknesses of leather, which absorbed the jolts from numerous chuckholes in the roads and permitted those inside to ride in reasonable comfort. An iron railing on the top allowed the stowing of passengers' baggage there as well as on a leather-covered platform in the rear. Of the three inside seats, that in the middle was considered the most desirable, it being the easiest to enter and leave and affording the best view; when there were women passengers, the gallant drivers customarily installed them there.

In pleasant weather the windows and the upper parts of the doors were opened so those within could admire the scenery; all openings were, however, provided with curtains that could be rolled down and fastened during rain storms or extreme cold. A second place of honor was the "dickey seat" just forward of the baggage rack and behind the driver's box; this accommodated two favored passengers. Those who occupied that lofty perch, however, assumed certain obligations, for it was long a California custom that at stops along the way they treat the driver to drinks or cigars.

The Concord stages were much-admired examples of the carriage-maker's art. They were made of hard, well-seasoned woods fashioned into graceful lines, and were customarily painted a shining red with an abundance of gold scrolls on wheels and body, usually including scenic views on the panels of the doors. The accessories reflected the same elegance, the harnesses having numerous brightly polished metal ornaments, either of silver or brass. When, at night, candles in the stage's three lamps— one on each side and the third in the back — were lighted, the effect was such that those who encountered it on the lonely mountain roads gazed with rapt admiration as it swept smartly past. The drivers were by no means unaware of this, and it was a matter of pride with them to keep their outfits in tiptop condition, never taking them out of the barns until they had assured themselves that the stable help had rubbed the horses' coats to a glossy smoothness and that no flecks of dust or mud marred the beauty of the coaches themselves.

Throughout the first years the matter of finding enough trained horses for the rapidly expanding stagelines presented a serious problem, for few of the native animals were broken to harness. One pioneer owner, H. C. Ward, thus described how he and a partner overcame that handicap:

At this time [1850] it was considered a disgrace by the Spanyards to use Mares for any thing but breeding. There was thousands of wild Mares in the lower part of the State. The price from $4.00 to $6.00 per head; but as we were pressed for time and wanted only the best we contracted with Don Juan Foster to give us the pick of all the wild Mares in the country and deliver them to us in Los Angeles for $20.00 per head.

We tried to get Mares about six years old and weight about eleven hundred. On March 1st 1851 Foster delivered to us five hundred Mares and fourteen Stallions. In twenty days we had them on Hall & Crandalls ranch and commenced to break them to harness. . . . They were coraled in the Morning, twenty or thirty were lassoed and tied down and the ballance turned out. Then a strong rope with a blind attached is put on and with about twenty feet of rope they are tied, a stake drove in the ground and they halter-break themselves. After a few days at the stake they are harnessed; and — three Mares with a gentle or broke horse in the Near lead, with the off Mare strapped to his hame ring — the Mares were blindfolded and hitched to [the] breaking wagon. When all was ready they raise this blind and let them go. They are frightened to Make a start, but when they find they can go they make things lively. As soon as they learn to start they are put together in four or six horse teams until they are used to the bits and to being guided by lines. They [are] then put in a line . . . with six horse Mustang stock with two drivers on each coach and no Stops between stations. They was kept at work in that way and by the Middle of June 300 or 400 was stage horses.

It was, however, neither the resplendent vehicles themselves nor the prancing animals out front that first captured the attention of onlookers as the early stages rolled by. Because of the aura of romance that came to be associated with these aristocrats of the Sierra highways, the man who sat in the box, nonchalantly holding the reins, was the envy of every other Jehu, to say nothing of the small boys of the period.

A considerable degree of skill was required to handle four spirited horses on the winding, tortuous mountain roads and to maintain the fast clip needed to bring passengers, mail, and express packages through on time schedules. Accordingly, only picked men were chosen for such posts and their pay was on a par with their qualifications.

Three hundred dollars a month was long the standard wage for drivers on the main-traveled routes. Moreover, in the earlier period, they frequently enjoyed substantial sources of additional income. For although post offices and express companies were in operation in the foothill towns from 1849 onward, many of the communities deeper in the mountains had to depend entirely on the stages for their contact with the outer world. Thus it was customary to pay the drivers for all letters, papers, or packages brought up

from below, as well as a fee — usually one per cent — on
gold dust carried down from the placers and deposited to
the owners' accounts in the newly established banks at Sacramento, Stockton, and other valley towns.

The speed at which the early stages had to travel in order
to maintain their schedules, together with the condition of
the early Sierra roads, sometimes resulted in accidents, notwithstanding the acknowledged skill of most of the drivers.
Hubert H. Bancroft, in his *California Inter Pocula*, relates
one somewhat typical instance:

> Upon the box of the coach leaving Forest City for Nevada
> [City] on the 23d of July, 1855, were seated two men, mem-
> bers of the Jehu brotherhood, one of whom was driving.
> Passing under the limb of a tree which seemed in some way
> to have . . . dropped down since the last trip, the top of the
> stage was torn entirely off, and the driver thrown to the
> ground. Of the eleven passengers one was thrown from the
> roof and three jumped to the ground. The crash of the
> breaking vehicle frightened the horses, which started off at
> full speed, dragging the driver some distance before they
> freed themselves from his grasp. The horses were now dash-
> ing along the road at a furious rate, wholly without control,
> and the inmates of the stage apparently helpless. At this
> juncture the man who occupied the seat next the driver
> deliberately got down upon the pole, walked to the end of
> it, gathered up the reins, returned safely to his seat, and
> finally succeeded in stopping the horses without further
> damage or loss of life.

Despite such feats as that, Bancroft's opinion of the California stage driver was not an altogether favorable one.
While admitting his skill with the reins and the fact that "in
places of danger [he] manages his team with the coolest dexterity," he deplored what he termed the other's callous atti-

tude toward the feelings of his more impressionable passengers:

> The road across the Sierra Nevada was fearfully picturesque, and going down the mountain sides was anything but quieting to unsteady nerves. Lighting a cigar and . . . lashing his snorting horses to a keen run, the skillful Jehu, with a diabolical leer, would send his coach dashing around precipice and craggy wall on a thread of chiseled-out road, swaying and sliding to within a few inches of death, and dodging the overhanging rocks and trees, diving in and out of ruts and whirling around on the verge of chasms where but for the timely cry of "Sit up to windward," horses, coach, and company would be hurled into the abyss below. More than once the thing has happened, when upon a drunken driver, a slippery road, a fallen tree or boulder unexpectedly encountered in rounding some sharp turn, was laid the blame.

In the early days the fares charged were by no means standardized, the owners fixing their prices on the principle of all the traffic would bear. Thus on routes where there was no competition the tariffs were high indeed, in some instances as much as fifty cents a mile, and with an extra charge for all baggage in excess of twenty-five pounds. On the other hand, when two or more lines were making the same run, there was likely to be spirited bidding for the patronage of the traveling public. Bancroft in this probably hypothetical story tells of one such occurrence:

> Before the United States Hotel, Nevada City, one morning in May 1855 stood two rival stages for Forest City. One passenger only had put in an appearance when the agents for the competing lines came up and opened the business for the day. The solitary passenger was found seated in the stage.

"What fare are you paying in there?" asked the agent for the opposition.

"Five dollars," was the ready reply.

"Get out, and I'll carry you for four." The passenger, thinking it an easy way to earn a dollar, complies and takes his seat in the opposite stage.

"Here, come back," exclaimed the other agent, "I'll take you up for three."

The passenger is but fairly seated in the first stage, when an offer of two dollars tumbles him out again, and an offer of one dollar sends him back. But the opposition is not to be beaten in this way.

"Well, old fellow," he finally puts in, "sorry to make you so much trouble, but get back here and I will carry you for nothing, pay for your dinner, and give you all the whisky you can drink on the way!"

Roadside Inns

Stories of the early stages, of their routes, their speed and comfort — or lack of them — and in particular of the colorful individuals who held the reins and cracked the whip, occupy a prominent place in the literature of the Sierra.

J. D. Borstwick, the English tourist quoted earlier, had this to say of the scene presented at one of the valley towns in the fall of 1851 as a score or more of coaches prepared to leave for as many points in the foothills or higher into the range:

The teams were all headed the same way, and with their stages, four or five abreast, occupied the whole of the wide street for a distance of sixty or seventy yards. The horses were restive, and pawing, and snorting, and kicking; the passengers were trying to navigate to their proper stages through the labyrinth of wheels and horses, and frequently climbing over half-a-dozen waggons to shorten their journey. Grooms were standing at the leaders' heads, trying to keep them quiet, and the drivers . . . were swearing at each other in a very shocking manner, as wheels got locked, and waggons were backed into the teams behind them, to the discomfiture of the passengers on the back seats, who found horses' heads knocking the pipes out of their mouths. In the intervals of their little private battles, the drivers were shouting to the crowds of passengers who loitered about in front of the hotel, exhausting all their persuasive eloquence in entreating them to take their seats and go . . .

"Now then, gentlemen," shouts one of them, "all aboard for Nevada City! Who's goin'? Only three seats left — last chance today for Nevada City — take you there in five hours. Who's there for Nevada City?" Then catching sight of some man who betrays the very slightest appearance of helplessness, or of not knowing what he is about, he pounces on him, saying "Nevada City, sir? — this way — just in time," and seizing him by the arm, he drags him into the crowd of stages and almost has him bundled into that for Nevada City before the poor devil can make it understood that it is Coloma he wants to go to, and not Nevada City. His captor then calls out to one of his brother runners who is collecting passengers for Coloma — "Oh Bill! — Oh Bill! where the —— are you?" "Hullo!" says Bill from the other end of the crowd. "Here's a man for Coloma!" shouts the other, still holding to his prize in case he should escape before Bill comes up to take charge of him. . . . There was certainly no danger of anyone being left behind; on the contrary, the probability was, that any weak-minded man who happened to be passing by, would be shipped off to parts unknown before he could collect his ideas.

Eventually, however, the last passenger was got safely aboard and the hubbub subsided — but only temporarily. Borstwick thus described the departure:

At last the solid mass of four-horse coaches began to dis-

solve. The drivers gathered up their reins and settled themselves in their seats, cracked their whips and swore at their
horses; the grooms cleared out as best they could; the passengers shouted and hurraed; the teams in front set off at a
gallop; the rest followed as soon as they got room to start,
and chevied them up the street, all in a body, for about
half a mile, when, as soon as we got out of town, we spread
out in all directions to every part of a semi-circle, and in a
few minutes I found myself one of a small isolated community, with which four splendid horses were galloping
over the plains like mad. No hedges, no ditches, no houses,
no road in fact — it was all a vast open plain, as smooth as
a calm ocean. We might have been steering by compass,
and it was like going to sea; for we emerged from the city
as from a landlocked harbour, and followed our own course
over the wide, wide world.

After a long, hot ride across the valley, with frequent stops
at roadside inns where horses were changed and passengers
fortified themselves at the bars, they pushed on through the
foothills and up into the mountains themselves. There the
roads, narrow, rutted, and rocky, skirted the sheer edges of
cliffs, dipped down alarmingly steep inclines into canyons,
and wound upward on their far sides. Now, the skill of the
lordly one in the box drew unstinted praise from the traveling Englishman:

To one not used to such roads or such driving [wrote he],
an upset would have seemed inevitable. If there was safety
in speed, however, we were safe enough, and all sense of
danger was lost in admiration of the coolness and dexterity
of the driver as he circumvented every obstacle, but without
going an inch further than necessary out of his way to save
us from perdition. He went through extraordinary bodily
contortions, which would have shocked an English coach-
man out of his propriety; but at the same time, he per-

formed such feats as no one would have dared to attempt
who had never been used to anything worse than an English
road. With his right foot he managed a brake, and, clawing
at the reins with both hands, he swayed his body from side
to side to preserve his equilibrium, as now on the right pair
of wheels, now on the left, he cut the "outside edge" round
a stump or rock; and then coming to a spot where he was
going to execute a difficult manœuvre on a piece of road
that slanted violently down to one side, he trimmed the
waggon as one would a small boat in a squall, and made us
all crowd up to the weather side to prevent a capsize.

Another early-day observer, Frank Marryat, was impressed
by the number of taverns that had sprung up beside the
main-traveled routes to the mountains. On his way by stage
from Stockton to Sonora in September, 1851, he commented:

> The immense traffic carried on the roads that lead to the
> mining regions affords an extensive field for profitable man-
> agement of houses of entertainment. These may be en-
> countered at almost every mile through out the whole coun-
> try, and they vary in size from a wooden two-story house to
> the very smallest kind of canvas shanty.

As for the services offered at these resorts, Marryat wrote:

> There seems to be a certain hour of the day for every
> traveler in California to breakfast, dine, or sup; and should
> he not arrive at a roadside house at one of these specified
> hours, he will get no meal; and could the traveler by any
> possibility be present at each and every hostel at the same
> moment, he would find a stereotyped bill of fare, consisting,
> with little variation, of a tough beefsteak, boiled potatoes,
> stewed beans, a nasty compound of dried apples, and a jug
> of molasses.

He would then sit down at the summons of a bell in com-

pany with all the ragtag and bobtail of the road who might
have congregated for the repast in question: and, if inclined
to follow the custom of the country, he would, with the
point of his knife (made blunt for this purpose), taste the
various condiments, butter included, that were ranged before him, and, selecting as many of these as were suited to
his taste, he would pile them on his plate, demolish them
with relish, and depart on his way in peace. Travel where
you will in California you may rest assured that of the fore-
going will your meal be composed, and in nearly such a
manner must you eat it.

"Keep Your Seat, Horace"

Of the hundreds of drivers who piloted stages over the
Sierra in the twenty years before the completion of the railroad by far the most celebrated was Hank Monk. The fact
that he, alone among the knights of the whip who daily
negotiated the mountain roads, is remembered today is due
to one of those combinations of circumstances that from
time to time project obscure men into lasting prominence.
For there is nothing in Monk's career, either before or after
the episode that brought him fame, to indicate that he was
of the stuff of which heroes are made. He was, by all accounts, an able enough driver, expert at piloting his teams
over the tortuous Sierra roads and maintaining the speed
necessary to bring his passengers, mailbags, and treasure
boxes through on schedule; but that was no more than was
daily done by scores of others.

The feat that elevated Hank Monk to legendary stature
took place in 1859. It was during the summer of that year
that Horace Greeley — who in the widely read columns of

his *New York Tribune* had long been urging young men
to go West — at length decided to follow his own advice.
Having arrived at Carson City in early August, he set off
early the next morning on the ride over the summit to
Placerville, where he had a speaking engagement that evening, and it so happened that the driver of his stage was the
soon-to-be-famous Monk. Evidently nothing out of the ordinary took place during the course of the seventy-five-mile
trip; at any rate, in Greeley's account of the ride that he
sent back to his paper, he made no mention of any untoward
happenings. To be sure, he made it clear that the crossing
was an exciting one and, to his eyes, not without an element
of danger.

Having crossed the summit at Carson Pass and started
down the American River canyon, he observed that the
road "is, for most of the way, cut into the side of a steep
mountain, with a precipice of from five to fifteen hundred
feet on one side and as steep an eminence on the other." He
went on to state that "along this mere shelf, with hardly a
place to each mile where two meeting wagons can pass, the
mail-stage was driven at the rate of ten miles an hour (in
one instance eleven), or just as fast as four wild California
horses, whom two men could scarcely harness, could draw
it."

Of the driver — whom he did not mention by name —
Greeley wrote in mildly critical terms, remarking that, although he handled his team skillfully, had he "met a wagon
suddenly on rounding one of the sharp points or projections
we were constantly passing, a fearful crash was unavoidable.
Now his horses seem fit to run away . . . I know that he could
not have held them, and we might have been pitched headlong down a precipice of a thousand feet, where all of the

concern that could have been picked up afterwards would not have been worth two bits a bushel. Yet at this breakneck rate we were driven for not less than four hours or forty miles, changing horses every ten miles, and raising a cloud of dust through which it was difficult at times to see anything." The editor then summed up the rough, jolting trip in these words: "I cannot conscientiously recommend the route I have traveled to summer tourists in quest of pleasure, but it is a balm for many bruises to know that I am at last in California."

Greeley's crossing of the range would, in the ordinary course of events, have passed speedily into the limbo of forgotten things. Indeed for a period of more than a decade it was to all appearances permanently buried in the past. However, when in the early 1870's he became the standard-bearer of the Democratic Party in the coming presidential election, supporters of his Republican rival — Ulysses S. Grant — not only resurrected the story but retold it in such a way as to make the editor a laughingstock throughout the bitter campaign. Among those who took a hand in the game were two leading humorists of the day, Mark Twain and Artemus Ward, both of whom so embroidered the tale as to picture Greeley as the timid Easterner, with the redoubtable Hank in the role of daredevil stage driver having his fun at the tenderfoot's expense.

By Ward's version of the tale Greeley was on his way from Sacramento to Placerville, where his supporters were planning a huge celebration in his honor. Somewhere en route, however, the stage was delayed and it was not until late afternoon that it rolled into Folsom, some forty miles from his destination. Faced by this emergency, officials of the Cal-

ifornia Stage Company ordered out extra relays of horses
and, putting Monk in charge, informed him that the great
man must be in Placerville by seven that evening — to
which Hank replied confidently: "The great man shall be
there!"

Ward's account went on to report that during the early
part of the trip the road was poor and the stage proceeded
at so slow a pace that Greeley became impatient, frequently
reminding the driver that it was imperative for his passenger to arrive on time. To this, Hank's invariable reply was
a succinct: "I've got my orders!"

> But the speed was not increased [Ward continued] and
> Mr. Greeley chafed away another half-hour; then, as he was
> again about to remonstrate with the driver, the horses sud-
> denly started into a furious run, and all sorts of encourag-
> ing yells filled the air from the throat of Henry Monk.

Greeley at first applauded this burst of speed; but, as the
stage moved ever faster — bouncing recklessly over the rocks
as it plunged down the inclines and about sharp turns —
the passenger, shuttled from side to side within the coach,
presently suggested mildly that it wasn't necessary, after all,
for him to arrive precisely on time. Again Hank's only comment was: "I've got my orders!"

After another few miles at this headlong clip, the by then
thoroughly demoralized Greeley again leaned out, and this
time announced that he didn't care if he never got there at
all. This time the only answer was a still greater burst of
speed that sent the passenger "bouncing from one end of
the coach to the other like an India-rubber ball." Presently came "another frightful jolt, and Mr. Greeley's bald
head suddenly found its way through the roof of the coach,

amidst the crash of small timbers and the ripping of strong canvas.

"Stop, you — maniac!" he roared.

Again answered Henry Monk: "I've got my orders! *Keep your seat, Horace!*"

Roaring into Mud Springs, a few miles from Placerville, the stage was met by a committee of prominent citizens who had come out to welcome the editor.

"Is Mr. Greeley on board?" asked the chairman. . . .

"He was a few miles back," said Mr. Monk. "Yes," he added, after looking down through the hole . . . in the coach-roof — "yes, I can see him! He is there!"

It was the committee's intention to have the guest descend there and make a triumphant entry into Placerville at the head of a torchlight procession. But the indomitable Hank had his orders, and he was determined to carry them out. Brusquely ordering the welcoming delegation to stand aside, he cracked his whip and the stage rumbled on.

Years hence [concluded Ward's tale] gray-haired men, who were little boys in this procession, will tell their grandchildren how this stage tore through Mud Springs, and how Horace Greeley's bald head ever and anon showed itself like a wild apparition, above the coach roof. Mr. Monk was on time.

Mark Twain's version of the exploit, while recounting the story of the ride in less detail, has this advantage: it at least has the editor traveling in the right direction; that is, from east to west. Twain, as he relates in *Roughing It,* first heard the tale in the early 1860's when he was journeying over the Overland Trail en route to Nevada.

Just after we left Julesberg, on the Platte [he wrote], I was sitting with the driver, and he said:

"I can tell you a most laughable thing indeed, if you would like to listen to it. Horace Greeley went over this road once. When he was leaving Carson City he told the driver, Hank Monk, that he had an engagement to lecture at Placerville and was very anxious to get through quick. Hank Monk cracked his whip and started off at an awful pace. The coach bounced up and down in such a terrific way that it jolted the buttons off of Horace's coat, and finally shot his head clear through the roof of the stage, and then he yelled at Hank Monk and begged him to go easier — said he wasn't in such a hurry as he was awhile ago. But Hank Monk said, 'Keep your seat, Horace, and I'll get you there on time!' — and you bet he did, too, what was left of him!"

Some days later, Twain goes on, a Mormon preacher boarded the stage at a way station beyond Salt Lake City, and, after conversing on various topics, Greeley's name came up and he proceeded to relate the identical story. Then while crossing the desert beyond the village of Ragtown, the stage stopped and picked up a foot-weary wanderer, the other passengers paying his fare and making him comfortable. Thereupon the grateful stranger, after remarking that he would never be able to repay these kind gentlemen for their generosity, added that perhaps he could "at least make one hour of your long journey lighter." On being encouraged, he began thus: "In this connection I can tell you a most laughable thing, if you would like to listen to it. Horace Greeley — "

He had got only that far when Twain broke in:

"Suffering stranger, proceed at your peril. You see in me the melancholy wreck of a once stalwart and magnificent manhood. What brought me to this? The thing which you are about to tell. Gradually but surely, that tiresome old anecdote has sapped my strength, undermined my constitution, withered my life. Pity my helplessness. Spare me just this once; and tell me about young George Washington and his little hatchet for a change."

It was by such means that Hank Monk, more than ten years after he had driven the eminent editor over the Sierra, found himself the hero of an exploit destined to occupy a permanent place in the folklore of the West.

At the time of his memorable ride, Greeley evidently harbored no resentment against his driver; indeed, he is said to have presented him with a gold watch upon arriving at Placerville. When, however, during the campaign of 1872, Monk wrote the candidate asking some favor, the other's reply was far from cordial. "I would," he stated, "rather see you 10,000 fathoms in Hell than ever give you a crust of bread, for you are the only man who ever had the opportunity to place me in a ridiculous light, and you willingly exercised that opportunity, you damned scamp."

Greeley, having been defeated for the presidency, died soon afterwards; Hank Monk, however, survived his illustrious passenger for more than a decade, basking in his reputation as the most widely known stage driver the West had ever produced.

The Ubiquitous Pack Mule

Although it was not long until roads of a sort were built to most of the Sierra gold towns, with daily stages and frequent trains of freight wagons keeping their inhabitants in reasonably close touch with the outer world, this was not everywhere the case. There were, indeed, certain diggings, high in the mountain canyons and separated by many miles of rugged country from the valley supply towns, that throughout the entire period of their activity had no means of communication with the outside save rough trails that wound upward, usually by steep and circuitous routes, from below. Thus the miners and merchants of such isolated communities — who in some instances numbered into the thousands — were obliged to transport every pound of food and other needed supplies on their own shoulders or on the backs of pack animals.

Throughout the early and middle 1850's, therefore, the hauling of merchandise to these mountain outposts was a large and flourishing business. Although horses were sometimes used in this trade, the favorite animal was the sturdy, dependable mule. Accordingly, large numbers of these were imported from Sonora, Sinaloa, and other Mexican provinces, together with Mexican vaqueros to serve as drivers.

To encounter one of these pack trains plodding up a winding mountain trail was, according to early-day observers, one of the most picturesque sights to be seen throughout the gold country. In the van of the procession was usually a horse, a youth mounted on its back and a tinkling cowbell suspended from its neck, the sound of which the animals behind had been trained to follow. Then would come the mules, numbering from ten to as many as fifty, each following closely on the heels of the one ahead and each carrying loads of from 200 to 400 pounds. Drawing up in the rear were several mounted vaqueros, rounding up stragglers, keeping an eye on the packs to see that the loads were secure and properly balanced, and in general supervising the operation.

The trains traveled from daylight to dark, maintaining a slow but steady pace and normally covering from twenty to twenty-five miles per day. Whenever possible, overnight stops were made at points along the trail where water and grass were available for the animals. There the mules were unloaded, their burdens of goods — sacks of flour, sugar, and beans, kegs of whisky, bales of clothing, and merchandise of many sorts — were stacked in piles, and the animals, after first having their backs inspected for evidences of chafing from the packsaddles, were each given its quota of barley and then turned loose to graze. These duties attended to, the vaqueros would then set about preparing their own supper, usually a highly seasoned stew and fresh-made *tortillas* washed down with red wine. This was followed by an hour or two about the campfire — a period that was often enlivened by songs and the thrumming of a guitar — after which the group wrapped themselves in their serapes and slept until dawn, when preparations got under way to take to the trail again.

Sometimes these operations were carried on by the storekeepers of the mountain towns or camps in order to keep their shelves stocked with goods; usually, however, they were managed by independent packers, their trains making regular trips over specified routes, transporting merchandise, mail, and sometimes passengers, and serving numerous customers along the way.

How such transportation businesses were conducted was thus described by a pioneer merchant who in the middle and late 1850's operated a number of general stores at St.

Louis, Poker Flat, and other now-vanished towns in the
northern mines:

. A fairly decent train [he wrote] consisted ordinarily of
twenty-five to forty pack and riding animals. Ours was usually comprised of thirty-five mules of which six were riding
animals, while the rest carried freight. Besides, every train
had a white mare with a bell around her neck to lead the
train. The crew consisted of the proprietor, the *cargador*
(supervisor and manager), four *arrieros* (packers and drivers), and a cook. Mexicans seemed to be best fitted for this
occupation. The cook on his white mare, the *yegua,* rode
ahead, followed by an animal carrying cooking utensils so
that he could begin preparing the meals as soon as a stop
was made. The *cargador's* business included the distribution
of the freight among the individual animals, the supervision
of his crew, and the maintenance of the harnesses. According to their ability to carry, the mules were packed at the
starting point for a four day trip with 300 to 425 pounds
each, including 50 pounds of fodder. The distance covered
in a day averaged about sixteen to eighteen miles.

During the winter period, when snow lay too deep, the
train was taken to the lowlands in Yuba County for grazing.
Once every summer a rest period of from four to six weeks
was inserted during which the animals grazed at a mountain
meadow and the equipment was overhauled. Carrying on
the transportation in winter was a difficult and strenuous
undertaking. We often had to start at two o'clock at night
when the snow crust was still hard and had to halt at eight
o'clock when the sun came out. At one time, in the fall, a
very severe snow storm took us by surprise, and despite our
most arduous efforts we were forced to stop and unload the
animals and to stay there throughout the night. Worn out
by hard work, I fell asleep. When I woke up at two o'clock
in the morning, I was covered by a blanket of several inches
of snow. After a wagon road had been laid out to Saint
Louis, our pack-train became unnecessary and we sold the

animals at an average price of $120. The departure of my two loyal Mexicans, the packer and *arriero,* Pedro, and the *cargador,* Juan, was a moving episode.

The little pack animals, sturdy and patient, had a far more important role in early-day mountain transportation than is generally recognized today. On them in large measure the residents of dozens of camps tucked away in remote Sierra canyons depended for the necessities — and luxuries — that made life there supportable. On their long treks up into the hills they carried not only stocks for the merchants but letters and newspapers, lumber, mining tools, even on occasion the costumes and props of barnstorming theatrical troupes.

Of the pack mule's exemplary behavior on the trail, Hubert H. Bancroft once wrote:

> He guards the load entrusted to him with intelligence and faithfulness, being careful not to knock it against the trunks of trees, stooping low to let it pass under an overhanging limb, planting his feet firmly in dangerous places, eyeing the rocks that jut out over the trail round the mountain side, lest in an evil moment his pack striking one, he be thrown from the narrow path, and hurled into the abyss below. The moment the pack is loose or anything drops from it he stops, and no matter how hungry or weary he may be he is allowed little time to eat until his work is finished.

Ships of the Desert

In 1861 a German emigrant named Edward Vischer, a substantial San Francisco businessman with a pretty talent for drawing, took a trip over the Sierra, following a route that wound upward via the Calaveras Big Trees, crossed the summit in the vicinity of Ebbetts Pass, and so down into the Carson Valley on the east side of the range. On this outing Vischer took his sketching materials along and at various stops on the way made a series of drawings; these he later published from lithographic plates in several albums, the first of which appeared in 1862 and the last in 1870.

His views of the Big Trees and other points of interest along the route were much admired by the public and his albums had a ready sale. Several of them, however, contained a feature that must have sorely puzzled those who examined them, for the objects depicted — a group of camels — seemed strangely out of place in a California landscape. The artist himself evidently foresaw that there might be some curiosity on that point, for in the text accompanying the last and largest of his albums, the *Pictorial of California,* he inserted a note of explanation:

> We must, however, account for the recurrence of camels, in sketches relating to the Big Tree Route, by the circumstances of our having traveled over that route, for the sake of studying their habits, with the little caravan of nine Bactrian camels, taken over the Sierra Nevada to Washoe in 1861.

The presence of the first of these ungainly beasts in the California of the day was the result of a suggestion made in 1848 by an army officer, Major Henry C. Wayne, to the Secretary of War that they be imported for use in carrying supplies to the widely separated military posts in the arid Southwest. Nothing came of the proposal at the time; however, when Jefferson Davis became Secretary of War in 1853, he petitioned Congress for funds with which to conduct the experiment. Finally, in March, 1855, the lawmakers voted an appropriation of thirty thousand dollars for "the purchase and importation of camels and dromedaries to be employed for military purposes."

A party, headed by Major Wayne, was thereupon dispatched to Egypt, where they bought thirty-five camels — paying an average price of two hundred and fifty dollars for them — and these were duly landed at a Texas port in mid-May of 1856. Later a second shipment arrived, which increased the herd to seventy-five. After some months, during which the animals became acclimated and the soldiers assigned to take care of them learned the difficult task of lashing loads to their high, humped backs, the first caravan was dispatched into the West. This train of twenty-eight animals, fully loaded, set off from San Antonio in the summer of 1858 and proceeded, by way of El Paso, across the plains and mountains of New Mexico and Arizona, forded the Colorado River and, five months later, reached southern California.

There the herd was divided, the greater number going to Fort Tejón and the others heading for the pueblo of Los Angeles. At the last-named place the creatures created something of a sensation, a correspondent for the *Alta California*, published in San Francisco, reporting that they "scared all the horses, mules and children." He added, however, that "when the docility of the animals was proved to the wonder-stricken senses of the natives, they were all anxious to take a ride upon the humps of these awkward locomotives, and as long as they remained in town, throngs of boys and men followed their motions."

Although the beasts had their ardent admirers, including

Lieutenant Beale, the officer in charge — who termed them "economical and noble brutes" and prophesied that they would eventually be employed on "every mail route across the continent" — the Westerners in general would have none of them. At the military posts the soldiers detailed to drive them were scornful, maintaining that the creatures were stupid and stubborn and that they would never supplant the tried and true army mule. Although Beale and others protested that the prejudice against the animals was due to unfamiliarity with their idiosyncrasies, their pleas were of no avail, and Secretary of War Davis presently ordered the herd sold at public auction.

At the time when these instructions were received — in the fall of 1863 — there were thirty-five army-owned camels in California, distributed among several posts in the southern part of the state. These were assembled at Santa Barbara, then driven up the coast and inland to Benicia, where the auction was held on the last day of February, 1864. All were knocked down to a single bidder, one Samuel McLeneghan. After selling off twenty-five of the animals, McLeneghan drove the remaining ten to Sacramento, it being his intention to use them to carry goods over the Sierra to the booming Nevada silver towns.

On reaching Sacramento McLeneghan learned that a state fair was about to open there and he saw an opportunity to raise funds to finance his freighting venture by putting the beasts on display at the fair's livestock division and by entering some of the fleetest in a race. Much was made of the novel contest in the newspapers, and on the day the race was held several thousand spectators gathered in the grandstand to witness it, paying fifty cents each for the privilege. The owner then drove his animals up the valley to Red Bluff, crossed into Nevada over the Lassen Trail and, having abandoned his plan of using them to carry freight across the range, sold them soon after he reached Virginia City. During the next year or two the new owners put them to use carrying salt from the saline lakebeds of western Nevada to the mills of the Austin area, where it was employed in refining the refractory ores. Later some — perhaps all — of the little herd were turned loose to shift for themselves on the barren plains and hills of central Nevada.

It was not these animals, however, that Edward Vischer depicted in his celebrated series of Sierra drawings. Those he had accompanied over the range in 1861 were another species of camel, the Bactrians, which had been imported, not from Egypt, but from the steppes of Mongolia. Their presence in California was due to the initiative of another San Francisco merchant, Otto Esche, who had journeyed to China in 1860 and bought thirty-two of the beasts, which he planned to use to conduct a fast express service between San Francisco and Salt Lake City.

On the long voyage across the Pacific in a sailing schooner the animals, crowded below decks and improperly fed, fared badly. Many died en route, and those that were hoisted onto the dock at San Francisco were in a deplorable condition.

On being put out to pasture, however, the herd, then reduced to thirteen, recuperated so rapidly that after only a few days they were placed on exhibition at a downtown music hall. Admission of fifty cents for adults and twenty-five cents for children was charged, the proceeds going to the German Benevolent Society of San Francisco, of which Esche was a member. Later the animals were put up at auction and after two had been sold — bringing 425 and 475 dollars, respectively — the owner withdrew the remaining eleven, contending that the bids were too low. Something less than a year afterwards these eleven were also sold to a San Francisco commission merchant who, like McLeneghan, planned to use them to carry goods and passengers over the Sierra to the Nevada towns. In order to prepare them for these arduous transmountain treks the new owner put them through a rigorous course of training, daily loading 650-pound sacks of sand on their backs and driving them along San Francisco's ocean beach and up and down the steep hills that ringed the town.

Their training completed, the herd set off — in September, 1861 — for the scene of their labors, Vischer accompanying them and producing the drawings that have kept their memory green ever since. The beasts appear in six of the views, forming a picturesque but highly incongruous feature of such Sierra scenes as the Mammoth Grove Hotel, Holden's Station on the Upper Mokelumne, Summit Lake, and the descent of the eastern side of the range, with the Carson Valley visible in the background.

In the text accompanying his drawings, Vischer made frequent mention of the animals.

Thus on Plate 6 of his *Pictorial of California* is this comment:

A drove of nine Bactrian Camels, imported from the Amoor River, in 1861, and destined for Washoe, for packing purposes, was, in the fall of the same year, taken over the Sierra Nevada, by the Big Tree route, and is here represented entering the mammoth grove.

Of the rugged mountain scenery at Summit Lake he wrote:

That nothing should be wanting to complete the awful grandeur of this solitary wilderness, the specter-like forms of several of our camels, having strayed from their encampment on an adjoining lake (forest-bound, yet encircled by rich meadow land) appear in the foreground, noiselessly grazing on the rich sward of the near shore, or nibbling on the branches of the over-hanging trees.

Accompanying Plate 47 — the encampment on the eastern slope of the range — is this more lengthy comment:

Bactrian camels, imported from the Amoor River, and brought over the Sierra Nevada (to convey salt from the Walker River District to Virginia for mining purposes) now halting in sight of the Carson Plains, and, for the first time since their voyage, snuffing the air of the desert. Their instinct enables them to recognize a congenial region, resembling their native wilds of Tartary.

Traveling with this drove on the occasion of our inspection of the Big Tree Route, we could not but observe with interest the peculiar habits of these sagacious and much-enduring animals. Seemingly listless, they notice everything, and are fond of overlooking a wide range of scenery. On a halt, though fatigued from a day's journey, if they discern any eminence near the camp, they like to climb it, to obtain a more extensive view, and, with their heads towards that direction, quietly kneel down, as though in contemplation. They are less fond of becoming themselves the subject of observation, especially from strangers, and when annoyed by their curiosity, give unmistakable evidence of impatience. Though usually slow in their movements, their attitudes are continually changing, rendering it difficult to sketch these animals from nature.

The Brief Reign of the Pony Express Riders

Although the contemplated use of camels as a means of speeding traffic across the Sierra failed to pan out, the fact that the experiment was tried is, in itself, evidence that the Californians were on the lookout for any practical substitute for the slow-moving stages and freight wagons then in use. As the decade of the 1860's opened, the growing tension between North and South and the ever-mounting threat of war pointed up to those on the West Coast the need for speedier communication with the rest of the nation. At Washington, too, this need was recognized, for Southern sympathizers were known to be both numerous and influential in California, and there were apparently well-authenticated reports that, should open conflict ensue, plans had been made to set up an independent republic there.

The result was the organization in the spring of 1860 of what many regard as the most romantic and picturesque venture in the entire annals of Western transportation. This was the famous Pony Express. Sponsored by W. H. Russell, whose firm of Russell, Majors & Waddell owned numerous freight and stagelines throughout the West, the new service was designed to operate on a semiweekly schedule, covering the nearly two thousand miles between Sacramento and St. Jo., Missouri, in nine days — less than half the time required by existing carriers.

In planning the new service and putting it into effect, speed was the prime consideration in every phase of the operation. Letters were carried at a flat rate of five dollars per half ounce — later reduced to two dollars and fifty cents — and arrangements were made for the prompt forwarding of messages over the newly strung telegraph lines at both ends of the run. The riders — all young men, many still in their teens — were selected not only on the basis of their horsemanship, stamina, and courage, but for their weight, 130 pounds being the maximum allowed.

Over the entire route stations were set up, at each of which the messenger paused only long enough to swing his mail pouch on to a fresh mount before pushing on to the end of his run, which was usually from sixty to seventy-five miles in length. From the eastern base of the Sierra to the Missouri River the stations were spaced about twenty-five miles apart; in the passage over the range, however, they were much closer together, three changes of horses being made on the sixty-mile stretch from Placerville to Genoa: at Strawberry Flat, Hope Valley, and Woodbridge.

The inauguration of the service, on April 3, 1860, was celebrated in California with great éclat. Although the official western terminus was at Sacramento, San Francisco was given an opportunity to join in the festivities. The rider and gaily decorated pony that were to make the first eastward run left the office of the Alta Telegraph Company, on Montgomery Street, promptly on the stroke of four in the afternoon, dashed through cheering crowds lining San Francisco's streets, and clattered aboard the fast river steamer *Antelope* which conveyed them to the capital city.

On arriving there — at three o'clock the next morning — the real trip began, the mail pouch being opened to receive additional letters; whereupon the pony, with Billy Hamilton in the saddle, set off on the forty-five-mile dash to Placerville. Having covered that distance in less than four hours, the first rider was replaced by a second — Warren Upson. Then came the first real test of the efficiency of the

new service, for spring storms had for three days been lashing the range, leaving heavy deposits of new snow on the
upper slopes. By the time Upson reached Strawberry the
trail had been all but obliterated; beyond that point frequent avalanches sweeping down the mountainsides added
a further element of danger. Nonetheless, pony and rider
and mailbag got safely through, Upson reaching his home
station at Carson City late that same night, having covered
some eighty-five miles without rest and with scarcely a pause.

Nine days later, on April 13, the first westbound rider
crossed the range, his pouch bulging with letters that had
left St. Jo. on the same day and hour the initial trip to the
east from Sacramento had begun. Arriving at Placerville in
mid-afternoon after a comparatively easy journey over the
hump, the messenger made a quick change of mounts and
sped on, aiming to reach Sacramento before nightfall. Meantime, news of his passing through the foothill town had
been telegraphed ahead and at the capital city preparations
for a rousing welcome got promptly under way. The state
legislature, then in session, adjourned in honor of the occasion; merchants festooned the fronts of their stores with
flags, mounted drill-teams were assembled to provide the
rider with an honorary escort, and military companies made
ready to fire their cannon to announce his arrival.

The rider — the same Billy Hamilton who had set off on
the first relay nine days earlier — hove in sight out of the
east at half-past five; and, to the booming of cannon and the
ringing of the town's bells, drew up before the local office
of the Pony Express. Pausing only to extract from his pouch
the letters destined for Sacramento, he hurried on to the
riverbank, where the *Antelope* was waiting to convey horse

and rider to San Francisco. There another gala celebration had been arranged.

Notwithstanding its festive inauguration, however, the Pony Express proved to be a short-lived enterprise, for it remained in existence only a little more than eighteen months. When it began operation, Congress had already appropriated funds for the building of a transcontinental telegraph line, and crews were presently in the field stringing the wires both east and west. As this work progressed, the trips of the express riders grew steadily shorter, covering only the narrowing gap between the outpost telegraph stations. By the middle of 1862 only a few hundred miles separated the crews of wire-stringers and when, on October 24, the two met, the Pony Express retired from the field, its brief period of usefulness at an end.

Snowshoe Thompson

For several months of each year, heavy deposits of snow — which on the higher elevations frequently reached a depth of twenty feet or more — caused the suspension of virtually all transmountain travel. This was, during the early years, a source of much inconvenience, and occasionally of genuine hardship, to residents on both sides of the range.

Throughout northern California this annual closing of the mountain passes was felt with particular keenness, for it meant that all communication with the rest of the nation had to be carried on by extremely roundabout means, either by slow side-wheel steamers that plied the waters of both oceans, with crossings at Panama or Nicaragua, or overland via the Santa Fe route which entered the state near its southern end.

The delays thus caused were burdensome to Californians of all classes: the merchants because they complicated the task of replenishing their stocks, and the populace in general — who at best felt that they were an unconscionably long way from home — because of the many weeks required for the exchange of letters with family and friends. The inconveniences involved were, however, felt with particular intensity by those who, from the mid-1850's onward, had settled on the east side of the range, both inhabitants of newly founded mining camps there and of farming communities in the Carson and Washoe valleys, the Honey Lake area, and elsewhere. These groups, shut off from needed supplies for many weeks each winter — on the east by hundreds of miles of semidesert and on the west by the snow-bound Sierra — frequently suffered downright privations.

It was not until the winter of 1856–1857 that residents of these areas received some measure of relief, and it came from an unexpected quarter. The one responsible was John A. Thompson, a thirty-year-old native of Norway, who was then operating a ranch in the Sacramento Valley. One day Thompson, a giant of a man with blue eyes and flowing blond hair and beard, read a newspaper story stating that all traffic over the Sierra had been suspended for the winter due to heavy snowfall on the upper levels. Although he had left his native Scandinavia while still a boy, he well remembered that snow had never been looked on there as a serious obstacle to travel. Accordingly he set to work making himself a pair of "Norwegian snowshoes," using the wood of an oak tree that he had recently cut down on his ranch. By present-day standards, the shoes, or skis, he fashioned were awkward in the extreme, they being, according to one account, ten feet long, four-and-a-half inches wide in front and four inches wide behind, and weighing twenty-five pounds.

Having completed them, Thompson made his way into the foothills and, on a steep slope above Placerville, proceeded to try them out. There the feats he performed astonished the residents, for the only snowshoes then known in California were the light, oval-shaped type, the webbed surface of which, while it permitted wearers to walk on the soft snow without sinking unduly, made progress slow and laborious. There was, however, nothing slow about Thompson's movements. Mounted on his odd-looking contrivances and maintaining his equilibrium by means of a long pole, he slid down the incline at what seemed to the onlookers a terrific speed.

After a few days of practice to accustom himself to his cumbersome skis, Thompson was ready to assay his first winter crossing of the range. With a well-filled bag of eastbound mail strapped to his back, and carrying little else except the clothes he wore, he set out from Placerville late in January, 1856, headed for the Carson Valley some ninety miles distant. The trip took him three days, in the course of which he crossed the seventy-three-hundred-foot summit, passing over snowdrifts that in places were as much as fifty feet in depth. On the journey he rested but two or three hours each night, choosing spots that were sheltered from the winds and — since he was without blankets — building fires to ward off the subzero cold.

Having proved the practicability of such winter crossings, Thompson on his return to Placerville a few days later found himself established in business. Thereafter, for the balance of that winter, he made regular trips, usually taking three days for the eastward crossing — mainly because of the long ascent to the crest from that direction — and on his return covering the ninety miles in forty-eight hours. As the novel service he was offering became more widely known, the amount of mail and other goods he carried increased to the point where the weight of his pack averaged from sixty to eighty pounds and sometimes exceeded a hundred.

Only a man of prodigious strength and endurance could have performed such feats, yet the sturdy Norwegian continued to cross the range each winter for many years, making the passage at regular intervals and in blithe disregard for the condition of the weather. When, as occasionally happened, he was overtaken after dark by blizzards so severe that he was unable to see, it was his habit to stop at a spot that the wind had swept clear of snow and there stand, waving his arms and stamping his feet to keep his blood circulating, until the coming of dawn provided enough light to allow him to proceed. One spot where he sometimes snatched an hour or two of sleep was a narrow cavern in the rocks at Strawberry Flat, a few miles to the west of the summit. There, on a bed of pine boughs and with a brisk fire burning at its entrance, he rested in what he termed luxurious comfort.

During the winter of 1862–1863, when he was crossing over a new route farther to the south — from Murphy's Camp to Genoa, via Markleyville and Hermit Valley — he sometimes sought temporary shelter in one or another of a group of deserted miners' cabins at the last-named place. Often, however, the snowdrifts were so deep at that point that the cabins were completely buried and he was able to locate them only by probing downward with his long ski-pole until it struck one of their roofs.

During most of his mountain treks Thompson passed through a completely deserted country, rarely encountering another individual, and then only as he neared the settlements at either end of his route. On one occasion, however, he came on another man, a circumstance that proved highly fortunate for the other. During an eastward trip from Placerville to the Carson Valley he one night stopped at a presumably deserted cabin in the vicinity of Lake Valley, on the east slope of the range, intending to rest a few hours there. On entering, however, to his vast surprise he found a man lying on the floor, having no covering other than the clothing he wore and with his boots frozen on his feet.

A dispatch that first appeared in the *Sacramento Union* and was reprinted in *Hutchings' California Magazine* for February, 1857, thus describes the scene:

> In this deplorable condition [the sufferer] had been lying for twelve days, with nothing to sustain life but raw flour. His feet were completely frozen, and will both have to be amputated below the knee. His sufferings must, according to the statement of Mr. Thompson, have been indescribable, and yet he . . . scarcely permitted a murmur to escape him. Although death would soon have terminated his agony, he still had a lingering hope that Providence might direct Mr. Thompson by his cabin, and thus save him. . . .
>
> The sufferer proved to be James Sisson . . . who had left for the Carson Valley some two weeks previous. The storm overtook him on his way, and his feet becoming frozen, it was with great difficulty that he reached his cabin. On arriving he found his matches so wet that he could not strike a light, and thus he remained for four days, when he discovered a box of matches in his cabin which furnished him with a fire. He then attempted to cut his boots off his feet, but could not succeed; and nothing remained for him but to await either succor or death.

On the 24th, Mr. Thompson started for Carson Valley,
and on Christmas Day got five men to accompany him back
to Lake Valley. He rigged them out with snowshoes, made
after the pattern of his own, and taking with them a sled
upon which to haul the sufferer, they started back on the
26th. They reached the trading post that night, and laid
over during the 27th, in consequence of the severe weather
— another snow being falling. On the 28th, they packed Mr.
Sisson on the sled, and thus, with great labor, succeeded in
conveying him safely to Carson Valley, where the sufferer is
now lying in the care of Dr. Dagget. Mr. Thompson, on his
return, will take with him some chloroform which will be
administered to the patient and his feet amputated, as it is
not deemed advisable to attempt the operation without this
agency.

Thompson maintained his unique one-man service across
the mountains for close to two decades. During much of
that period he followed the route over the summit from
Placerville to the Carson Valley settlements. Later, after the
completion of the railroad over the range in the late 1860's,
he shifted farther to the south, making regular winter crossings between the foothill towns of the southern mines and
the camps on the eastern slopes. On his trips he carried not
only letters and newspapers, but, when the occasion arose,
merchandise urgently needed on the far side of the range,
including medicines. Toward the end of 1858, when the *Territorial Enterprise* — destined to become one of the West's
leading newspapers — was about to be launched at Genoa,
Thompson is credited with having carried on his back much
of the type and other material needed to permit it to begin
publication.

Ironically, although the valuable services Thompson performed each winter were widely recognized and served to

make his name a household word throughout the area, he profited little from them in a material way. It has been stated that the rate he customarily charged for carrying goods over the range was fifty cents a pound — little enough considering the time and effort involved, to say nothing of the danger. During one two-year period he each winter carried the United States mails on a regular schedule across the Sierra, not waiting for a formal contract that he had been assured would presently be forthcoming. Month after month, however, dragged by without any action from the postal authorities at Washington and in the end he, in the words of one commentator, "got nothing but promises."

"Snowshoe Thompson," as he had come to be known, continued to make his hazardous crossings each winter as long as he lived. For most of that period he spent the summers cultivating a 160-acre farm he had bought in the Diamond Valley on the eastern flank of the Sierra, close to the California-Nevada line. There he died in May, 1876, at the age of forty-nine, and was buried at the nearby town of Genoa. His gravestone, still standing in the little cemetery there, has carved on its marble surface a highly appropriate symbol: a pair of crossed "Norwegian snowshoes."

Rails over the Range

At the time California became a part of the United States, and for a full two decades thereafter, an overwhelming majority of its residents were convinced that the chief obstacle standing in the way of the full development of the new state's resources was the lack of a fast, cheap, and dependable means of transportation linking the two coasts.

What they had in mind was, of course, a railroad. For railroads were then enjoying a great period of expansion all over the east, with thousands of miles of new rails being laid each year, and everywhere it was believed that the coming of the iron horse would usher in an era of unprecedented prosperity. The Californians fully shared that belief, and from the time of the state's admission to the union its representatives at Washington lost few opportunities to urge on the Federal government the desirability of authorizing — and financing — the building of a Pacific Railroad.

By 1853 this hoped-for road seemed about to materialize. In that year Congress directed the Secretary of War to assign a board of army engineers to the task of locating the most practicable route for such a line, and appropriated $150,000 to cover the cost of making the survey. The engineers carried out their assignment with commendable thoroughness, devoting several years to the task and examining five different routes, with their western termini ranging from Vancouver, Washington Territory, on the north, to San Pablo, California, far to the south.

However, the Westerners' early enthusiasm for this project gradually ebbed away. For aside from the engineers' report of their findings — embodied in thirteen bulky volumes, handsomely illustrated with views of Western scenery — no tangible results of the survey were forthcoming during the next several years. Meantime the Californians, impatient to hear the sound of a locomotive's whistle, had in 1856 built a railroad of their own, a twenty-one-mile line connecting Sacramento with the foothill town of Folsom. Six more years passed before the long-projected transcontinental line got actively under way, for it was not until late in 1862 that

Congress authorized its construction and granted liberal subsidies to its builders.

The Central Pacific Railroad Company was awarded the contract to build the western part of the road and, under the direction of a brilliant young engineer named Theodore D. Judah, promptly set to work on what was recognized to be a truly herculean labor. For athwart the route the line would have to take loomed the massive bulk of the Sierra, recognized to be an extremely formidable obstacle to railroad builders even today, and one that seemed virtually unsurmountable to workmen using the primitive tools and materials available ninety years ago.

The story of the laying of rails over the lofty crest of the Sierra Range has often been told and need not be repeated here. Suffice to say that the route laid out by Judah — leaving the foothills at Auburn and following the course of the American River up to the heights, crossing lofty Donner Summit and winding down the steep eastern escarpment to the Truckee River Canyon — took five years of unremitting effort on the part of the hard-bitten construction crews and their overseers. Among the unsung heroes of the enterprise were the thousands of Chinese coolies imported from Canton by contractor Charles Crocker: put to work trundling wheelbarrows to make the earth fills; spending snowbound winters patiently chipping tunnels through the hard granite of the upper ridges.

When the line was opened to through traffic in 1869 travelers had for the first time an opportunity to view the wonders of the Sierra crossing without having to endure the dust and jolts and tedium of the trip by stage. They made the most of that privilege. During the first few years the tourist traffic was heavy; not only did numerous individuals and small groups make the trip, but large parties of excursionists also were organized in cities throughout the East and headed westward in special trains.

Seated in comfort before the windows of the Central Pacific's ornate little Silver Palace cars, passengers fresh from day-long passages of the sage-covered plains farther east took on a new animation as their train, drawn now by two diminutive, wood-burning locomotives, entered the Truckee River Canyon and wound slowly upward, presenting an ever-widening panorama of pine-covered meadows and towering cliffs. The approach to the summit was marked by a series of tunnels and long stretches of snowsheds through which the train passed with a continuous, rumbling roar, the confined smoke from the engines ahead filling the coaches.

This latter discomfort, however, was speedily forgotten as a stop was made at Summit Station and passengers scrambled out to breathe deeply of the cool air and admire the scenery, the mountains dropping sharply away on the eastern flank — with tree-ringed Donner Lake glistening in the valley below — and, to the west, descending in a series of ridges until lost in the distance. An hour or so later a second stop was made at a spot called Cape Horn. There the roadbed had been cut into the face of a vertical cliff, over the edge of which the awestruck tourists peered straight down upon the turbulent surface of the American River some two thousand feet below.

It was not long, though, before the Californians — like some people in other parts of the country — began to realize that the coming of a railroad did not necessarily usher in a period of universal prosperity. The freight and passenger rates charged by the new road presently came to be consid-

ered excessively high by shippers and travelers alike, and
during the next several decades strenuous efforts were made
to break the Central Pacific's control of the transmountain
traffic. Throughout that period companies were regularly
organized to build competing roads, and although the public
subscribed liberally to their stock, and substantial cash subsidies were voted by residents of the counties through which
the proposed lines were to pass, for more than half a century none of these ventures got beyond the paper stage.
The cause of their failure was not far to seek, for the limited
number of passes in the central part of the range, plus the
extremely rugged nature of the country through which their
rails would have to pass on both the eastern and western
approaches to the summit, made the cost all but prohibitive.
It was, indeed, not until well after the turn of the century
that a second road, the Western Pacific — which follows a
more northerly course up the canyon of the Feather River
— was built over the range, and there have been no others
since.

During those early years, before the installation of air
brakes, automatic signals, and other safety devices, the operation of trains over the steep and winding Sierra grades
was fraught with considerable danger. In the level country
to the east and west, if the light locomotives and coaches of
the day left the tracks little damage resulted — the passengers customarily suffering no inconvenience save a delay
of a few hours while the rolling stock was eased back on the
rails. At numerous points on the mountain division, however, a like mishap could well have resulted in a major catas-
trophe. For over many miles of its course the roadbed wound
about the sides of steep canyons, and there was the ever-

present danger that should the cars leave the rails they would plunge to the bottom of the gorge below.

In view of that hazard, many precautions were taken by the Central Pacific during the early years of its operation. While crossing the mountains the trains moved at a moderate speed, rarely exceeding twenty miles an hour; the hand-operated brakes were kept in efficient condition, and wheels and brake shoes were inspected at each stop. The result of such precautions was that during the first several decades of its operation the line experienced few serious wrecks in the mountain division and none involving heavy loss of life.

There were, however, some narrow escapes. One such took place in the early 1870's, when a freight train — Number 5 — eastbound across the range, stopped at Colfax. There the brakeman left the caboose, at the end of the string of cars — and the engineer up ahead, unaware of the other's absence, pulled out, leaving him behind. Number 5 continued up the grade to Cape Horn Mills, where another stop was made to take on wood and water for its locomotive. As it started up again, a coupling parted and the last seven cars of the train started rolling back down the incline.

With no one on board to set the brakes, the runaway rapidly gathered speed, swayed around Cape Horn, rumbled across the high trestle over Long Ravine, and approached Colfax with a roar that could be heard throughout the town. There the brakeman who had been left behind quickly realized what had happened and at the same time grew aware of a new danger that threatened. For the road's crack passenger train, the eastbound Overland, had by then left Auburn, a dozen miles below, and the intervening stations had no telegraph operators to warn those on board of their peril.

Knowing that he himself was responsible for any tragedy that might ensue, the brakeman shed his coat, stationed himself at the trackside and, as the string of cars flashed by, made a desperate lunge at the handbar of the caboose.

Onlookers later stated that on clutching the bar he was jerked forward so violently that for a moment his body was parallel with the ground. However, he managed to maintain his grasp and, as the racing cars disappeared from view, he was seen to scramble forward to set the first of the series of hand brakes.

The next half-hour was an anxious one for the group gathered at the Colfax station. Only if the brakeman could succeed in stopping the runaway would a disastrous collision be averted, and, in view of the steepness of the grade and the fast-narrowing distance between the two trains, that possibility seemed a remote one.

As the minutes dragged on — to half an hour, to forty-five minutes — the suspense increased. Then, a full hour after the maverick cars had swept through the town, came the sound of the Overland's whistle from far down the track. Ten minutes later the train hove into view, pushing the seven freight cars on ahead, with the brakeman standing on the steps of the caboose signaling the engineer that the track ahead was clear. At Colfax the Overland made its regular dinner stop, and, while the brakeman was helping shunt his cars on to a spur-track, the passengers gathered at the station eating-house took up a collection as a reward for his heroism. Men contributed liberally of coins and currency, and the women passengers, not to be outdone, removed their rings, brooches, and other jewelry and added them to the pile on the counter. It is said that the gift turned over to the courageous trainman had a value in excess of three thousand dollars.

V

Gold Lake, Nataqua, and Other Delusions

The Source of the Sierra's Gold

By AND LARGE, California's pioneer miners were firm believers in the maxim that "gold is where you find it." Accordingly, on making their way up into the hills, new arrivals staked out their claims at whatever spots seemed to their unpracticed eyes most likely to yield color.

From the beginning, however, there were a few to whom this hit-or-miss method of trying to locate a fortune seemed much too uncertain, and a week or two spent prospecting the barren hillsides or creekbeds of the foothills served to confirm them in that opinion. It was not long before certain of their number, having given thought to the matter of how the gold was distributed over so wide an area — being found from Mariposa in the south to the Feather River diggings far northward — came up with an ingenious theory.

This was that all the Sierra's gold had once been concentrated in one spot, and that through the ages it had, by the action of streams, glaciers, and other natural forces, been carried down toward the lowlands. In support of that belief, its adherents laid much stress on the fact that the metal washed out at the lower elevations was predominantly gold dust — that is, minute flakes or fragments — whereas the higher one progressed into the mountains the greater the likelihood of finding pieces of larger size and value. This, by their logic, constituted proof that all the gold had come from a central point; that it had been broken into ever smaller pieces during its long, slow descent toward the valley.

This widely held belief that somewhere in the upper reaches of the range lay hidden one or more great concentrations of the precious metal was naturally a source of roseate daydreams on the part of miners while they worked their unproductive foothill claims. Even the fact that those parties that from time to time had penetrated up to the heads of the mountain canyons had invariably returned empty-handed failed to dampen the ardor of those who believed that somewhere in the area fantastically rich bonanzas lay concealed. It was this widespread assumption on the part of the rank and file of the miners that presently resulted in one of the most picturesque episodes of the entire gold rush.

The Gold Lake fiasco — as it came to be known — had its beginnings in the spring of 1849, and the man who gave it its initial impetus was Caleb Greenwood, the grizzled frontiersman — then well past eighty — who a few years earlier had served as a guide for the Donner Party on their tragic journey into the mountains. Greenwood, having survived that ordeal, was taking his ease one day at Sutter's Fort, listening while a group of miners just in from the diggings were relating their experiences and exhibiting specimens of their gold.

At sight of the nuggets the ancient aroused himself and related to his suddenly interested companions a yarn to the effect that a few years earlier he and several of his numerous offspring had camped beside a lake, high in the Sierra, the edges of which were thickly strewn with bright yellow objects very like these. On being asked if he had carried any away with him, he shook his head. No, the children had amused themselves playing with them during their stay, but it was obvious that they had no value, there being so many.

His listeners exchanged glances, meanwhile asking themselves if it were possible that the old man, now far gone in senility, had unknowingly stumbled on the source of all the Sierra's gold. They began plying him with questions as to the lake's location. This information he seemed by no means loath to share with them. It was, he stated, high in the mountains to the northeast. One approached it by way of Bear Valley, crossed a divide to the east into a second valley, and from there passed over a succession of ridges — and so reached the little depression in which the lake lay. It was, he added, not at all difficult to find; however, if any of the group wished to visit it and felt that they needed a guide, he would give one of his sons instructions as to the route, asking in return only a modest cash payment for the information.

The little group at the Fort talked the matter over. It was a gamble, of course; but the stakes were high indeed, and the cost of fitting out an expedition would be moderate. The result was that a few days later thirteen men, including young John Greenwood, with several weeks' supplies loaded on pack mules, set off in quest of the golden lake. Something less than a month later the party made its way back to the Fort, its members discouraged and travel-worn — and convinced that they had been duped.

When one of the backers of the expedition, Henry De

Groot, charged Greenwood with having deliberately sent them off on a wild goose chase, the ancient replied mildly that his son must have failed to follow the directions he had given him, for the lake really existed, he having personally camped on its golden shores. However, when the angry De Groot continued his abuse, terming the other a swindler and fraud, Greenwood got deliberately to his feet and, leading the way to an arsenal of rifles leaning against a nearby tree, remarked brusquely:

"Take yore choice, stranger, and measure off yore ground. I ain't particular 'bout distance."

This was an invitation the younger man was by no means inclined to accept, for the frontiersman was widely renowned for his marksmanship. He protested that the oldster would be at a disadvantage in such an encounter because of his failing eyesight; and besides, he himself was opposed on principle to fighting duels. As a gesture toward restoring friendly relations, De Groot produced a plug of tobacco and proffered it, inviting the offended one to have a chew. Greenwood accepted it, bit off a generous quid, stowed what remained in his pocket, and indicated that the affront to his honor had been forgiven. Later De Groot further soothed the old man's feelings by presenting him with a bottle of whisky, whereupon complete harmony again prevailed.

This episode might have marked both the beginning and end of the Gold Lake saga, except that in the California of that day no tale involving the precious metal, regardless of how fantastic it might be, failed to find ardent believers. Thus the news that a party had set out from the Fort bound for the gold-strewn shores of a remote mountain lake had spread quickly through the northern mines.

The result was that during the remainder of 1849, and

much of 1850, a whole series of like yarns became current, virtually all of which had their warm adherents. In consequence, that part of the Sierra that lay to the north of the main-traveled emigrant trails — constituting one of the most complex and broken areas of the entire range — was overrun and thoroughly explored much earlier than would otherwise have been the case. Miners, singly and in groups, made their way up the canyons of the Yuba and Feather rivers, followed their numerous branches to their sources, and hopefully searched the shores of the many mountain lakes that lay beyond. Although the great treasure trove for which they were looking failed to reveal itself, not all these laborious treks were wasted effort, for a number of rich placers were found along the way, some of which continued to produce handsomely for years after.

Of the many versions of the Gold Lake tale following Caleb Greenwood's original yarn, a few only need be outlined here. Several were based on stories allegedly told by the California Indians, of how wonderfully rich deposits of the metal had been seen at one or another of the hundreds of lakes in the high back country. Thus, in the spring of 1850, a man named Marks appeared at Marysville and told of having learned from the Indians the location of a mountain stream of surpassing richness and, with a partner, of having reached the spot, which proved to be all his informants had promised. However, he continued, after having gathered an abundant store of the gold, they had been set on by a band of bloodthirsty savages and had had to flee for their lives, leaving it all behind.

Evidently this stranger's story was convincingly told, for a party of thirty miners promptly joined forces and, with Marks as guide, set off for the mountains, spurred on by a fear that others might stumble on the treasure before they reached it. During the first part of their journey Marks radiated confidence, leading the group up from the valley into the higher reaches of the mountains and there turning into the rugged, largely unknown region that lay to the north. There, however, he grew hesitant and uncertain, turning first in one direction and then in another until at last his followers, tired out from the fruitless search and with their supplies all but exhausted, abandoned the quest entirely and made their way back to Marysville.

Another such venture — this one with a happier termination — had its beginning, not in the gold country, but in far-off Valparaiso, Chile. According to this tale, a Chilean ship had docked at San Francisco soon after gold was first discovered, and a Negro crew member had deserted and joined the rush to the new diggings. Not long thereafter, the Negro and a companion had appeared at one of the valley towns bearing a fortune in nuggets and then had dropped from sight. The next California heard of him was the arrival early in 1850 of a letter from Valparaiso stating that the Negro had reached that city with his new-found wealth, adding that he had gathered it on the shores of Caleb Greenwood's Gold Lake, he having learned its location from the old frontiersman whom he had met by chance at Sutter's Fort.

Such stories circulating through the gold towns always aroused widespread interest, for a gambler's atmosphere pervaded all phases of life in the diggings and, although many were skeptical, none was inclined to rule out entirely the possibility that such tremendous hordes of treasure might somewhere exist.

It was not, however, until midsummer of 1850 that the

quest for the much-talked-of golden lake reached the pro-portions of a stampede. The man to whom belongs the distinction of having set off that mass migration was one J. R. Stoddard. In the spring of that year, Stoddard, an English-born ex-sailor, appeared at Nevada City and other foothill towns, where he displayed a considerable quantity of nuggets, most of them of greater size and value than the general run of those found in the local claims.

It was, however, not his possession of these that aroused the interest of onlookers — for many of the local placers were then yielding abundantly, and such sizable pokes were by no means uncommon. What created a genuine sensation was his story of how he had come by his horde. He and a friend, he related, had set off on a hunting trip to the north-east of Nevada City and, having lost their bearings in that wild and rugged country, had chanced on a little mountain lake, the shallow, moss-covered borders of which were thickly strewn with gold. A sudden attack by hostile redskins, he added, had driven them away, and during their flight he had become separated from his companion and had made his way back to the camps on the Yuba carrying only these few samples of the lake's abundant treasure.

Stoddard's yarn — which closely paralleled that told by Marks a few weeks earlier — seemed to many of his listeners proof that the golden lake really existed. Accordingly, when he made known his intention of organizing a party and returning to the spot, there was no lack of volunteers eager to join up. In fact, so many were determined to take part that when Stoddard's group headed into the mountains they found themselves followed by a crowd of hangers-on said to number in the hundreds.

Starting from Nevada City, the motley caravan proceeded

up Deer Creek and, turning toward the northeast, entered the high, broken country drained by the headwaters of the Yuba and Feather rivers. Here, as had Marks before him, Stoddard began to exhibit signs of indecision, backtracking on his course and setting off first in one direction and then another. By some this was regarded as proof that their leader was hopelessly lost. Others, however, suspected that his behavior was merely a clever ruse designed to deceive the horde of uninvited followers and that, once these got discouraged and left, the wily Stoddard would head for the fabled lake. In any event, only a few abandoned the quest and those who did had their places taken by late-comers who had caught the infection and hurried up from the foothills.

Presently a further complication developed, for the wooded region into which the expedition had penetrated was thickly strewn with lakes of all sizes and descriptions. Confronted by a superabundance of these, Stoddard grew more hesitant than ever, indicating first one and then another as the true Gold Lake. When all these proved barren, Stoddard led his followers still farther north into a country equally rough but with fewer lakes, and there at last his long-patient disciples rebelled. Having charged him with deliberately hoodwinking them, his followers ordered him forthwith to lead the way to his elusive lake, warning him that if he failed to do so within twenty-four hours he would be strung up to the nearest tree as an object lesson to other impostors. Faced by this ultimatum, Stoddard slipped out of camp that night and, no longer confused as to what direction to take, made a beeline back to safety in the valley.

Curiously, by the time the fugitive reached the lowlands the great Gold Lake stampede was just getting fully under way. For by then word of the purported discovery of the immensely rich lake was heralded not as an unsubstantiated rumor, but as an accomplished fact, its location known, with hundreds already at the scene industriously scooping up its limitless treasure. The rush that followed all but emptied the towns and camps of the northern mines, causing prospectors to abandon scores of rich claims on the Yuba and its tributaries, and converting Marysville, Nevada City, and other settlements into virtual ghost towns. One participant stated that not since the first great rush had got under way in the fall of 1848 had so concerted a mass movement been seen.

Efforts of calmer heads to stem the tide all proved fruitless. Newspaper editors at Sacramento and elsewhere heaped ridicule on the movement, pointing out that the misguided dupes were abandoning claims of known richness in order to pursue this fraudulent will-o'-the-wisp. When their appeals to logic and common sense failed to slow down the movement, the editors resorted to satire, one gravely reporting that the Indians living in the vicinity of the golden lake were using that metal not only for arrowheads and personal ornaments but had fashioned it into beds, chairs, and other furnishings for their wigwams. Carrying the horseplay still further, he wrote that one miner returning from the lake had carried with him a thin sheet of gold he had found floating on its surface, and that another, having located an immense chunk on the lake's floor, had succeeded in attaching a rope to it and at last reports was still futilely trying to drag it ashore.

Despite such valiant attempts to puncture the bubble, the search went on throughout most of the summer, to the detriment of business in numerous towns and camps, including even Sacramento, the chief trading and distribution point for the northern mines. The only ones who profited by the exodus were certain shrewd traders in provisions and mining tools, who loaded their merchandise in wagons or on muleback and followed the fortune hunters into the back country, finding there a ready market for their goods, at sky-high prices.

Presently, though, the excitement subsided and the adventurers, travel-worn and empty-handed, commenced straggling back to the settlements. Thus, after a hectic three months, the Gold Lake fiasco — a now all but forgotten chapter of the story of the gold rush — passed into history.

Hunt for the Lost Cement Mine

Gold Lake was by no means the only one of the Sierra's elusive treasure troves to haunt the dreams of the gold-hungry forty-niners. One of the most widely renowned of these was the "Lost Cement Mine." This was supposedly located somewhere in the craggy mountains of what is now Mono County, and was popularly believed to be so rich that, in the words of Mark Twain, "lumps of virgin gold were as thick in it as raisins in a slice of fruit cake."

The story of its discovery, and of subsequent efforts to find it again, follows closely the traditional pattern of all lost mines. Two men, making their way over the Sierra in the early days of the rush, got off the trail and paused briefly to rest in a narrow mountain gorge. While thus taking their ease, one chanced to notice "a curious vein of cement" underfoot and on examining it discovered that its entire surface was liberally sprinkled with gold.

After each had dug out some twenty-five pounds of the

fabulous ore — which they estimated would yield at least two hundred dollars a pound — and after carefully covering up the vein, the new-rich emigrants resumed their westward trek. But then disaster befell them. The haphazard route they took over the summit was rugged in the extreme; one man fell down a declivity and was killed, and when the survivor, after incredible hardships, finally emerged into the lowlands he was ragged, half starved, and with his mind clouded as a result of his ordeal. However, through all his wanderings he had retained a few samples of the ore, the surpassing richness of which aroused the awe of all who beheld them.

Of the subsequent story several versions exist. One states that the second man lived only a short time after he came down out of the mountains and that before he died he gave his ore fragments to the physician who had attended him, together with a rough map showing the location of the outcropping. The doctor thereupon set out to find the treasure, taking with him a prospector named Whiteman. When the long and arduous search proved fruitless, the medico grew discouraged and withdrew. Whiteman, however, was made of sterner stuff. For years thereafter he continued the quest, making many trips into the complex canyons and peaks to the west of Mono Lake, always alone.

Eventually the legend of the Lost Cement Mine became a part of the heritage of all the mining camps on the east side of the range. The result was that the appearance of Whiteman at any settlement in that area to buy supplies before setting forth again was a signal for scores of miners to organize parties and follow him into the hills. Aware of this, the wily prospector took to donning disguises whenever he visited the towns, hoping thus to outwit any possible spies.

One day in the early 1860's, Mark Twain's path briefly crossed that of the elusive Whiteman, and the story of what happened next forms one of the most hilarious chapters in the humorist's *Roughing It*. By this account, Twain's partner Higbie — with whom he was working a promising, but ultimately barren, claim at Esmeralda — one evening rushed into their cabin and in high excitement announced that he had recognized Whiteman in the town, despite the fact that the prospector was "disguised and in a pretended state of intoxication." At once the two, plus a few others who had been let in on the secret, began laying plans to follow him.

> We were [wrote Twain] to leave town quietly, after midnight, in two or three small parties, so as not to attract attention, and meet at dawn on the "divide" overlooking Mono Lake, eight or nine miles distant. We were to make no noise after starting, and not speak above a whisper under any circumstances. It was believed that for once Whiteman's presence was unknown in the town and his expedition unsuspected. Our conclave broke up at nine o'clock, and we set about our preparations diligently and with profound secrecy.

Since they assumed that their stay in the mountains would likely be a lengthy one, it seemed prudent to take along a considerable amount of supplies and provisions. These were duly assembled and loaded on a pack horse, Twain being assigned to the task of leading the animal. In deepest secrecy the group mounted their own horses and set off, Mark bringing up in the rear. But the pack animal had been inexpertly loaded and before they were well out of town disaster came.

> As the ascent grew steeper [the horse] grew proportionately less satisfied with his cargo, and began to pull back on his *riata* occasionally and delay progress. My comrades were

passing out of sight in the gloom. I was getting anxious. I coaxed and bullied the pack horse till I presently got him into a trot, and then the tin cups and pans strung about his person frightened him and he ran. His *riata* was wound around the pummel of my saddle, and so, as he went by he dragged me from my horse and the two animals traveled briskly on without me. But I was not alone — the loosened cargo tumbled overboard from the pack horse and fell close to me. It was abreast of almost the last cabin.

The commotion caused lights to appear in the adjacent cabins; miners rushed out to investigate, and although Twain, by lying silent and motionless at the roadside, was able to avoid discovery, he heard one of the awakened men shout excitedly to a companion:

"I'll tell you what! Welch knew what he was talking about when he said he saw Whiteman today. I heard horses — that was the noise."

The pair passed out of earshot, and presently Twain's fellow conspirators, having come back to learn what had detained him, helped him gather up their outfit and stow it again on the pack horse. The group then resumed their journey up to the divide and, passing into the next valley, paused and cooked breakfast, they being by then, in Twain's words, "tired and sleepy and hungry."

While so occupied, and while congratulating themselves on having slipped out of town unobserved, they perceived a depressing spectacle: the entire population of Esmeralda, in a long procession, came trooping over the divide above them. Aware that the jig was up — for surely Whiteman would never lead the way to his mine with a horde of that size at his heels! — Twain and his companions made their way back to town, their dreams of riches rudely shattered.

Summit City: Its Rise and Fall

However, not all the treasure in the upper reaches of the range was of the chimerical nature of that at Gold Lake and the Lost Cement Mine. Almost from the beginning of the rush, parties of prospectors each spring pushed higher up the Sierra's western slopes, following the receding snowline through the maze of canyons toward the lofty crest. To be sure, all but a few of these returned from their laborious, weeks-long treks empty-handed, for the granite ridges and swift-flowing streams of the area rarely showed any traces of color. Successive disappointments, however, failed to discourage the optimists who believed that somewhere high on the range were the fabulously rich deposits that were the source of all the metal found lower down. So for a decade more the quest went on.

Moreover, from time to time rich enough strikes were made to give rise to hopes that one of the long-hidden treasure troves might at last have been found. One such was at Meadow Lake, a small, shallow body of water that lay close to the crest of the range, a few miles to the northwest of Donner Summit and at an elevation of more than seven thousand feet.

The Meadow Lake excitement began mildly enough. In the summer of 1860, one Henry Hartley, a sufferer from tuberculosis, settled there in the hope that the altitude would stay the progress of the disease. This proved to be the case, and three years later Hartley, restored to health, came on a ledge of gold-bearing quartz that looked highly promising. Taking in two partners, the discoverer continued the search,

with the result that the three staked out claims, organized a
company, and spent the next few months making borings to
determine the extent and richness of their property. While
the result of these samplings was encouraging enough to
draw a few others into the area, and caused the staking out
of a number of other claims, the little camp that sprang up
on the shore of the lake grew slowly, showing few signs of
developing into a boom town.

Not until 1865 did the belated rush get under way, and —
curiously enough — a majority of the newcomers came, not
from the towns of the California foothills, but from the far
side of the Sierra. For Nevada's Comstock lode, having experienced its first great boom, was now in the doldrums,
with most of its mines and mills closed down and hundreds
of miners tramping the streets of its towns. When rumors
of rich new strikes at Meadow Lake, high on the western
slope of the Sierra, began circulating through the Comstock,
a wholesale exodus promptly got under way.

It is said that during the single month of June, 1865 no
less than three thousand people poured into the little settlement. They were convinced that the camp would be a permanent one, so a town site was laid out, complete with broad
streets and a central plaza, and to it was given the name
Summit City. By September the place boasted some seventy
houses, with as many more building, and with daily stages,
offering express and mail service, connecting it with the
outside world.

That, however, was only the beginning. With new mining
companies being formed daily, with the first stamp mill already under construction and others planned, the new community seemed well on its way to becoming, as its citizens
jubilantly predicted, "a second Comstock." Even the coming

of winter — always severe at that altitude — failed to bring activity to a complete halt. While most of the residents prudently retired to the lowlands until spring, several hundred chose to remain. As luck would have it, these enjoyed mild and sunny weather during the normally frigid months of December and January, only to encounter violent storms and heavy snowfall all through February, March, and April.

With the arrival of the long-delayed spring a new rush got under way, some four thousand arriving in May. These set off a new building boom, which this time included brick stores, hotels, a school, a newspaper office, and scores of other substantial structures, all evidences of the citizens' belief in their town's future. By midsummer of 1866, Summit City's closely built central district had an estimated two hundred business houses. Nearly half of these were bars, but they included, too, a bank, an express office, a mining exchange, and two breweries. Nor were facilities for recreation — genteel or otherwise — lacking. For the musically inclined, a brass band, a choral society, and a string quartette were organized, and a theater was planned. Moreover, one entrepreneur provided a steam-driven launch on which parties were carried on summer cruises about the lake, one of its regular ports of call being a cluster of resorts on the far shore known euphemistically as "hurdy-gurdy houses."

The next winter, that of 1866–1867, proved as severe as the preceding one had been mild. This time the several thousands who remained behind felt the full fury of the High Sierra storms, all roads being blocked by snowdrifts and communication with the outer world limited to messengers on snowshoes, who made infrequent trips from Dutch Flat or Cisco carrying mail, drugs, and other urgently needed supplies. Meantime the residents, their houses buried under twenty-five feet of snow, lived a curious, molelike existence, digging a maze of tunnels to get from place to place and, thrown on their own devices, organizing debating societies, amateur theatricals, and discussion groups to while away the hours.

By the spring of 1867 a dozen mining companies had finished preliminary work and were about to begin full-scale production, and no less than eight stamp mills stood ready to reduce their ores. The town seemed about to realize the high hopes of its founders. This feeling of confidence, however, was short-lived. For it presently grew clear that the gold-bearing quartz of the region was of a composition that made it extremely difficult, and costly, to extract the metal. Long delays ensued while mining engineers struggled with the problem, trying one by one every process known to the profession. Eventually a workable method was evolved, but it was a hollow victory, for the process was so complex, and expensive, that only the richest ores could be profitably worked; the rest would show only a loss.

The consequence was that the mines of the area — with a single exception — one by one closed down and the jobless miners moved on to more active districts, most of them heading back to the Comstock, which was then enjoying its second boom. Once under way, the exodus proceeded at a rate that exceeded even the headlong rush into the district two years earlier. By the fall of 1867 the number of residents — which three months earlier had exceeded four thousand — had shrunk to less than a tenth that total, and by the time winter again shut down fewer than a hundred remained.

A picture of the flight — in the van of which were the card-sharpers, prostitutes, and others of their ilk — was thus presented in the *Overland Monthly* of November, 1874:

All the miserable riff-raff, the indolent, worthless, and profligate adventurers, who have no capital, no industry, no brains, and who expect to make their living by fleecing honest men; all the gamblers and the harlots . . . the lily-livered counter-jumpers, measurers of tape and wearers of cheap jewelry; all the sutlers, thieves, pickpockets, and toughs were gone. There was a mighty purging and cleansing of the mountaintops before they were given back as clean and wholesome granite to the pure embrace of the snow.

Each year thereafter saw fewer remaining, the number dropping until the time presently came when Summit City boasted a population of one — the same Henry Hartley who had been the first to settle there thirteen years earlier. In the *Overland* article quoted above appears this graphic description of the abandoned town as it looked to a winter visitor. Approaching it on skis over the snow, he "glided through its empty streets on a level with the second-story windows, and hove to before one of the commodious hotels."

Peering through the chamber windows, he beheld sleeping compartments comfortably furnished: chairs, washstands, mirrors, and beds smoothed down . . . all inviting to luxurious repose. He was tempted to go in and take a cozy sleep . . . but the sepulchral solitude chilled his heart and blood. It was like to things beheld by divers who . . . look through portholes of sunken argosies into luxuriously upholstered rooms. . . . Not a living soul did he behold.

Today hardly a trace of the town remains.

The Honey Lakers Secede from California

During most of the first two decades after California's admission to the union, the precise location of the state's eastern boundary was unknown and remained so until the line was surveyed and marked in 1872. The consequence was that those pioneers — mainly miners and ranchers — who had taken up residence on the eastern slopes of the Sierra were often left in doubt as to which political body they owed allegiance, whether to California on the west, or to the expansive Utah Territory — the headquarters of which were at Salt Lake City, some five hundred miles farther east.

In the early years, this uncertainty, plus the isolation of their position, had both advantages and disadvantages. On the one hand, being separated from the centers of authority by many miles of waterless desert in one direction and by the lofty wall of the Sierra in the other, they were free to conduct their affairs very much as they pleased, without interference from official sources — and in particular without visits from tax-collectors and like nuisances. But at the same time the situation had its drawbacks. These included not only a lack of regularly constituted law enforcement officials and the machinery for settling differences, but residents lacked, too, the means of obtaining secure titles to their property and representation in the law-making bodies of California and Utah to foster legislation designed to further their interests.

During the latter 1850's this situation led to some extraordinary developments. On April 26, 1857, a group of settlers in the Honey Lake Valley, at the eastern base of the range to the southeast of Mount Lassen, met in conclave and solemnly drew up a document declaring that "inasmuch as Honey Lake Valley is not within the limits of California . . ." they were setting up a new territory. They then proceeded to draft rules and regulations.

On this new political entity they conferred the name of "Nataqua Territory" — Nataqua being, so they stated, the name for "woman" in the dialect of the local Indian tribe. Next they fixed Nataqua's boundaries, generously taking in an area some 250 miles long and 150 miles wide. This embraced a large slice of the most fertile land of western Nevada, together with a population of between 500 and 600. However, in laying out the boundaries of their territory, the Honey Lake pioneers fixed its western border at the 117th meridian of longitude. This proved to be a serious mistake, for the 117th meridian lay some thirty miles to the east of where they lived. In other words, in creating the new territory its sponsors failed by a wide margin to include their own property within its borders.

When word reached California that the Honey Lakers had "seceded" from that commonwealth, the news aroused more amusement than concern. The San Francisco newspapers and most of those of the interior dismissed it as a hairbrained proceeding, terming it "nonsensical, absurd, and preposterous." There is every evidence, however, that the men who launched the project did not regard themselves as crackpots or their new territory as a fit subject for ridicule. All the signers of the document had pre-empted land in the fertile Honey Lake Valley and all were concerned with the matter of securing firm legal title to their domain. And, since the high barrier of the Sierra rendered them remote from the California courts, and the capital of Utah Territory was an impossibly long distance away, it seemed prudent and logical to set up locally the facilities for self-government.

All this is borne out by the series of laws they had drawn up. These specified, among other things, that any adult male resident of the territory could file a claim for a square mile

(640 acres) of land, and specified the means by which he could register his title. Other sections dealt with water rights, the laying out of town sites, trading with the Indians, the orderly settlement of disputes, road building, schools, and a variety of other practical matters.

That Nataqua's residents took their territory with complete seriousness is further evident from the way they proceeded to abide by the provisions of its Magna Carta. To govern its affairs, two officials were chosen, both men of standing; Isaac Newton Roop being named Recorder and Peter Lassen, Surveyor. Roop's still-existing record book — now preserved in the Lassen County courthouse at Susanville — reveals that nearly 300 land claims were filed with him between April 29, 1856, and October 18, 1862, each recording the name, or names, of the applicants and precisely fixing its boundaries. In a second book, which has since dropped from sight, Lassen entered the minutes of meetings, together with accounts of resolutions adopted, the settlement of disputes by arbitration, the administration of estates, and other official business of the territory.

Meantime the population of the Honey Lake area — which in some quarters was facetiously termed "the Territory of Roop" — had been growing to the point where it presently began to attract official attention on the far side of the Sierra Range. Accordingly, in the summer of 1857, the board of supervisors of Plumas County, meeting at Quincy and on the lookout for new sources of tax revenue, announced the organization of the easternmost extremity of the county, terming it "Honey Lake Township." The action signally failed to find favor in the eyes of the Nataquans, who promptly met in conclave, declared that no proof existed that their valley was within the boundaries of California, and denounced the decree of the Plumas County supervisors as "an unwarrantable assumption of authority."

At the same time, the new territory began to gain adherents not only in the Honey Lake area but in the Carson and Washoe valleys farther to the southeast. On August 8, 1857, a convention was held at Genoa — in what is now Douglas County, Nevada — at which it was decided to dispatch a delegate to Washington, D.C., bearing a petition to Congress urging the creation of a new political entity, and pointing out that the region's geographical position made impractical its affiliation either with California or with Utah.

Subsequently, a second meeting was held at Honey Lake at which a resolution was adopted stating that "it is the unanimous opinion of the people inhabiting Honey Lake Valley that they are not living within the limits of the State of California," and maintaining that the officials of California counties had never shown any interest in the "spurs, foothills and valleys east of the Sierra Nevada" until after groups of pioneers had settled in the area and made it productive.

Warming to their task, delegates to the convention appointed a committee to draw up and forward to the California legislature a request that that state relinquish any "real or supposed" claims to lands on the east side of the Sierra. The resulting document concluded with the threat that, should such an effort be made to impose the authority of California upon them, "we shall resist such attempt with all the power we can command."

A contemporary account of the proceedings states that the resolution was enthusiastically adopted, and that at the conclusion of the roll call a brass band in attendance played a medley of "martial airs."

In California, this latest evidence of truculence on the part of residents of the small trans-Sierran communities was greeted in much the same spirit as before, although a few editors felt that this time the Nataquans had gone a bit too far, and such words as "treason" and "insurrection" were applied to their activities. Most journalists, though, chose to treat the resolution humorously, the San Francisco *Alta* commenting: "We should never be led to suspect that they emanated from a 'Honey region,' as they are particularly vinegarish."

A few weeks later the California editors were presented with another opportunity to poke none too mild fun at the Honey Lakers. For in late October, the Indians of the region went on the warpath and the whites, fancying themselves in serious danger, sent urgent appeals across the mountains for military aid. Although the California authorities responded by sending a supply of arms and ammunition, plus a small contingent of men, the *Sacramento Union* could not forbear recalling that the beleaguered settlers had recently passed a resolution proclaiming their complete independence from the Golden State. The editor added that "it looks a little strange to see the same men applying to the State of California to assist in protecting them. . . . Men of such independence and self-reliance, we should naturally conclude, would feel abundantly able to protect themselves."

Such gibes, however, served only to strengthen the determination of the Honey Lakers to govern themselves, without interference by anyone, and in particular by politicians on the far side of the Sierra. Moreover, it must be granted that during the first few years of their self-proclaimed independence they did a thoroughly workmanlike job of it.

Thus, early in 1858, the original laws adopted two years earlier having proved inadequate in some respects, the settlers again met in conclave to overhaul them. One section of the resulting new statutes provided that persons taking up public lands in the valley must make certain improvements on the property within a specified period of time, in order to retain title to it. Other revamped regulations pertained to water rights, to the methods of effecting changes of ownership, and to the recording of certain legal transactions.

Nataqua's method of maintaining peace and harmony within its borders — that of requiring residents to submit their differences to boards of arbitration and to abide by their findings — having proved satisfactory in practice, that system was retained and expanded. Nataqua Territory was now divided into several districts, each of which was authorized to choose three arbitrators to hear complaints. Should, however, litigants be dissatisfied with the arbitrators' decisions, appeal could be made to a special board composed of seven men — three of whom were to be chosen by each party to the dispute, who in turn would select the seventh.

Meantime, petitions urging the legalizing of this new territory continued to be presented at each session of Congress, with what their sponsors believed to be ever brighter chances of success. In mid-February of 1858 the delegate they had sent to Washington, a former California journalist named James M. Crane, sent back a highly encouraging report. President Buchanan, he jubilantly announced, was favorably disposed, and Crane expressed himself as confident the lawmakers would promptly pass the bill.

A bill creating the new Territory of Sierra Nevada — the

name Nataqua had been dropped somewhere along the line
— and fixing its western boundary on the crest of the Sierra,
was favorably reported on by the House Committee on Territories on May 12, and Crane sent home word that it was
"in the bag."

At this juncture, however, unexpected opposition developed on the floor of the House. It presently grew clear that
the growing bitterness over the slavery question had made
the admission of any new territories a bone of contention
between adherents of the North and those of the South. The
result was that the bill never came to a vote.

This, however, was only a temporary defeat. For the discovery, in 1859, of rich silver deposits on the slopes of Sun
Mountain — and the resulting influx of thousands of miners
into the region — made certain that the granting of territorial status to the wide area lying between California and
Utah could not be long delayed. When a bill creating "the
Territory of Nevada" was signed by President Buchanan
during the closing days of his administration, on March 2,
1861, the Nataqua agitation — which for five years had enlivened politics on both sides of the range — came to an in-
glorious end. For, ironically, when the dividing line was
determined the rambunctious Honey Lakers found themselves on the California side of the border.

Bodie, Lundy, and God

Another of the long-drawn-out political tugs of war between California and Nevada revolved about an extensive
region in the vicinity of Mono Lake. For in the late 1850's
parties of miners, in their ever-widening quest for gold, had

made their way, over Sonora Pass and over Ebbetts Pass, from the foothill towns on the west side of the range; and when pay dirt was struck in Mono Gulch, and elsewhere in the eastern region, a considerable rush into that district resulted. The discovery a year or two later of rich silver ledges on Sun Mountain enormously stimulated this transmountain migration, with prospectors overrunning the entire region in the hope of uncovering other bonanzas. Strikes of considerable promise were made in the area to the north and east of Mono Lake and a number of settlements sprang up there. The most important of these was Aurora, which by the spring of 1861 possessed, among other conveniences, bakeries, meat markets, shoemakers, blacksmith and carpenter shops, hotels, saloons, gambling houses, and restaurants.

Aurora was believed to lie quite close to the still unsurveyed California-Nevada boundary, and both commonwealths promptly laid claim to it — Californians maintaining that it was inside the borders of Mono County, while Nevada's first territorial governor, James W. Nye, was equally certain that it lay within that territory's newly created county of Esmeralda. The result, according to Myron Angel's *History of Nevada,* was that Aurora became "the seat of justice of two counties, under the laws of one State and one Territory."

While there is little evidence that this divided allegiance greatly inconvenienced the Aurorans — since neither claimant seems to have made any serious effort to assert its authority — it was none the less lively a topic of conversation in the town's bars and other gathering places. Opinion there was sharply divided along political lines — the Republicans favoring Nevada, and the Democrats, who were far outnumbered, pulling for California. It is said that on occasion the arguments waxed so hot that a number of duels resulted, during one of which the editor of the local newspaper, the *Aurora Times,* received a pistol ball in his foot, from the effects of which he acquired a permanent limp.

Partly with the idea of averting further bloodshed, but mostly in order to end the uncertainty that existed not only in the Mono-Esmeralda area but elsewhere on the long boundary, the California legislature early in 1861 appropriated ten thousand dollars to finance a survey of the border, and to that sum the Nevada lawmakers contributed an additional thousand. It was not until two years later, though, that the surveying parties took to the field. Proceeding down the 39th parallel from the Oregon border, and planting sturdy posts marking the line, each bearing the symbol CAL on one side and NEV on the other, the surveyors presently discovered that the spot where that parallel intersected the 120th meridian — at which point it was to turn southeast — was in the middle of the lake now known as Tahoe.

When that had been determined, the Nevadans regarded it as positive proof that Aurora lay on their side of the line, and the territorial governor proceeded to appoint temporary Esmeralda County officers to serve at Aurora, and called an election to select their permanent successors. A few weeks later the chief justice of the territory was dispatched to the town to open court there. Since a California judge was already on the scene dispensing justice, Aurora's litigants during the next several months enjoyed the privilege of being able to choose whether they wished their differences settled according to the laws of California or those of Nevada.

On the same day in September, 1863, elections were held to select officials for the two counties: California's Mono and Nevada's Esmeralda. In Aurora rival voting booths were set up — one in the police station and the other at the local armory — and the citizens had a busy day casting their ballots first at one place and then at the other, with frequent stops at bars conveniently located between the two. The Republican slates won a sweeping victory in both elections, and the residents settled down to await the coming of the surveying parties making their way down from the Lake Tahoe area.

Three weeks later the surveyors reached the Mono-Esmeralda district, and great was the jubilation of the Nevada partisans when it was learned that the line passed some three miles to the west of Aurora, placing that town well within the boundaries of the territory. On the other hand, there was considerable discontent on the part of the opposing faction, and charges that, because of political pressure, the line had been made to deviate from its true course. However, despite rumors that certain die-hards had armed themselves and were preparing to descend on Aurora and hold it for California by force, the crisis passed off without violence. Instead, the dispossessed Mono County officials docilely loaded their records into wagons and, carrying them across the line, deposited them at Bodie — population twenty — which became Mono's new seat of government. Some nine months later, as a result of a bitterly contested special election, the county seat was moved twelve miles farther west to Bridgeport, where it has remained ever since.

Of the numerous camps that sprang up on the east side of the Sierra Range during the late 1850's and after, one of the best known was Bodie, named for W. S. Body who, with four partners, had crossed over Sonora Pass in the fall of 1859 and, having found promising gold and silver ores in one of the foothill gulches, staked out their claims. The following spring, while Body and a companion were on their way to the town of Monoville for supplies, they were overtaken by a violent storm and Body perished, his body not being recovered until the snows melted some months later.

During its heyday — in the mid-1870's — the settlement that sprang up on the site of Body's discovery became known all over the west for its lawlessness and general tendency toward hell-raising. It was, however, not without its defenders. When the owner of a newspaper published in a rival town on the same side of the range told of a child who was about to be taken to the raucous new camp having offered up this prayer: "Good-by, God, I'm going to Bodie!" a Bodie editor promptly charged that the girl had been grievously misquoted. What she had really said, he maintained, was: "Good, by God, I'm going to Bodie!"

Throughout the late 1870's and early 1880's extensive quartz-mining operations were carried on in the rugged mountains to the west of Mono Lake. These resulted in the founding of two other once-populous towns, Tioga and Lundy, both close to the eastern boundary of the Yosemite National Park. Their remote sites made the transportation of supplies, in particular the heavy machinery needed for their stamp mills, an extremely difficult and expensive operation. But the companies developing the properties were amply financed — mostly with Eastern capital — and for some years cost was a lightly regarded detail.

Typical of these prodigal spenders were the managers of the Tioga Mine, who, early in 1882, had a huge amount of mine and mill equipment dragged over the summit from the west side of the range. "The transportation," wrote a local editor admiringly, "of 16,000 pounds of machinery across one of the highest and most rugged branches of the Sierra Nevada mountains in mid-winter, where no roads exist, over vast fields and huge embankments of yielding snows and in the face of furious wind-storms laden with drifting snow, and the mercury dancing attendance on zero, is a task calculated to appall the sturdy mountaineer."

The machinery, consisting of steam engine, boiler, air compressor, and other equipment — the heaviest item weighing well over two tons — was loaded on six specially constructed snowsleds. "Ten or twelve men," continued this editor's account, "two mules, 4500 feet of Manila rope, heavy double block and tackle, and all available trees along the route were employed in 'snaking' the machinery up the mountain." The most difficult part of the trip was near the crest, where the heavily laden sleds had to be "hoisted straight up to the summit of Mount Warren ridge from the southwest shore of Lake Oneida, an almost vertical rise of 2160 feet."

The following year, 1883, this company spent an additional $60,000 blasting out a road over 9941-foot-high Tioga Pass so as to gain more convenient access to the western side of the range. Such prodigal expenditures, however, seem to have discouraged the backers of the enterprise, for these refused to provide further capital. The result was that the mine shut down permanently the next year, after having spent some $300,000 without milling a single ton of ore.

On the other hand, some properties in the same general area produced handsomely, notably the May Lundy Mine, which commenced operations in 1879 and during the next three years yielded three million dollars. The long-since-vanished town of Lundy was for a time the liveliest in that part of the mountains, boasting among other metropolitan conveniences a weekly newspaper, the *Mining Index*. That the task of getting out this journal was not without its difficulties — particularly during the frigid winters — is indicated by the following, which appeared in its columns toward the close of 1880:

> The *Index* wears a cadaverous aspect this week. It is the unavoidable result of a concatenation of congruous circumstances. The boss has gone to Bodie on special business. The devil has been taking medicine, so that his work at the case has been spasmodic and jerky. The printing office is open on all sides and the snow flies in wherever it pleases. In the morning everything is frozen solid. Then we thaw things out and the whole concern is deluged with droppings. It is hard to set type under such conditions. When the office is dry it is too cold to work. When it is warm the printer needs gum boots and oilskins. In fact, it has been a hell of a job to get this paper out.

The ups and downs of such early-day Sierra mining towns is well illustrated in the case of Bodie, which lay some miles to the northeast of Lundy and close to the Nevada border. Although, as stated earlier, valuable ores were discovered there in 1859 and a sizable camp sprang up on the site, within a year or two all but a few of its residents pressed on to Aurora, Esmeralda, and other points beyond the state line, where still more promising ledges had been uncovered. The result was that throughout the next decade and a half Bodie was far overshadowed by its more active neighbors, having so few inhabitants that rarely were more than twenty votes cast at the town elections.

Then in 1878 an extremely rich strike was made in one of the properties of the Bodie Mining Company — whereupon its shares, which a few weeks earlier had been offered at fifty cents, with no takers, promptly jumped to fifty-four dollars. A year later — the town having meanwhile grown prodigiously — a movement was launched to recover the body of its founder, W. S. Body, from its lonely grave and transfer it to the camp's then flourishing cemetery. This was accordingly done in the fall of 1879, the prospector's bones being ceremoniously exhumed and, after being placed on public display, given an elaborate reburial, complete with eulogies by prominent citizens. Ironically, the spot to which the remains of the town's founder were transferred is today quite as weed-grown and neglected as was their original resting place, for Bodie's renaissance proved but a brief one, and all but a few of its population again drifted away, this time permanently.

VI

Some Sierra Superlatives

Mount Whitney — or Fisherman's Peak?

AT THE EASTERN EDGE of the Sequoia National Park, in the upended country that forms the headwaters of the Kings and Kern rivers, looms Mount Whitney, the highest point in the continental United States, having an elevation of 14,495 feet. It was, however, not until some twenty years after California came under the American flag that Whitney's pre-eminence in that respect was generally recognized. In the meantime, the perpetually snow-capped bulk of Mount Shasta, standing athwart the northern end of the Sacramento Valley, had been accorded that distinction.

The reason why Shasta's claim went so long unchallenged is easily understood. For from whatever direction it was viewed, its lofty 14,161-foot cone stood out in lonely grandeur, shouldering high above its neighbors. Thus inevitably it became a landmark familiar to all who passed that way, being plainly visible to pioneers following the main-traveled routes over the Sierra, and directly in the path of those journeying between California and Oregon.

Whitney, on the other hand, was in a region little frequented during the early days. Located well beyond the southernmost of the gold camps, it towers above an area then so remote that throughout the pioneer era few indeed ventured to penetrate far into its maze of lofty peaks and deep canyons. It was, in fact, not until 1864 that the outer world gained its first detailed knowledge of the topography and spectacular scenery of the Kings-Kern district.

In the summer of that year, a field party of the California State Geographical Survey, the chief of which was Josiah Dwight Whitney, made its way from the San Joaquin Valley up the course of the South Fork of the Kings, and, in early July, found itself at altitudes far greater than its members had expected. "We were not on the highest peak," wrote William H. Brewer, leader of the party, "although we were a thousand feet higher than we anticipated any peaks were. We had not supposed there were any over 12,000 or 12,500 feet, while we were actually up over 13,600, and there were a dozen peaks in sight beyond as high or higher!"

One member of the group, twenty-two-year-old Clarence King, got Brewer's permission to climb one of the most lofty of these neighboring peaks. With a single companion, King set off from the main camp and during the six days that followed, the pair made their way to the top of the one they had selected — only to find on reaching its summit that several higher peaks were visible just beyond, the tallest of which they christened Mount Whitney in honor of the chief of the survey.

King — who later gave a detailed account of the climb in his book, *Mountaineering in the Sierra Nevadas,* published in the early 1870's — stated that on returning to the base camp he urged Brewer to allow him to climb that peak too. Permission being granted, he — this time with two soldiers, members of a troop of cavalry stationed in a San Joaquin

Valley town — set off in mid-July, choosing a route that
took them to the southeastern side of the mountain of their
choice, only to find the ascent so precipitous that they were
forced to abandon the attempt while still several hundred
feet from its crest.

This failure, however, was far from discouraging the persistent King. Some half-dozen years later — he having meantime been placed in charge of a party sent out by the U.S.
Geological Survey to run the line of the fortieth parallel —
the opportunity came to make a new try. Setting off from
Lone Pine in Inyo County at the eastern base of the range
he, in company with a French packer named Pinson, made
his way up the intervening canyons, "keeping to the granite
as much as possible," and eventually came out on the crest
of what he assumed to be the goal he had been aiming at so
long. "I dared not think it the summit till we stood there,"
he concluded, "and Mount Whitney was under our feet."

It presently developed, however, that it was not Whitney
that he and his companion had climbed with such effort but
a considerably lower peak, then called "Sheep Rock" and
later "Mount Langley." But it was several years before the
mistake became known, and in the meantime King's published account of the perils he and Pinson had overcome to
gain the mountain's "terrible crest" had had a wide reading.
Hence, King — and the rest of the world — had no doubt
that he had in truth stood on the apex of the nation's highest mountain that summer afternoon in 1871.

Then, in August, 1873, he learned that, because of storm
clouds that had obscured his vision during the ascent, he
had mistaken the lower peak for Whitney and had climbed
that instead. Far worse was the revelation that the summit
he had reached with so much effort was in fact not at all

hard to climb; that if, instead of scaling its clifflike south-eastern face, he had approached it from any other direction, he would have had little difficulty.

This last was made abundantly clear by two parties that made the ascent of the pseudo Mount Whitney subsequent to King's climb in 1871. Both groups — the first in 1872 and the second the following year — reached the supposedly "terrible crest" after a quite easy climb, both making the entire trip without once having to dismount from their horses. One of the parties, that of Sheriff Mulkey of Inyo County, had included two women, the sheriff's wife and daughter. On gaining the summit the Mulkey group had been puzzled by the fact that off to the northeast, distant some five or six miles, loomed a peak that to them appeared far higher than the one on which they stood. However, since the latter had been officially designated the loftiest point in the area — and indeed in the entire United States — they doubted the evidence of their own eyes.

Not so the second party, however. For one of its members, W. A. Goodyear, was an experienced mountaineer and a former employee of the State Geographical Survey, and he was not so easily deceived. On his return from the crest of this obviously lower peak he addressed a letter to the California Academy of Sciences at San Francisco. This read in part:

On the 27th day of July, 1873, Mr. W. W. Belshaw, of Corro Gordo, and myself, rode our mules to the peak south-west of Lone Pine, which, for over three years now, has been known by the name of Mount Whitney, and which was ascended and measured as such by Mr. Clarence King, in the summer of 1871. . . . It is by no means the highest among the grand cluster of peaks which form this culminating portion of the Sierra Nevada; nor is it the peak which was discovered by Professor W. H. Brewer and party, in 1864, and then originally named by them Mount Whitney.

On learning that the mountain he had climbed with so much difficulty three years earlier was not "the" Mount Whitney, but one of its lesser neighbors, King lost no time. He promptly made his way back into the region, determined to scale the right mountain. This time he was successful, reaching his goal in mid-September of 1873. However, if, as seems probable, he had hoped to be the first to stand on its lofty summit, he was doomed to disappointment. For on the crest he found unmistakable evidence that others had been there before him; namely, a pyramid of stones within which were written records making it clear that at least two parties had preceded him. These were, he wrote, "save for Indian hunters, the first, so far as we know, who achieved this dominating summit."

To whom rightfully belongs the distinction of having first stood on this loftiest spot within the confines of the forty-eight states has long been a matter of doubt. During the mid-1870's, a number of candidates for the honor appeared, and their respective claims were hotly debated in the newspapers of the area, notably in the *Inyo Independent*. Its editor, in the issue of September 13, 1873, set off the hassel by announcing that three residents of Lone Pine — A. H. Johnson, C. D. Begole, and John Lucas — had made the pioneer ascent, his account going on to state that the trio, having reached the top of the pseudo Mount Whitney on August 17 and spied the higher peak to the northwest, had resolved to climb that too. "The next day they started," the editor continued, "and passing over two deep canyons, spending the entire day in the labor, they finally succeeded in reaching its highest point, and have the honor of being the first to stand on the greatest elevation in the United States."

This claim was promptly challenged by a member of a rival group. The next issue of the little weekly printed a letter from one Tom McDonough in which he declared flatly that Johnson, Begole, and Lucas had never climbed the peak, and that his own party — whose names King later found in the little cairn on its crest — were the true discoverers. In the same issue, however, was a second letter upholding the claims of the Johnson-Begole-Lucas contingent, which stated that the three had been members of a party of fishermen encamped high on the Kern River and that while there they "took a trip to the summit of the highest mountain in the range and christened it 'Fisherman's Peak.'"

This writer, who signed himself "Fisherman," continued thus:

> Some people are now trying to take the credit of their being the first there away from them, but they won't succeed. Prof. Whitney's agent has just returned from the mountain, and finds fault with the people here for their lack of romance in calling it "Fisherman's Peak." Ain't it as romantic as "Whitney"? The fishermen who found it looked mighty romantic on their return. . . . Wonder who the old earthquake sharp thinks is running this country, anyhow? [This last was a reference to the fact that Professor Whitney had recently been in the area tracing an earthquake fault.]

During the next several months the wordy battle continued, with, of course, neither faction succeeding in convincing the other. In the end, however, both sides scored a partial victory: the peak retained its name of Mount Whitney, and the party of fishermen were quite generally accorded the honor of having been first to climb it. Not until some years later, however, did the fishermen give up their efforts to have their name conferred on the peak. In the spring of 1878 the state assemblyman from Inyo County introduced into the lower house of the California legislature a bill providing that the mountain "shall be known as Fisherman's Peak, and the same is hereby declared to be the official name of the said peak, and the only name to be rewarded as legal in official documents, maps, or other instructions in writing, to be placed on State or county records, or used in reports made by State, county, or municipal officers."

The assembly unanimously passed the bill on March 28, and three days later it came up before the upper house. There the state senators, having due regard for the date — April 1 — voted to amend the document, substituting for Fisherman's Peak the name of the senator from the district where the mountain was located, rechristening it Fowler's Peak. In this form the bill was duly passed by that body; however, when it came before the governor, he — feeling that the joke had gone far enough — refused to sign it. Thus the country's highest mountain today bears the name of Whitney rather than that of the Lone Pine fishermen or of the latters' champion, Senator Fowler.

The Sequoias on Broadway and the Strand

Among the Sierra's natural attractions perhaps the most widely celebrated are the great redwoods, members of the sequoia family and to many known simply as the "Big Trees." Termed by scientists the oldest living objects on the planet, these venerable giants are to be found in some twenty-five groves extending from the Lake Tahoe area in the north to the canyons and meadows of the Kings and Kern rivers far to the south. Growing on the western slopes of the range at altitudes of from 4500 to 8000 feet, the trees vary in number widely in the different groves, ranging from as few as half a dozen to many thousands. Among the better known and most frequently visited of these are the Calaveras Grove on the North Fork of the Stanislaus, the Tuolumne and Mariposa groves in the Yosemite National Park, and, farther to the south and most spectacular of all, the Giant Forest in the Sequoia National Park.

So far as is known, the first white men to catch sight of these monarchs of the forest were members of Joseph Reddeford Walker's party which, in 1833, made the pioneer east-west crossing of the range. In Zenas Leonard's narrative of that journey, published six years later, appears this passage:

> In the last two days travelling we have found some trees . . . incredibly large — some of which would measure from 16 to 18 fathoms round the trunk at the height of a man's head from the ground.

The precise route followed by this party on their historic first crossing has, as stated earlier, long been a matter of debate. The most widely accepted opinion, however, is that on their journey down from the summit they kept to the high ridges above the Tuolumne Canyon, skirted the north rim of the Yosemite Valley, and so eventually reached the floor of the San Joaquin. In that case the "incredibly large" trees they encountered along the way would have been those in either the present Merced or Tuolumne groves.

Oddly enough, although the existence of the giants was thus known as early as 1833, more than twenty years passed before knowledge of them became general, either to the world at large or to the Californians themselves. Then, in 1854, the Calaveras Grove, being near one of the heavily traveled routes over the range, began to attract attention. A resort was established there during that year and each season thereafter visitors journeyed to the grove to view its wonders.

Among the earliest of these was a Captain W. H. Hanford, who conceived the idea of stripping the bark from one of the giants, shipping it in sections to the East Coast, and there reassembling it so as to give the Easterners a graphic demonstration of the tree's prodigious size. This he proceeded to do, removing the bark in ten-foot sections to a height of sixty feet above the ground, transporting the pieces to San Francisco, and there stowing them in a clipper ship for the long voyage to New York, via Cape Horn. On his arrival in that city he seems first to have tried to interest Phineas Barnum in exhibiting the tree at his American Museum, then at the height of its fame. Failing in that, Hanford rented a building at 596 Broadway, cut an opening in the two upper floors and, having set up his sequoia, invited the public to come and view its wonders, the admission price being twenty-five cents for adults and twelve and one-half cents for children.

In order to publicize his venture, Hanford prepared an eight-page brochure bearing the impressive title *Description of the Great Tree, Recently Felled Upon the Sierra Nevada, California, now Placed on Public Exhibition*. . . . The text gave the height, diameter, and other dimensions of the giant, told something of its native habitat, and conferred on the specimen the name *Americus gigantea*. This last was in the nature of a patriotic gesture, for a story of the California sequoias had appeared earlier that year in the *Illustrated London News,* in which the tree pictured was referred to as the *Wellingtonia gigantea,* with the accompanying text stating that "Wellington stands as high among his contemporaries as the California tree above all the surrounding foresters."

However, despite its designation, plus its other attractions, few came to see Captain Hanford's giant, and after a few weeks the Broadway exhibit was closed. The owner thereupon announced that the tree would be shipped to Paris and put on exhibition there; before that plan could be carried out, though, the warehouse in which it was stored took fire and it was consumed.

But soon New Yorkers — and later the residents of London — had an opportunity to view another product of the Sierra forests, one that, in the words of the New York *Daily Express,* made "the 'big Tree' exhibited in this city, several months ago . . . almost a pigmy in comparison with this mastodon." This second specimen, like the first, came from the Calaveras Grove, and for his purpose the exhibitor, George L. Trask, selected a mighty sequoia known as the Mother of the Forest. That giant had an estimated height of 365 feet, a diameter of 31 feet a dozen feet above the ground, and its massive trunk rose some 140 feet before throwing out its first limb.

About it scaffolds were erected to a height of 116 feet, and the bark — which at the base was eighteen inches thick — was carefully removed in sections, boxed, and shipped to the East Coast. There it was reassembled and placed on exhibition, on July 4, 1855, at the Crystal Palace — "the only building in New York," stated the *Tribune,* "large enough to contain it." Incidentally, the tree itself, though denuded of its bark over the lower third of its length, to all appearances continued to thrive for the next dozen years. Eventually, however, after standing for several decades in Calaveras Grove, a gaunt skeleton, it finally crashed to the ground during a winter storm.

After the New York showing — which was better patronized than that of the earlier tree had been — Trask took his exhibit to London. There a sixteen-foot-high section of the bark was placed on view, first at the Philharmonic Rooms on Newman Street and later at the Adelaide Gallery on the Strand. "Unfortunately," commented the *Morning Advertiser,* "in London no building could be found high enough to permit the monster being exhibited to the full height of 116 feet." The paper went on to suggest that "this vegetable wonder" be set up under the great transept of the Crystal Palace — which had been erected in Hyde Park for the Exposition of 1851 and removed to Sydenham three years later — "where the public could see it to advantage." Later this proposal was carried out and the "colossal specimen of Transatlantic vegetation," as the *London Times* termed it, remained one of the prime attractions of the Crystal Palace until that great building and most of its contents were destroyed by fire in 1866.

Meantime, while the sequoia was exciting wonder in far-off New York and London, Californians were given ample opportunity to familiarize themselves with their home-grown giants. By the mid-1850's the trees had become recognized as among the Sierra's major attractions, and thereafter each summer they drew ever-increasing crowds to one or another of the groves. For the accommodation of the visitors hotels were built and campsites laid out, and as a further means of attracting tourists the owners resorted to various means of dramatizing the immense size of the sequoias. Thus the proprietor of the hotel at the Calaveras Grove had one of the biggest trees cut down, and converted its stump into a dance floor and the fallen tree into a bowling alley. At the Mariposa Grove, a few miles to the south of the Yosemite Valley, a six-horse stage was driven up on to a fallen giant, known as "the Father of the Forest," and a photograph of the exploit was for years thereafter a favorite view with visitors to the grove, few of whom failed to carry a copy away with them.

Hardly less spectacular was the Wawona Tree, also in the Mariposa Grove, into the base of which a tunnel was cut large enough to permit stages to pass, thereby affording visitors the novel privilege of riding, not around the giant, but through it. Several of the groves had on exhibition cross-sections sawed from the trunk of one of the fallen giants, the theory being that by counting the closely spaced rings extending outward from the center the tree's age could be determined, each ring constituting a year of growth.

One such section on display at the Sequoia National Park portrayed the tree's estimated age in dramatic fashion by placing across its surface a series of cards indicating the sequoia's age at various periods of history. Thus events of comparatively recent times, such as the Civil War and the admission of California to the Union, were listed near the outer rim; a bit farther in toward the center were the Napoleonic Wars and the American Revolution; beyond these the Landing of the Pilgrims; and so, through the happenings of the Renaissance and medieval times, on to the birth of Christ, and finally to Hannibal's crossing of the Alps and other notable happenings of ancient history.

Nor were such estimates pure guesswork, for scientists

state that by a count of the rings the age of the trees can be determined with reasonable accuracy, often indeed with a margin of error not exceeding fifteen or twenty years in a specimen 2000 or more old. The diameter of the trunks of living trees has been found to increase on an average of one inch every twenty years. However, this varies widely in different groves and with individual trees in the same grove. Willis Lynn Jepson, long Professor of Botany at the University of California and a recognized authority on the subject, stated that one of the monarchs of the Calaveras Grove, which at its base had a diameter of twenty-seven feet inside the bark, would by the above rule-of-thumb have had an age of 6480 years, but was found on being cut down to be only 1300 years old. On the other hand, a tree in the Converse Basin, slightly less than twelve feet in diameter, was found by a ring-count to have been growing more than twenty centuries.

Although several of the groves lay claim to the distinction of possessing the "oldest" tree, such a claim can be established only by cutting down the contending trees, and, since all but a few stands are now in state or national parks, it is unlikely that this event will ever come to pass. When, some years ago, loggers were felling sequoias in the Converse Basin, a count of the rings of one giant revealed that it had been growing for approximately 3150 years. That makes this tree the oldest specimen of which authenticated records exist, although most authorities maintain that many of those still standing are in all probability even more venerable, some having perhaps been growing as long as 5000 or 6000 years.

In several of the groves, notably at Calaveras, Merced, and in the Sequoia National Park, it has long been the custom to confer names on individual trees, thereby honoring places or national heroes or distinguished visitors to the areas. Thus the Mariposa Grove has sequoias bearing the names of Massachusetts, Ohio, and several other states, as well as a number of cities, including St. Louis and Philadelphia. Elsewhere stand the General Grant and General Sherman — both tremendous specimens having diameters of 35½ and 34½ feet respectively — together with those perpetuating the names of General Lafayette, Theodore Roosevelt, John Muir, and a host of others.

Efforts to preserve the stands of sequoias from the axes of the loggers were for many years a major concern of nature lovers. Although their campaigns eventually turned out to be successful, results were achieved only after long-drawn-out and frequently bitter struggles. For the great trees — many of which would yield in excess of half a million board feet of lumber — were highly prized by the millmen, and during the 1860's and 1870's several of the finest groves, particularly those in the Converse Basin adjacent to the Kings River, were logged over.

Other magnificent stands farther to the south were, throughout the late 1870's and well into the next decade, the subject of prolonged contention, and with the lumber interests ranged on one side and the conservationists on the other. Long a leading figure in that battle was George W. Stewart, editor of a newspaper in the San Joaquin Valley town of Visalia. In the columns of his journal and elsewhere Stewart waged an unremitting campaign which played a decisive part in the creation, in 1890, of the Sequoia National Park, the boundaries of which enclose many of the largest and most stately examples of the species. In appreciation of his efforts, one of the lofty peaks dominating that portion of the range was named Mount George Stewart.

Few of the writers who visited the groves during the early days failed to leave a record of their impressions. One such was William Wright, who under the nom de plume of Dan De Quille, was for many years the leading historian of Nevada's great Comstock Lode. Wright, on an eastward crossing of the range in the fall of 1859, passed through the Calaveras Grove, and in a letter to a friend in his home town in the Middle West he commented thus:

> You have no doubt heard of the Big Trees, but you can form no idea of their size without visiting them. Why, Ben, if one of the smallest of them stood in front of Bishop's Drug Store and should be cut down, the butt would be lying on the ground so long as to be perfectly rotten before the top got to the ground. A large tree called the Father of the Forest . . . is supposed to have been blown up by the roots about the time of the big blow . . . and the top of it lacked four feet of being on the ground when we got there. These stories may look large to folks back home, but I can't help it. They were not nearly so big when I first wrote them, but this infernal climate is so moist I see they have swelled a good deal since. . .

John Muir, who termed the sequoia "king of all the conifers in the world, the noblest of a noble race," never tired of describing their manifold attractions, which to his eyes lay not alone in their size but in the beauty of their "exquisitely harmonious and finely balanced" proportions. He advised visitors to the groves, after having had a near view of the bases of the giants, "to stand back far enough to see the massive columns from the swelling instep to the lofty summit dissolving in a dome of verdure [and] rejoice in the unrivalled display of combined grandeur and beauty." He added that "a hundred feet or more of the trunk is usually branchless, but its massive simplicity is relieved by the bark furrows, which instead of making an irregular network run closely parallel, like the fluting of an architectural column. . . ."

With the then widely held belief that, because few young trees were to be seen in many of the groves, the species was dying out, Muir strongly disagreed. It was his opinion that, under normal circumstances, the life-span of many of the monarchs then standing was past estimating. "I never," he once wrote, "saw a Big Tree that had died a natural death; barring accidents they seem to be immortal, being exempt from all the diseases that afflict and kill other trees. Unless destroyed by man, they live on indefinitely until burned, smashed by lightning, or by the giving way of the ground on which they stand." Moreover, although it was true that young sequoias were a rarity in the then better-known northern groves, he pointed out that farther to the south near the lower end of the range all the great stands had an abundance of new growth, ranging from tiny seedlings to those a hundred feet or more in height. From this he concluded — logically enough — that, given protection from the saws and axes of the loggers, the great groves would continue to flourish for centuries to come.

The "Rape" of Hetch Hetchy

Although Muir and other nature-lovers of his day had little fear that the sequoias were doomed to early extinction, they were deeply concerned at what they conceived to be other serious threats to the beauty of the range. High on their list of what they termed "despoilers of the mountains," taking rank with the lumbermen's axes and the carelessly thrown matches of campers, was, surprisingly enough, the lowly sheep. For throughout the final decades of the last century these normally inoffensive animals — which Muir once termed "hoofed locusts" — having eaten every blade of grass on their foothill ranges, were each summer driven higher into the range, where they waxed fat on the lush mountain meadows, reducing them to much the same barren condition.

During his first summer in California, Muir had shepherded one of these ravenous bands "in the high grassy forests north of Tuolumne Meadows." There he had ample opportunity to see the destruction they wrought, for not only did they consume every plant within reach but stripped the foliage from the young trees, particularly from the mountain fir, for which they had a special liking.

Oddly enough, it was in large measure because of the damage done by these woolly despoilers that the Yosemite National Park — one of the most extensive and varied recreation areas in the entire range — came into being. For following the passage, in 1864, of an Act of Congress granting the Yosemite Valley to the State of California for park purposes, a movement got under way to have many square miles of the surrounding area set aside, for the same purpose. Proponents of this measure pointed out not only that through the annual invasion of tens of thousands of sheep all plants and flowers in the meadows were being consumed, but that through the carelessness of herders, many destructive forest fires were also being started.

Throughout the 1870's and early 1880's bills were regularly introduced into Congress designed to create this great national park. These were, however, violently opposed not only by the sheepmen, but by the lumbering and mining interests, and these opponents were able to marshal sufficient strength to defeat the measures.

The turning point in the long-drawn-out contest came in the summer of 1889 when Robert Underwood Johnson, ardent conservationist and one of the editors of the *Century Magazine,* visited Yosemite Valley and, in company with Muir, took a camping trip through the high country to the north and east. On that outing Muir did not fail to point out the damage done by the ravenous bands of "hoofed locusts," and both agreed that the only way to avoid further destruction was to have the region set aside as a national park.

The result was that Muir undertook to write for the *Century* a series of articles describing the numerous scenic attractions of the district, and at the same time Johnson busied himself enlisting the support of men of influence at Washington and elsewhere. This double-barreled campaign proved so successful that when a bill setting aside that extensive region came before Congress in the fall of 1890 it passed with flying colors and promptly received President Harrison's signature. Thereafter sheep were admitted to the area in far fewer numbers than formerly, and only to certain designated spots where the damage they might do was deemed negligible.

This successful fight to keep the canyons and meadows and lofty peaks of the region in their unspoiled, natural state, free from exploitation by sheep-raisers, lumbermen, and other commercial interests, was, however, only the prelude to a far more lengthy and bitterly contested struggle. This historic hassel began mildly enough in the summer of 1900 when the Board of Supervisors of San Fran-

cisco, which city had for years been contending with a woe-
fully inadequate water supply, instructed the city engineer
to make a survey of northern California for the purpose of
locating a new source sufficient for its present and future
needs.

After an examination of more than a dozen possible sites,
City Engineer O'Shaughnessy selected as the most desirable
for the purpose a spot, within the boundaries of the Yosemite
National Park, known as Hetch Hetchy Valley; he recom-
mended building a dam across the Tuolumne River at that
point, thereby converting the valley into a vast storage reservoir. Accordingly, Mayor James D. Phelan, after having
made the necessary filings, applied the following year to the
Secretary of the Interior for permission to construct the dam
and other works, including a series of stations for the generation of electric power.

This was a signal for the conservationists, the mountain
climbers, and nature lovers of all degrees to join forces and
loudly voice their opposition. For the Hetch Hetchy, although
it lay only a few miles from the Yosemite Valley, was situated in so rugged a terrain that few had ever laid eyes on it;
it was none the less regarded by those who had had that privilege as one of the most beautiful places in the entire Sierra,
one admirer describing it as "a Yosemite in miniature."

Among the earliest to sing its praises had been John Muir,
who had come on the valley some thirty years earlier and
had written glowingly of its attractions. Muir was, naturally,
in the front rank of those who opposed its being taken over
as a storage reservoir by the San Franciscans, and in a long
series of public pronouncements he denounced the sponsors
of the project as "temple destroyers" and "devotees of rav-
aging commercialism" who "instead of lifting their eyes to

the God of the mountains, lift them to the almighty dollar."
Warming to his task, he thundered: "Dam Hetch Hetchy!
As well dam for water tanks the people's cathedrals and
churches, for no holier temple has ever been consecrated by
the heart of man."

Replying to this barrage, San Franciscans pointed out that
the growth of their city and the health of its quarter of a
million residents were dependent on obtaining an adequate
supply of pure mountain water, that competent engineers
had pronounced Hetch Hetchy the most desirable and practical of the available sources; they added mildly that the
creation of a mountain lake there was, in their opinion, unlikely seriously to mar the beauty of the region. These arguments, however, found little favor with Muir or his cohorts,
who spoke eloquently of the stately pine and fir groves and
the flower-strewn meadows that would be inundated, and
sent fervent appeals to Washington to prevent the proposed
desecration.

In this the nature lovers were at the offset uniformly successful. In 1903, the then Secretary of the Interior, Ethan
Allen Hitchcock, denied the city's application; and when
two years later it was re-presented in modified form, he again
rejected it. Undiscouraged, the San Franciscans — whose
water supply by then had reached the critical stage — tried
yet again in 1907. This time the new Secretary, James R.
Garfield, after long hearings both at Washington and in California, granted the city the long-deferred rights, but with
certain restrictions. Among these was a proviso that the
municipality develop to its full capacity the Lake Eleanor
project, lower down in the mountains, before damming the
Hetch Hetchy canyon, and should dam Hetch Hetchy then
only if the amount of water in the first lake proved insuf-

ficient to San Francisco's needs. It also specified that the rights of two irrigation districts in the valley below — those of Modesto and Turlock — be fully recognized and protected.

Secretary Garfield's action by no means ended the matter, for his order specified:

> The city and county of San Francisco will, within two years after the grant . . . submit the question to the vote of its citizens . . . and within three years thereafter . . . commence the actual construction . . . and carry the same to completion with all reasonable diligence. . . . Unless . . . said work is commenced, carried on, and completed within the time herein specified, all rights granted hereunder shall revert to the Government.

At the time, it was freely predicted by opponents of the measure that an engineering work of such magnitude, involving as it did not only the construction of great dams and auxiliary works in the mountains but the conveying of water through tunnels and aqueducts for a distance of over 160 miles, was beyond the financial capacity of the city, particularly in view of the fact that its citizens had recently suffered heavy losses in the 1906 fire that had laid to waste virtually the entire central business district.

While the city authorities prepared to submit to the voters a formidable bond issue — its amount was $45,000,000 — to carry the work through, the conservationists continued to fight the measure, their chief argument being that abundant water was available much closer to San Francisco, and that this, by means of filterization, could be made as pure and palatable as that from the Sierra streams, and at far less expense. One such statement, widely publicized at the time, was that of an eminent Pennsylvanian who, having explained the efficiency of modern methods of filtration, ended with these words:

> I have been drinking every day for two and a half years filtered Susquehanna River water, crystal clear and sparkling, free from injurious organisms, which twenty-four hours previous to the time of drinking was culm-infested, filth-filled, and full of disease organisms. I see every time I go to the filtration plant the sullen, turbid flood of the river which more than a half-million people have used as a sewer, and I see the delightful results of the scientific and carefully guarded filtration under which at one cent a hundred gallons we get a result quite equal to Apollinaris at twenty-five cents a pint.

Oddly enough, San Franciscans were so little impressed by this argument that they went to the polls and voted approval of the whopping bond issue. That, however, by no means ended the long fight. Early in 1910, after work had begun on the Lake Eleanor phase of the project, so much pressure was brought on the new Secretary of the Interior, Richard A. Ballinger, that the whole question was reopened and the city was directed to show cause why the permit to dam the Hetch Hetchy Valley should not be revoked. During the next several months another lengthy series of hearings were held, with both sides presenting voluminous reports. Eventually, the Interior Department having found the matter, as one San Francisco newspaper stated, "too hot to handle," the whole question was dumped on the lap of Congress. Accordingly, the Riker Bill — so named for John E. Riker, the California congressman who sponsored it — was introduced in the summer of 1913, and — despite fierce opposition on the part of conservationists, nature lovers, and mountain climbers' clubs — the measure passed both House and Senate and received President Wilson's signature on December 12 of that year.

Thus, after more than a dozen years of contention, the issue was finally settled, with San Francisco emerging the victor on all fronts. However, it was not until after the passage of more than two decades that the vast project was completed. Meantime the costs mounted steadily: the building of the great O'Shaughnessy Dam across the lower end of the valley, of a series of hydroelectric plants, and of the many miles of tunnels and steel conduits through which the water was brought to the city necessitated a number of new bond issues, the total of which exceeded $100,000,000.

Moreover, it presently grew clear that the dire results opponents of the measure had foreseen had not come to pass. For the transformation of the Hetch Hetchy Canyon into a mountain lake did not materially lessen the scenic attractions of the region; indeed, in the opinion of many, it served rather to enhance them. In addition, the city-built roads rendered easily accessible a section of the range that formerly could be reached only on horseback or afoot over rough, winding trails.

To be sure, this opening of the area to those who traveled by automobile was also deplored by many nature lovers, who maintained that a true appreciation of the mountain solitudes could be had only by passing at a leisurely pace over its picturesque trails and at nightfall camping in some grassy meadow or beside a stream or tranquil lake, far from the cares and stresses of the outside world. Others, however, pointed out that the building of such roads permitted many thousands each year to visit the area and to gain some appreciation of its scenic wonders, fleeting and superficial though this might be, and that for those who wished to commune with nature on more intimate terms there were great areas of the park far removed from these or other works of man.

But although the conservationists and mountain lovers lost this long-drawn-out battle, it presently came to be regarded not as a defeat but as a moral victory for their cause. For it served notice that future attempts to gain like concessions within the boundaries of the national parks would be fought tooth and nail. It was, indeed, a turning point in the long-standing feud — there is no other word for it — that for close to a century has revolved about the question of to what uses the vast resources of the Sierra should be put.

On one side are ranged those who maintain that the high Sierra country, because of its outstanding scenic attractions, should be reserved in perpetuity in its natural state, and thus form a spacious setting in which present and future generations may know and enjoy nature in its grandest and most picturesque aspects, and under its benign influence shunt off the trials and distractions of urban life. Opposing this group are those who, while few of them deny that the region is a desirable and extremely attractive place of healthful recreation, feel that the primary consideration should be the full development of the resources of the mountains, thereby promoting the economic well-being of the state as a whole.

During the quarter-century following the gold rush those who held this last view had things very much to themselves. Private enterprise was in the driver's seat; and the result, more often than not, was a reckless waste of the area's resources and the spoliation of its natural beauties. As we have seen, great herds of sheep were driven into the mountain meadows each summer and so overgrazed them that for a generation they remained barren, and logging crews invaded the forests of sequoias, felling the biggest trees and carting off only a few logs sawed from their bases, leaving the rest to rot. Elsewhere hydraulic miners washed away whole mountainsides with powerful jets of water, causing the debris to clog the mountain streams for miles below.

These and other abuses, together with the realization in some quarters that the resources even of the sprawling Sierra were not inexhaustible, presently led to a demand that some sort of curb be put on the work of the despoilers. One of the earliest and most effectual of these was that of withdrawing federal lands in certain parts of the range from private ownership and making them a permanent part of the public domain. In this manner groves of sequoias were saved from the onslaughts of the woodmen, the grazing of sheep in the upland valleys was sharply restricted, and vast areas both to the north and south were set aside by the Federal and state governments as forest reserves, parks, or game refuges.

This far-sighted movement had, in theory at least, the approval and support of an overwhelming majority of the people. It was only on the scale and manner in which it was carried out that conflicts arose. For the conservationists were of the opinion that far too little of the high mountain area had been so set aside, whereas those who advocated the fullest development of the range — for lumbering, for mining, and presently for irrigation projects, hydroelectric plants, and sources of water supply — took an opposite view.

The result, naturally enough, was that both sides went to extremes. Those who advocated keeping the mountains in their natural state strenuously opposed the building of roads or of tourist resorts in the back country, contending that making such areas accessible to those who preferred to ride in automobiles would spoil them for the true mountaineers who preferred to walk in, carrying their supplies and camping equipment on muleback. On the other hand, spokesmen for the opposition heaped none too gentle ridicule on the more extreme of the nature lovers, terming them dreamers, visionaries, and impractical idealists, and charging that, in order to preserve unsullied by man the setting for their de luxe summer pilgrimages, they were making determined efforts to prevent the carrying through of enterprises essential to the well-being of the citizenry as a whole.

Today, after many years of violent contention, both sides maintain an uneasy truce, and an unwonted peace prevails over the Sierra's snow-clad peaks and flower-strewn meadows. It will surprise no one, however, if the conflict presently breaks out again, and with all its old-time fury.

From Bonpland to Bigler to Tahoe

One of the caprices of Far-Western exploration lies in the fact that Lake Tahoe, by far the largest body of water within the confines of the range, and today widely celebrated for the beauty of its setting, remained all but unknown to the tens of thousands who streamed over the Sierra in the days of the gold rush.

It was not until the beginning of the 1860's that Tahoe's attractions — or, indeed, its very existence — became known to a great majority of the Californians. This is all the more puzzling when one considers its geographical position. For this by no means small lake — some twenty-three miles long and thirteen wide — is not tucked away in one of the more remote and inaccessible parts of the Sierra. Instead, it lies close to the middle of the range and in the very area over which the bulk of the Argonauts crossed during the 1840's and 1850's. Only a few miles to its north lay the historic Donner Trail, a route that had seen a heavy traffic since the beginnings of the rush and earlier, and but a little distance to its south was a second much-traveled route over the mountains, that via Carson Pass.

In point of fact, the thousands of emigrants who made their way over one or another of these trails passed within an easy half-day's journey of the lake as they followed up the course of the Truckee River to the north or the Carson to the south. Yet if any considerable number of them visited the spot during the gold rush days they left no record of the fact. This last, however, is not so strange as might at first sight appear. For on their westward crossings, the intervening ridges and tall pine forests effectually hid the lake from view. Moreover, the early overland parties were far too eager to scale this final barrier that lay between them and the gold fields to waste time exploring the country adjacent to the trails.

The consequence was that although, as we have seen, Captain John C. Frémont as early as 1844 got a distant view of the lake from the top of a peak near Carson Pass, it remained for more than a decade and a half thereafter but little known to the world at large. To be sure, from 1850 onward, it was visited at intervals by certain far-ranging prospectors who hoped to locate new diggings on the steep eastern flank of the range. One of the earliest of these was William M. Stewart, later a United States Senator from Nevada. In his reminiscences, published in 1908, Stewart tells of crossing the divide from the Grass Valley district in the summer of 1850 and spending several days on the shores of the lake.

He was followed the next spring by a party from Hangtown, who, having been taken in by one of the then-current stories of fabulous gold lakes in the back country, headed to the northeast and, after a difficult crossing of the snow-covered summit, descended to its shores. There the group met up with a band of Indians, to whom they exhibited samples of gold they had brought with them, indicating by signs their wish to be shown where more of the metal might be found. However, the Indians stared at the shining particles without showing any sign of recognition and the disappointed whites, after some half-hearted prospecting in the vicinity, headed back over the mountains.

During the winter of 1852, an expedition of a different sort reached the lake, one that resulted in bestowing on it a name it was to bear for some years — that is, Lake Bigler. The circumstances were as follows:

Word having reached Sacramento that a group of emigrants had strayed from their trail to the shores of the lake and had become snowbound there, a party of volunteers was assembled and set off to their rescue, the state's newly elected Governor, John Bigler, riding at the head of the caravan. When, having accomplished their mission, the group was on its way back to the capital city, the citizens of Placerville — ex-Hangtown — tendered its members a banquet, and during the speech-making that followed, the proposal was made that Lake Bonpland, Frémont's name for the spot, be discarded — Bonpland being a foreigner of whom few Californians had heard, besides being a name hard to pronounce — and that of the expedition's leader be substituted. This suggestion was accepted with enthusiasm, with the result that the pretty sheet of water became Lake Bigler and so remained for the better part of a decade.

The change was, however, by no means universally applauded, some dissenters charging that the rechristening had been no more than a political trick designed to glorify the current occupant of the governor's chair, while others took the stand that a locale of so much natural beauty deserved a more euphonious designation.

As time passed this question of what name should be applied to the lake became an increasingly lively one. The argument reached its climax in the mid-1860's, for Bigler, a Democrat, had earlier made no secret of the fact that his sympathies were with the South in the fast-developing crisis over the slavery question, and he had been suspected of plotting to deliver California to the Confederacy should war ensue. Moreover, it was rumored in some quarters that the governor was overfond of the bottle.

Something of the bitterness engendered by all this is reflected in this comment by the historian Bancroft:

> The name and naming of Lake Tahoe have first and last caused no little discussion. In his report of 1845–6 Frémont called this sheet Mountain Lake, but on his map of 1848 he lays it down as Lake Bonpland. There were those who sought to do John Bigler further honor than making him governor of California, by setting on foot the name Lake Bigler. Nothing could have been in worse taste . . . than in applying to a liquid so beautifully clear and cool the name of one who so detested water. A legislature might make the name legal, but no statute-book could render the proceeding respectable.

But although by far the greater number of the Californians were in favor of discarding Bigler as a name for the lake, there was no such unanimity when it came to choosing a successor. The story is told that when, early in 1862, a San Francisco publishing firm was about to issue a new map of the state, a sketch of the proposed map was shown to two local authorities, Henry De Groot and John S. Hittell. When Hittell called attention to the fact that the lake bore no name, its compiler, William H. Knight, stated that the omission of Bigler's name had been intentional and invited the pair to suggest an appropriate substitute.

De Groot, who was regarded as something of an authority on the Indian place-names of the Sierra area, came up with "Tahoe," which he maintained was a word used by the Washoe tribe and meant "water in a high place." This seemed to the others a singularly melodious and fitting designation for the spot — the lake's surface being more than 6000 feet above sea level — and it was accordingly entered on the drawing, thereby giving it a degree of official approval, for the map was being published with the endorsement of the General Land Office.

This, however, by no means ended the matter. No sooner had the map been issued when objections began to be heard from many quarters, mostly on the ground that De Groot had been in error in claiming that the word was known to the Indians of the region. One stated that if Tahoe was an Indian name — which he doubted — "it must be an importation from the lingo of an extinct tribe in Massachusetts or some other Eastern state." Even Mark Twain, who, because of his brief visit to the spot in the early 1860's, looked on himself as an authority on all things pertaining to the lake, presently got into the act, writing in 1869:

> People say that Tahoe means "Silver Lake" — "Limpid Water" — "Falling Leaf." Bosh! It means grasshopper soup,

the favorite soup of the Digger tribe — and of the Piutes as well.

As time passed, however, these outbursts were heard less frequently; the new name gradually came into general use and its former designations of Bonpland and Bigler passed into the limbo of forgotten things.

Advice to Skeletons

Tahoe's deep-blue waters, together with its picturesque setting, made a lasting impression on Twain — as on countless other visitors from his day down to the present.

Having arrived at Carson City in the summer of 1861 as private secretary to his brother Orion, who had been appointed Secretary of the newly formed Nevada Territory, and having, as he stated, found his office a sinecure with "nothing to do and no salary," time hung heavily on Twain's hands. Accordingly, in August of that year he and a companion, after listening to tales of the attractions of the lake, decided to go out and view these for themselves.

Since they had been told that the trip was a short and easy one, they made no very extensive preparations for the journey; in Twain's story they merely "strapped a couple of blankets on our shoulders and took an axe apiece" and set off. The axes were to be used to build themselves a shelter, for they planned to combine business with pleasure by staking out claims to some of the public woodlands on the lake's shore.

"We were told that the distance was eleven miles," he relates in *Roughing It*.

We tramped a long time on level ground, and then toiled laboriously up a mountain about a thousand miles high and looked over. No lake there. We descended on the other side, crossed the valley and toiled up another mountain three or four thousand miles high, apparently, and looked over again. No lake yet. We sat down, tired and perspiring, and hired a couple of Chinese to curse the people who had beguiled us. Thus refreshed, we resumed the march with renewed vigor and determination. We plodded on, two or three hours longer, and at last the lake burst upon us — a noble sheet of blue water lifted six thousand three hundred feet above the level of the sea, and walled in by a rim of snowclad mountain peaks that towered aloft full three thousand feet higher still! It was a vast oval, and one would have to use up eighty or a hundred good miles in traveling around it. As it lay there with the shadows of the mountains brilliantly photographed upon its still surface I thought it must surely be the fairest picture the whole earth affords!

Having located a skiff hidden in the bushes on the shore by friends in town, the pair set off across the lake, with his companion at the oars and Twain seated comfortably in the stern — "not," he explained, "because I mind exertion myself, but because it makes me sick to ride backwards." Arriving on the far shore, "very tired and wolfishly hungry," Twain sat down on a convenient boulder and "superintended" while his partner built a fire and prepared their supper. "Many a man who had gone through what I had," he commented, "would have wanted to rest." Refreshed by a meal of hot bread, fried bacon, and black coffee, the hardworking Twain waxed poetic, describing the beauty and serenity of the scene in these words: "As the darkness closed down and the stars came out and spangled the great mirror with jewels, we smoked meditatively in the solemn hush and forgot our troubles and our pains."

After spending a night rolled in their blankets on the sandy shore and awakening in the morning completely refreshed and free of all aches, Twain was convinced that the mountain air possessed remarkable curative qualities. "Three months of camp life on Lake Tahoe," he wrote, "would restore an Egyptian mummy to his pristine vigor." After adding cautiously that "I do not mean the oldest and driest mummies, of course, but the fresher ones," he went on:

> The air up here in the clouds is very pure and fine, bracing and delicious. And why shouldn't it be? — it is the same the angels breathe. I think that hardly any amount of fatigue can be gathered together that a man cannot sleep off in one night in the sand by its side. Not under a roof, but under the sky; it seldom or never rains there in the summer time. I know a man who went there to die. But he made a failure of it. He was a skeleton when he came, and could barely stand. He had no appetite, and did nothing but read tracts and reflect on the future. Three months later he was sleeping out of doors regularly, eating all he could hold, three times a day, and chasing game over mountains three thousand feet high for recreation. And he was a skeleton no longer, but weighed part of a ton . . . I confidently commend his experience to other skeletons.

Washing Made Easy

Another Sierran lake visited by Twain during his stay at Carson City is Mono, which lies some sixty miles to the southeast of Tahoe. He was, however, far from impressed by the natural beauties of the spot, terming it a "solemn, silent, sailless sea" set in the midst of a "lifeless, treeless, hideous desert."

Nonetheless he and his companion — this time a Mr. Higbie — presently discovered that the lake, the waters of which are so heavily impregnated with salt that almost no marine life exists in its depths, had qualities that in a measure compensated for its lack of picturesque features; namely, that its alkaline properties made the task of washing clothes preposterously easy. It was, he stated, necessary only to dip the most disreputable looking garment into the lake, swish it about a bit, and on wringing it out it would be "as clean as if it had been through the ablest of washerwomen's hands." Having made that welcome discovery, the pair — who were ever on the lookout for laborsaving devices, even in the wilderness — "tied the week's washing astern of our boat, sailed for a quarter of a mile, and the job was complete."

But while the caustic qualities of Mono's waters were gratifying to Twain and Higbie, they were considerably less so to a third member of the party, a stray dog that had attached himself to the travelers and which one day plunged into the lake with the aim of ridding himself of swarms of bothersome flies. This was, commented Twain, lamentably bad judgment on the dog's part, for the animal had a great many bruises, abrasions, and scratches on his hide, and in that state "it would have been just as comfortable to jump into a fire." For on coming in contact with the water all his raw spots began stinging simultaneously and he regained the shore with all possible speed. Although he was, according to Twain, "not a demonstrative dog, as a general thing, but rather of a grave and serious turn of mind," his behavior during the next few minutes was completely out of character. He raced about in ever-widening circles, turned back-ward and forward somersaults, barking loudly all the while, then disappeared over the nearest mountain at a speed that the onlookers estimated to be in the neighborhood of 250 miles an hour.

One day Twain and Higbie rowed out to the center of the lake — the dog prudently remaining behind — and explored one of the several islands on its surface, Higbie doing the rowing while Twain sat in the stern and charted their course. The expedition proved to be something less than the pleas-ure jaunt they had anticipated. The day was extremely hot and their destination more distant than it had appeared from shore. Moreover, on reaching the island — a barren cone of volcanic ash and pumice stone — they found the water in the canteens they had brought with them too warm to be drunk with pleasure and they accordingly poured it out and set off for the spring they had been told was to be found there. But the spring — if it existed at all — proved highly elusive, for the pair, by then possessed of monumental thirst, scrambled over several square miles of the island's surface without finding any trace of it.

"Finally," Twain's account continues, "we noticed that the wind had risen, and we forgot our thirst in a solicitude of greater importance; for, the lake being quiet, we had not taken pains about securing the boat." They hurried back to their landing place, only to find that the boat had pushed off — "it was drifting along, leisurely, about fifty yards from shore, tossing in a foamy sea." Some gloomy moments ensued while they pictured themselves marooned on the island, with-out food or water, and with little chance of rescue since their boat was the only one on the lake.

Presently, however, it was observed that the little craft,

driven by the wind, was moving parallel with the shore, and that if it continued on the same course it would pass close to the end of a small promontory some distance ahead. Higbie, urged on by Mark, hastened to the spot and stationed himself on the very tip of the headland. With mounting suspense the pair watched the tantalizingly slow progress of the boat, unable to decide whether or not it would pass within reach. As it turned out, the craft cleared the point by several yards, and when the distance between boat and shore began to widen again and Higbie still made no move, Twain confessed that his heart stood still. Then he added: "But when he gave a great spring . . . and lit fairly in the stern, I discharged a war-whoop that woke the solitudes!" A long, hard pull back to camp followed, with Higbie again at the oars and Twain offering advice and encouragement, all the while expecting their little craft to be capsized by the storm-lashed waters; in which case, observed Mark, "in less than five minutes we would have a hundred gallons of soapsuds in us and be eaten up so quickly that we could not even be present at our own inquest."

They were, however, spared that fate. The boat remained right side up until they were close enough to wade ashore before it was finally overturned. The adventurers, notwithstanding severe pain resulting from the caustic waters coming in contact with their numerous bruises, scratches, and blistered hands, ate and drank with gusto and promptly fell into an exhausted sleep.

One further incident of their stay at the lake so impressed Twain that he recalled it ten years later. This was the fact that although the place was well over a hundred miles from the ocean, great flocks of seagulls flew there each season to lay their eggs and raise their young. This circumstance caused him to reflect in this fashion on what he called "nature's wisdom":

> The islands in the lake being merely huge masses of lava, coated over with ashes and pumice-stone, and utterly innocent of vegetation or anything that would burn; and the sea-gulls' eggs being entirely useless to anybody unless they be cooked, Nature has provided an unfailing spring of boiling water on the largest island, and you can put your eggs in there, and in four minutes you can boil them as hard as any statement I have made during the past fifteen years. Within ten feet of the boiling spring is a spring of pure cold water, sweet and wholesome. So, on that island you get your board and washing free of charge — and if Nature had gone further and furnished a nice American hotel clerk who was crusty and disobliging, and didn't know anything about the time-tables, or the railroad routes — or — anything — and was proud of it — I would not wish for a more desirable boarding-house.

R. K. Culcord, who in the 1890's served several terms as governor of Nevada, was an early-day resident of the Mono area and a frequent visitor to the lake. In a reminiscence written many years later he recalled that its waters — "as strong as a whiskey cocktail in a country hotel" — supported no life save millions of tiny insects the names of which were unknown to him but which he described as "about the same color and just as useful as a rusty nail." Each season, he continued, great flocks of wild ducks flew in from the west and fed on them, and from time to time newcomers to the district would hasten down to the shore and shoot a number of the plump birds. It was an experiment they rarely tried a second time. For, stated Culcord, "after these birds have feasted on that kind of food for a couple of weeks, the aroma rising from them while being roasted is not that of a camomile bed." Later, recalled this authority, the water of Mono's "Little Dead Sea" was found to be an excellent preservative of wood, and cross-ties and other timbers used in building a railroad into the area in the early 1880's were floated on the lake's surface for several weeks before being put to use, with the result that more than thirty years later they were found to be as sound as the day they were laid.

New Times, New Methods

During the early months of the gold rush, mining in the Sierra creekbeds was almost entirely a hand operation, the prospectors working their claims with no other tools than picks, shovels, and shallow metal pans. Soon, however, more formal equipment came into use in the form of homemade rockers and sluiceboxes, and by these means the bulk of the metal in the surface workings was gathered in.

It was not long, however, before miners in the foothill camps and higher on the range adopted more elaborate methods. One of the first of these was the building of dams across the mountain streams by which their waters were diverted from their normal channels and the gold extracted from the gravel of their exposed beds. Such projects were often of considerable magnitude, and to carry them through groups of miners joined forces, frequently devoting weeks to building the stone or wooden barriers and attendant dikes and ditches.

Such enterprises were commonly undertaken in the late summer or fall, when the streams were at their lowest levels, and they had to be carried through with all possible speed, for with the coming of the winter rains floods would pour down the canyons and sweep their dams away. Works of that type were ever a gamble, with the miners risking long periods of hard work in the hope that the storms would hold off long enough to permit them to scrape the exposed sections of the streams down to bedrock. Sometimes these ventures paid off handsomely, with the lucky ones finding rich pockets of the metal that yielded them small fortunes. Just as often, however, unseasonable rainstorms fell higher in the hills, transforming the placid streams into roaring torrents and washing away the labor of weeks.

A variety of other engineering projects, some quite extensive, were carried through during the 1850's and later. One was the building of flumes and ditches to convey water to the dry diggings so their gold could be washed out in sluice-boxes, commonly called Long Toms. Such operations, like those of damming the mountain streams, were usually too extensive to be carried out by individuals or small groups; accordingly, considerable numbers of claim-holders banded together, each contributing his labor to the venture.

Among the earliest of such ditches was one dug in the spring of 1850 in present Nevada County, which carried water from Mosquito Creek to diggings at Old Coyote Hill, a distance of a mile and a half. Many others followed until, by the close of the next decade, more than 300 were in operation in the gold country, their total length running into thousands of miles. Perhaps the more ambitious of these was one built in the Yuba River area in 1859 by the Eureka Lake Ditch Company, one lengthy section of which — a flume over a deep gorge called Cherry Hill Gap — was widely heralded on its completion as an engineering feat of the first importance.

Moreover, this work seems to have deserved the encomiums heaped upon it, for the trestle supporting the six-foot-wide aqueduct rose to a height of 125 feet from the canyon's floor, and its other dimensions were in proportion. "The timbers employed in its construction," stated the *Hydraulic Press*, published at nearby San Juan, "were all hewed from pines growing directly on or near the spot, and the uprights are all single pieces. It is not probable that unspliced timbers 125 feet long, 16 inches square at one end and tapering to 9 inches at the other, could be procured anywhere else . . . yet the mountain ridges of California are crowded with trees that would yield even larger timbers." This account went on to record that the pairs of lofty uprights had a spread of thirty feet on the ground, narrowing to eight feet at the top, and that "the entire structure, as one views it from a short distance, looks massive yet graceful, and as though it could not be overturned by anything less . . . than a hurricane."

The spectacular Cherry Gap crossing was, however, only a small section of the Eureka Lake Ditch, which carried a large volume of water from lakes high in the Sierra to a score or more of foothill mines, the distance covered being some thirty miles and the cost $600,000.

This and many other elaborate water systems were made necessary by the fact that, in the latter 1850's, the industry entered a new phase: that of hydraulic mining. By that method, jets of water under high pressure were played on the claims, washing the debris down into a system of sluices where the gold was extracted. Because such operations not only called for an abundant supply of water but required that it be delivered with sufficient force to disintegrate the hillsides against which it was directed, new techniques had to be devised by the mine owners.

One such project that attracted wide attention in the technical journals of the day was the Cherokee Siphon on the North Fork of the Feather River, built in 1870. It was said to have been the first use of iron pipe of large size — this one was thirty inches in diameter — under extremely high pressures. In this enterprise, instead of conveying the water across an intervening canyon by means of a flume, an inverted siphon was used, which dipped down to the bottom — a drop of some 800 feet — and was forced up to the far side. Because the pressure put a severe strain on the lower sections of the pipe, there was much concern when the time arrived to turn the water into the conduit.

> It was calculated [stated a writer in the *Butte Record* for December 24, 1870] that it would take four hours to fill the pipe so that it would commence to discharge, and it might take much less time to cause it to break. A period of tense waiting followed, the faces of those in charge plainly revealing their anxiety. Then at last from its mouth pours a stream which takes its way into the ditch, around the graceful curve, and rushes down the hillside into the reservoirs commanding the mines of Cherokee. Men shout with gladness, and, jumping into the receiver, drink from the mouth of the pipe . . .

Further evidence exists that mine owners of the area were quick to adopt the newest technical advances of the time. Because some of the systems of flumes and ditches were many miles in length, and because prompt means of communication between various points along their routes were necessary for their proper operation, the owners were not slow to grasp the significance of Alexander Graham Bell's recent invention, which had been demonstrated at Philadelphia's Centennial Exposition in 1876.

Accordingly, two years later, several large mining companies operating in the vicinity of North San Juan joined forces and built what is generally credited with being the world's first long-distance telephone line. The wires, strung at a cost of six thousand dollars, had a total length of sixty miles, with twenty-two instruments spaced at intervals along the ditch from its outlet in the foothills to the storage dam well up toward the source of the Middle Fork of the Yuba. It is said that the line, which remained in operation for more than two decades, paid its cost many times over by making it possible to regulate the flow of water at all times, thereby preventing its wasteful and inefficient use.

Once the value of this pioneer line had been demonstrated, numerous others were put into operation throughout the northern mines. Thus by the end of the 1870's — and long before the new device had come to be widely adopted in other parts of the country — a network of wires had been strung on the high ridges and deep canyons of the area and were in daily use.

Hydraulic mining, which had been primarily responsible for the building of numerous dams, flumes, siphons, and like projects, flourished for less than three decades, then came to an abrupt and permanent end. For almost from the beginning determined efforts had been made to have the lawmakers at Sacramento pass legislation prohibiting the practice, on the ground that the vast amount of debris washed into the mountain streams and carried down into the central valley was not only hampering water transportation on the Sacramento and San Joaquin rivers but was causing them to overflow their banks and ruin wide areas of fertile agricultural land.

By the early 1880's this long-drawn-out controversy between the mine owners and the agriculturists had reached a stage that bordered on open warfare. On a number of occasions the embattled farmers were suspected of resorting to direct action to gain their ends. These were said to include the destruction of company flumes and ditches and, on June 18, 1883, the blowing up of one of the high Sierra dams, releasing a flood of water that caused widespread destruction on its course down to the lowlands.

Further violence was averted, however, by the passage in 1883 of a law drastically limiting hydraulic operations, and by a court decision the following year upholding the validity of the legislation. The statute prohibited miners from allowing the rubble washed down from the hillsides to flow into the streams. Other methods of disposing of the debris being impractical in most instances, the consequence was that all but a few of the owners were forced to suspend operations. In certain instances, however, something was salvaged from the wreck. For while many of the systems of reservoirs, dams, and ditches were abandoned, others were converted to a new use: that of carrying water to the parched lands on the floor of the central valley. Thus they became forerunners of the great irrigation projects developed during the next several decades.

VII

A Gallery of Bad Men

Black Bart, Road Agent Par Excellence

*F*ROM THE DAYS of the gold rush down to the turn of the century, rare indeed was the Californian who did not take a close interest in the doings of the state's bumper crop of outlaws. The reason for this is fairly obvious, for by and large the Argonauts were themselves an adventurous lot — else they would hardly have embarked on so hairbrained an enterprise — and although the passing of the years dampened their youthful ardor for excitement, tales of the daring of the hooded knights of the road served to stir in them the embers of their own reckless pasts.

Thus for more than fifty years there was hardly a time when the residents, ably abetted by the area's newspapers, were not busy at the congenial task of making folk heroes of one or another of the highwaymen then at large within the confines of the state. The great majority of these, having enjoyed a few days or weeks of notoriety and come to their just rewards — usually at the end of a rope — have long since been forgotten. A select few, however, are still remembered. The earliest of these was Joaquin Murieta, a half-legendary Sonoran youth who, with his hard-riding band of

confederates, ranged the length of the Mother Lode, leaving
behind a trail of robbery, pillage, and bloodshed so impressive that an incurably sentimental age dubbed him "the
Robin Hood of Eldorado."

In general, the early-day road agents preferred to confine
their attention to stages that were carrying passengers, for
in such cases the drivers and express company messengers
were reluctant to engage in gun duels.

Aware of this liking for well-filled vehicles on the part of
the highwaymen, George Hackett, one of the most courageous of the Wells Fargo messengers, made a point whenever
large amounts of specie or gold dust were to be transported,
of stowing the box in a stage on which only himself and the
driver were riding.

On more than one occasion this strategy paid off. In the
summer of 1879, a stage plying between Forbestown and
Marysville was held up, the two robbers making off with
some six hundred dollars in gold dust and an undetermined
amount of coin. On the following day the pair struck again,
stopping a coach on the way from Forest City to Marysville.
This time, however, Hackett was in the box beside the driver,
and there were no passengers.

The messenger had his shotgun to his shoulder the moment the masked men appeared, and the latter, nonplussed
at this prompt show of opposition, turned and fled back into
the roadside bushes. Hackett leaped from the stage and set
off in pursuit. After proceeding some distance he came on
the spot where the pair had camped the night before. There
he found not only a pile of their clothing but a satchel containing the gold dust and coins taken the day before. Moreover, on going through the clothing, he gathered in an additional two hundred and fifty-six dollars.

Having carried the recovered loot back to the road and sent the stage on its way, Hackett returned to the camp and, concealing himself in the nearby bushes, awaited further developments. When one of the pair presently appeared to recover their property, the messenger stepped forth, gun in hand, slipped handcuffs on the bandit, and marched him to the nearest jail. The culprit got fifteen years; his more cautious confederate escaped.

Another of Hackett's feats is recorded in the Wells Fargo Company's bulky file dealing with that firm's long battle with the state's road agents. In July, 1882, some three years after his encounter with the frustrated pair on the Forbestown-Marysville run, the messenger was again conveying a well-stocked treasure box, this time on a stage out of La Porte, high in the Sierra. When, on the rise of a hill a short distance from that town, a lone man, masked and armed, stepped into the roadway ahead, Hackett's shotgun went into action, the charge, states the report, "grazing his head." The man raised his own weapon but before he could use it the messenger fired another barrel, knocking the gun from the bandit's hands. Thereupon the robber turned and scurried back into the woods, leaving behind his hat and mask. He was not found there and it was not until some time later that his identity became known. Late the following year, when an elusive operator known as Black Bart — whose exploits are recorded later in this chapter — was captured, he provided the authorities with a complete list of his robberies. Then it was revealed that he had been the lone bandit on the La Porte road that day. The affair stood out clearly in Bart's memory: it had been the one failure in all his twenty-eight attempts.

While banditry of many sorts was far from uncommon

during the first years of the gold rush, it was not until the mid-1850's that stage robbing came into its own. The first practitioner of that art to gain wide renown was one Tom Bell. Bell was a physician who, having served with distinction in the Mexican War, joined the migration to California. But, failing to find a fortune in the diggings, he took to gambling and drinking and ended by joining a gang of cattle rustlers operating in the northern mines.

After being briefly jailed on a horse-stealing charge, Bell returned to the mountains and began laying the foundations of his career as a road agent. Although he and his gang continued to keep their hands in by petty thievery, stopping teamsters or lone wayfarers and relieving them of their valuables, ransacking inns or isolated farmhouses and the like, Bell all the while was preparing to embrace the more dignified and lucrative calling of stage robbery.

Bell's first — and last — big test came one day in the summer of 1856 when the down-stage out of Camptonville, on the North Fork of the Yuba, was set on, at a point in the foothills only a few hours' travel from its destination, Marysville. The stage bore not only a full load of passengers, eight in all, two of whom were women, but on this trip it carried an armed messenger as well. The reason for the latter's presence was that Camptonville's leading dealer in gold dust had chosen that day to ship recent purchases down to Marysville; the horde, said to have a value of close to a hundred thousand dollars, was in a strongbox under the driver's seat.

Tom Bell and his confederates, numbering six in all, met with a decidedly warm reception. As the first three members of the gang — which had divided into two parts — appeared in the roadway ahead, the messenger, Bill Dobson, brought his gun into action. The bandits promptly returned the fire and for the next few seconds the air was full of flying lead, more than forty shots being exchanged. The resulting carnage was considerable. One of the two women passengers was killed, the other was shot in the leg, and the driver, John Gaer, received a wound in the arm.

But the casualties were not all on the side of the attacked. One of Dobson's slugs struck the horse on which the gang's leader was mounted, throwing Bell to the ground, whereupon he and his two companions fled into the bushes at the roadside. Then, the stage having hastily got under way again, the other three bandits — who had been thrown off their timing by pausing to rob a lone horseman — appeared on the scene, but too late to do more than send a fusillade after the fast-disappearing vehicle.

Bell and several of his companions, having been recognized, were soon rounded up, the leader being apprehended as a result of information supplied by one of his confederates. Bell was granted a brief reprieve by his captors to permit him to write a farewell letter; then a noose was slipped over his head and he was unceremoniously hoisted to the branch of a nearby sycamore.

By the end of the first quarter-century after California's entry into the Union, there were many who believed that the era of the state's road agents had at length drawn to a close. That belief, however, was rudely shattered by the appearance on the scene of the highly picturesque individual known as Black Bart. For the most part, Black Bart operated in the lowlands, making only occasional forays into the higher reaches of the Sierra. There was a sound reason for this, for by the time he took up his calling — in the late 1870's — the mining boom had long since passed its crest;

all but a few of the Mother Lode settlements had already taken on the aspect of ghost towns.

Black Bart — who, whatever his other shortcomings, was no fool — recognized that the stages plying between these down-at-the-heel mountain communities were unlikely to be carrying any considerable amount of treasure. Accordingly he devoted a major part of his time and talents to holding up those operating between more prosperous towns.

It appears, however, that he did not at once reach that conclusion. For quite early in his career of crime — on July 25, 1878 — at a spot high in the American River Canyon he stopped a Quincy-Oroville stage, making off with some three hundred and eighty dollars in coin from the express box, together with a diamond ring and silver watch, the two last-named having been contributed by passengers. This, so far as known, was only his second offense — the first having been the robbery of a stage traveling between two lumbering towns in the Coast Ranges north of San Francisco; but already he had attained a renown overshadowing that of nearly all the state's earlier practitioners of the art.

For Black Bart had introduced into that prosaic and tradition-bound profession a novelty that had at once captured the attention of the populace. On each occasion, after relieving the driver of his mailbags and express box, he had left behind a bit of handwritten doggerel, to which he had signed not only the name Black Bart but below it the words: "The PO8." The first of these read thus:

> I've labored long and hard for bread,
> For honor and for riches,
> But on my corns too long you've trod
> You fair-haired sons of bitches.

This was enough of a novelty to raise his first exploit well above the common run of stage hold-ups, and when on his next appearance he left behind a second, and longer, verse, his place in the folklore of the West was secure. This doggerel ran as follows:

> Here I lay me down to sleep
> To wait the coming morrow,
> Perhaps success, perhaps defeat,
> And everlasting sorrow.
> Let come what will I'll try it on,
> My condition can't be worse;
> And if there's money in that box
> 'Tis munney in my purse!

There was, of course, no question in the minds of the authorities that the two jobs — although there was an interval of some eleven months between them — were the work of the same man. The handwriting of the "poetry" — to say nothing of its quality — was in itself proof of that, but in addition there were other points of similarity. In both cases the robber had appeared at the roadside clad in a long linen duster, with a flour sack — into which eye-holes had been cut — over his head, and in a deep, authoritative voice had directed the driver to "Throw down the box," the shotgun at his shoulder lending urgency to the command. Moreover, in neither case had he made a thorough search of the passengers, confining his chief attention to the express boxes and mail pouches, which he hastily looted after sending the stages on their way, taking only coin and other easily negotiable objects and leaving the rest behind.

At first it was assumed that the verse-writing bandit would not remain long at large, and that belief was strengthened when rewards totaling eight hundred dollars were posted for his capture and conviction, the sum being made up of three hundred dollars put up by the state of California, a like amount by the Wells Fargo Express Company, and two hundred dollars by the Post Office Department.

Black Bart, however, proved far more elusive than anyone had anticipated. Such clues to his identity as turned up were one by one run down; all, as the detective-story writers say, ran up against a blank wall. Meanwhile he continued his lucrative, one-man campaign, at some periods pulling as many as half-a-dozen jobs in the course of a single week, at others lying low for as long as six months. In all, he is credited with having during the next six years held up no less than twenty-seven stages, from each of which he escaped scot-free — but not always obtaining anything of value for his trouble — and without having once fired his gun.

Long before that time he had captured the imagination of many thousands all over the West Coast. Moreover, most of these looked on his exploits with open approval — for after all it was not the common people who were the losers by his machinations, but the plutocratic Wells Fargo Company — and the newspapers co-operated by printing reams of copy describing his achievements and theorizing as to his identity.

Then, in the fall of 1883, on a hillside near Copperopolis in the Sierra foothills, the by then legendary figure, complete with duster and flour-sack hood, stepped from behind a clump of bushes and leveled his gun at the driver of a Nevada Stage Company coach. It was his twenty-eighth robbery and also, as events were to prove, his last. For this time the express company, having learned its costly lesson, instead of leaving the treasure box loose had bolted it to the floor of the passenger compartment.

On discovering this, Black Bart ordered the driver to un-hitch his horses and drive them over the crest of the hill above; then he busied himself breaking open the box. This he finally accomplished, but the task took valuable time. In the interval the driver, having met up with a hunter friend armed with a rifle, crept back to the crest of the hill and took three pot-shots at the sweating bandit. None of these found its mark, but in the haste of his departure he left behind a number of highly important clues. These included a derby hat, a case that had contained binoculars, two empty flour-sacks, and a handkerchief.

It was the last-named that brought about his downfall. For when the law officers and a Wells Fargo detective reached the scene and scrutinized the evidence, the handkerchief was found to bear a laundry mark: the mystic symbols FXO7. It was concluded, logically enough, that in all likelihood the mark was that of a metropolitan laundry, and the search accordingly turned to San Francisco. That city at the time had close to a hundred laundries, and the task of checking them was a time-consuming operation. Something over a week later, however, the express company detective who was conducting the search struck pay-dirt. At the shop of a tobacco dealer on Bush Street — who operated a laundry agency as a sideline — the owner not only identified the marking as that of one of his customers but supplied his address.

The rest was mere routine. The handkerchief's owner was picked up, taken to the Wells Fargo office and questioned at length, then lodged in the city jail charged with having held up the Copperopolis stage. The prisoner — who was soon enmeshed in a net of highly incriminating evidence the detectives had uncovered while searching his hotel room — bore little resemblance to the dashing, romantic figure that had been building up in the public's mind over the past half-dozen years. Black Bart in the flesh proved to be a mild-mannered, dapper little man, with graying hair and drooping mustache. He was looked on by his acquaintances as a reserved but amiable mining man who, although it was his habit to keep his affairs much to himself, was known on occasion to display a very pretty wit.

In San Francisco, where he had resided for some eight years, he was known as "Charles E. Bolton," although it presently developed that his true name was Boles and that he had been born fifty-five years earlier in upstate New York. Still stoutly maintaining his innocence, he was taken to the foothill town of San Andreas, the county seat of Calaveras County where the crime had been committed. There, seeing that the jig was up, he confessed the robbery and led the officers to a hollow log in which he had hidden the major part of his swag — all in the hope that co-operation of that sort would win him a mild sentence.

This last expectation, however, failed to work out. He was committed to San Quentin for a term of six years. There he proved himself a model prisoner and on his release, in January, 1888, he returned briefly to San Francisco and then dropped from sight, this time permanently. That the little man's incarceration had not dulled his wit was, however, made clear before he vanished. For on reaching the city from San Quentin he was met at the ferry slip by a group of reporters and plied with questions. Asked if, now that he was free again, he planned to resume his old occupation of stage robbing, he replied that his law-breaking days were finally and definitely over. When this was followed by a second query as to whether or not he intended to write any more verses, the erstwhile "PO8" terminated the discussion with:

"Young man, didn't you hear me say that I would commit no more crimes?"

Latter-day Robin Hoods

At the time of Black Bart's capture one of the San Francisco journals, in a moment of optimism, referred to him as "the last of the California bandits." It was not long, however, before convincing evidence to the contrary presented itself. This was the rise — and eventual fall — of a brace of gunmen who were to take rank in the public mind with Murieta and the ineffable Bart. The names of these latter-day Robin Hoods were Chris Evans and John Sontag.

In order to account for the place this pair came to hold in the esteem of a great many Californians of their day, some background is necessary. During the period in which they operated — the late 1880's and early 1890's — the Concord coaches of the pioneers had, in all save the more remote corners of the state, been supplanted by the Iron Horse. For a quarter-century the promotion and building of railroads had been a major industry; and, to a man, the inhabitants of farms and towns and villages along their routes had looked to their coming as ushering in an economic millennium. By the mid 1880's, however, that belief had been severely shaken. This was particularly true in the San Joaquin Valley, where in the first year of that decade a longstanding feud between the Southern Pacific and a group of farmers, over the price to be charged for railroad lands that the settlers had bought and put under cultivation, flared into open war.

This Battle of Mussel Slough, in which seven men were killed, opened a breach between the railroad and residents of the area that was a long time healing. The hard times that soon gripped the valley during the latter 1880's and early 1890's were, in the minds of many residents, laid to the greed of the corporation, which, by excessive freight rates, kickbacks to favored shippers, and other practices, was believed to be filling its own bulging coffers at the expense of the valley's farmers and merchants.

It was on this situation that, some years later, Frank Norris based his widely read novel *The Octopus*. It was, too, because of this widespread antirailroad sentiment throughout the valley that, when the company's trains there presently began to be boarded by masked men who overpowered the engine crews, dynamited the express cars, and made off with whatever coin they contained, public sympathy was firmly on the side of the unknown brigands.

The general opinion was that those responsible were local people who, like so many of their neighbors, had suffered wrongs at the hands of the railroad and had taken that means of settling old scores. Thus from the beginning conditions were favorable for the creation of a new set of folk heroes, with Robin Hood overtones, worthy successors to the romantic road agents of an earlier day.

The manner in which the robberies were conducted did much to foster the growth of that belief. The bandits conducted themselves with coolness and determination, carrying out their assignments with a speed and efficiency that indicated careful planning, and making clean getaways which for many months defeated all efforts to pick up their trails. Moreover, it soon became clear that the pair were concerned only with the contents of the express car strongboxes, and that passengers would not be molested provided they remained inside the coaches and refrained from interfering.

The robberies followed a fixed pattern and there was never much doubt that the same men were responsible for all of them.

The first of the series took place on the evening of February 22, 1889. Number 17, southbound from San Francisco, had stopped at the town of Pixley while the passengers had their supper at the station eating-house, diners having not yet been added to the company's trains on the San Francisco-Los Angeles run. As Number 17 was getting under way again, two men were seen to slip from the shadow of a water tank and swing aboard the front end of the express car. A mile or two farther on, the pair — the upper parts of their bodies concealed beneath black hoods — climbed over the wood-filled tender, jumped into the cab and, covering engineer and fireman with revolvers, ordered the train stopped at a point that had obviously been fixed in advance.

That done, they forced the engine crew to lead the way back to the express car and order the messenger to open the door. That, however, was a highly irregular proceeding and the man inside refused to comply. Thereupon the bandits brought forth a number of sticks of dynamite, lighted a short fuse, and tossed the homemade bomb under the car. The resulting explosion shattered the car's windows and extinguished its lights. The messenger, badly shaken, thereupon opened the door; while one of the robbers stood guard outside, the other climbed within and forced the messenger to unlock the Wells Fargo treasure box.

Meantime the train's unscheduled stop, followed by the heavy explosion, had aroused those in the coaches and a number of passengers hurried forward to investigate. That proved a serious error of judgment, for the highwayman standing guard outside brought his sawed-off shotgun into action against the approaching group, and with telling effect. The constable of a nearby town was seriously wounded and a second passenger received the full force of a charge of buckshot and was instantly killed. The others thereupon scurried back into the cars, and the robbers, their guns still covering the train crew, backed into a neighboring wheatfield and disappeared in the darkness.

Within a few hours a full-fledged manhunt was under way, with Wells Fargo and Southern Pacific detectives joining the sheriffs of Fresno and Tulare counties and their deputies in the pursuit. California newspapers made much of the matter — train robberies being highly newsworthy events — and for days thereafter stories of correspondents on the scene told of the unearthing of important new clues and forecast the speedy capture of the fugitives. But in spite of a two-thousand-dollar reward posted jointly by the express and railroad companies, it presently grew clear that the bandits had effectually covered their tracks. Numerous suspects were rounded up, questioned, and then released. At length it came to be recognized that the pair — with their three thousand dollars in loot — had disappeared into what the reporters called "thin air." The public's interest gradually simmered down.

It flared up again some eleven months later. On the night of January 21, 1890, the pair struck again. This time they boarded another southbound passenger train, Number 19, at Gothen, a village thirty miles north of the site of the first robbery and close to the spot where the Mussel Slough battle had been waged a decade earlier. Again the masked bandits climbed into the locomotive cab, forced the engineer to stop at a designated spot and, with the fireman, to go back and order the messenger to open the express car. Once more there were gunfire and carnage, the victim this time being an itinerant who had been riding the rods beneath one of the forward cars. On seeing the four men approaching, he had evidently thought they were intent on routing him out; accordingly, he had left his perch and started running into the darkness when one of the robbers sent a lethal charge of buckshot into his back. A second shot from the same gun caused curious passengers who had been disembarking to scramble back into the coaches.

This time it was unnecessary to dynamite the express car. The sound of gunfire and the urgings of the captive engineer combined to persuade the Wells Fargo man to unlock the door and turn over to the outlaws the substantial amount of gold coins — most estimates placed the sum at eight thousand dollars — in the strongbox. After forcing the engine crew to carry this weighty swag some distance up the track, the pair again set off across the fields. Once more they covered their trail so well that the weeks-long efforts of scores of valley police officers, Federal agents, and company sleuths failed to pick it up.

Following this lucrative Gothen raid, nothing further was heard of the outlaws for more than a year and a half. The public and the law enforcement officers alike had about concluded that the pair had abandoned their career of crime when, on the night of September 2, 1891, they had convincing proof to the contrary. This third of the series took place in the northern end of the valley, near the town of Ceres. Once again the bandits confronted the engine crew and ordered the custodian of the express car to open up. This time, however, the enterprise failed to work with its accustomed smoothness. One reason was that a veteran railroad detective chanced to be on board, and, on learning what was afoot, he had hurried forward, shooting as he ran. The bandits returned his fire and, after several exchanges, the detective fell, seriously injured from buckshot wounds in his head and neck.

Meanwhile the express messenger had defied orders to unlock the door, and the outlaws had tossed a bomb through a window, which on exploding tore a sizable hole in the car's side. At this juncture the train's conductor, too, entered the fray, opening fire from farther down the train; thereupon the bandits, without entering the wrecked car, turned and fled into the darkness, this time empty-handed.

Once again swarms of detectives, sheriffs, deputies, Federal agents — and reporters — converged on the scene, and again, after weeks of intensive effort, no clues of value turned up. Thus, after nearly three years, the identity of the bandits remained as deep a mystery as it had been in the beginning. In the meantime, many residents of the valley — and elsewhere throughout the west — were openly expressing their admiration of the pair, and heaping ridicule on their would-be captors.

A Leisurely Getaway

The next — and last — of the series took place on the night of August 4, 1892. Again the train was Number 17, the Southern Pacific's night express, southbound from San Francisco to Los Angeles. It was stopped near Collis, a village some nine miles north of Fresno, and the by then familiar drama was re-enacted. While the occupants of the coaches behind slept, the express car was bombed and the messenger, injured by the blast, handed over "three large sacks" containing coins of an estimated value of five thousand dollars. The loot would have been larger except that the express company, having grown tired of its losses, had installed time-locks on the car safes which prevented their being opened en route. Before they fled, the bandits disabled the locomotive by exploding a stick of dynamite beneath its drivers.

Again the man hunt got under way, and for a time it appeared that the wily pair had once more made a clean getaway. But not for long. The officers, scouring the countryside, presently came on a highly promising clue. At dusk on the night of the robbery a passerby had observed a buggy and team of horses in a shed on the grounds of a rural school a mile or two from the scene of the holdup. On examining the horses' hoofprints, it was discovered that one of the animals had lost a part of the shoe on its left hind foot. Within a few hours a check of adjacent towns disclosed that the horse was one of a team belonging to a Visalia livery stable. Further inquiry brought out that the team had been rented several days earlier by one George Sontag, and that, on the morning following the robbery, it had been returned by Sontag's elder brother John and another Visalia resident named Chris Evans.

That was the first break in the case, but others followed rapidly. Probing into the behavior and movements of George Sontag, it was learned that that young man had been much in evidence about Visalia since the robbery, which he claimed to have witnessed at first hand. His story was that he had been visiting in San Francisco and was returning on Number 17 when the holdup occurred; that he had continued on to Fresno when the damaged locomotive was repaired and then had taken a local train to Visalia, which was on a branch line. Questioning of the livery stable owner, however, brought out that when young Sontag had rented the team he had stated that he planned to drive to Simpson Flat, high in the mountains east of Visalia, and there pick up his brother John and Chris Evans, who were supposedly working a mining claim they owned there. It soon developed, however, that this announced plan had not been carried out. Instead, the team George Sontag had rented at Visalia had been put up that night at Fresno by John Sontag and Evans, and the same pair had taken it out again the next morning; that is, on the morning of the robbery.

The result was that two law officers, railroad detective William Smith, and George Witty, deputy sheriff of Tulare County, drove out to the Evans cottage on the edge of Visalia where, so they later stated, they planned to question Evans and John Sontag concerning their whereabouts on the night of the holdup. If such was their intention they had no opportunity to carry it out. Having tied their horse outside the gate, they knocked on the door and were admitted by fifteen-year-old Eva Evans, the eldest of six Evans children. They asked for John Sontag, and were told by the girl that he was not there. Evans, who had been chopping wood in the back yard, had in the meantime been told of the visitors and entered the house through a back door. He stepped into the front room just as the railroad detective, Smith, revolver in hand, strode over and thrust aside a curtain screening an alcove of the room. Standing inside was John Sontag, a sawed-off shotgun held in readiness. At that moment the other two men — Evans and Witty — drew their revolvers. A brief running battle ensued as the officers beat a hasty retreat, returning the fire of Evans and Sontag.

No fatalities resulted from this sudden eruption of gunfire, although both Smith and Witty received wounds. But the day was not to end without a second and more deadly encounter. Having decided to head for the rugged mountain country to the east — which both men knew well — Evans and Sontag made methodical preparations for the journey. Taking possession of the buggy left behind by the officers and loading into it a small arsenal of weapons, they drove to a farmhouse on a little-frequented country road. There they bought barley for the horses, turned the team out to pasture, and themselves lay down in a nearby haystack and waited for nightfall before venturing forth again. In the evening they drove back to the Evans house, to pick up there such food and clothing as they felt would be needed during their stay in the mountains. The fugitives put up the stolen team in the Evans barn and having, as Evans later recalled, "decided to go up town and hear the news," walked into the center of Visalia. "There seemed to be a lot of excitement around the hotels and saloons," he continued, "and we discussed the situation with a lot of our friends. About midnight we went back to the house and had lunch."

Around one o'clock in the morning this singularly deliberate pair decided that they might as well be on their way. They went out to the barn, hitched the horses to the buggy and were about to drive off when they were hailed by a dimly seen figure standing in the yard, some thirty yards distant. "Who's there?" the stranger shouted. Sontag replied, directing the other to approach and identify himself. Receiving no reply, Sontag asked: "Have you got a gun?" The answer was four rapid flashes in the darkness, two from a shotgun followed by two from a revolver.

"The first shot hit the nigh horse," according to Evans in

his account of the fracas, "which fell at once, and the next moment the off horse staggered over on top of it. . . . I was entangled by the struggling horses, but managing to free myself I joined Sontag and we emptied our shotguns into the man." The latter fell to the ground and Evans, shouting to his partner, "We've got him!" hurried toward the spot. The shooting, however, was not yet over. As Evans drew near, the prone man raised himself on an elbow and at point-blank range fired the remaining shots from his revolver. They failed to reach their mark and an instant later the battle was over. "We," remarked Evans, "emptied our other two barrels into his body and walked away." The dead man was Oscar Beaver, one of the corps of railroad detectives.

The horses they had planned to use in their flight having been killed, the pair then started off on foot, leaving behind the supplies they had gathered and carrying only their weapons. Some hours later they stopped at a farmhouse and aroused its owner, who was a casual acquaintance. The latter, understandably, was none too happy to see his early-morning callers. On being told that the pair wanted a horse and buggy with which to flee to the mountains, the farmer protested that he had none that were fit to use. "All right," Evans replied, "the posse's coming along pretty soon and we would just as leave fight it out here as any place." That did it. "For Heaven's sake, No!" cried the badly frightened farmer. "We want no fighting at this house. . . . Have breakfast and take my rig and get into the mountains as quick as you can, gentlemen!"

Evans, however, made it clear that he and his partner were in no hurry to leave. They sat at their ease in the farmhouse kitchen while what Evans described as "a very decent breakfast" was prepared by their unwilling host; then, as dawn was breaking, the two made ready to depart. But the harassed farmer was to have another scare before he saw the last of his guests. As he started for the barn to harness his mule to a cart, he spied two men galloping down the road. He ran back into the house and, wringing his hands, announced that a gunfight was imminent. Evans advised him, should there be trouble, to take his wife into the back yard where they would be out of the line of fire. As it happened, the two officers rode past the house without stopping. Once they were out of sight, the relieved farmer watched his guests, sitting in his cart and driving his mule, turn into the country road and jog off at a sedate pace toward the mountains.

"Petey" Bigelow's Interview

Having successfully made their way into the high Sierra country, the pair were reasonably safe, notwithstanding the fact that rewards for their capture — which presently reached around ten thousand dollars — induced first scores and then hundreds to join in the man hunt. There, living in secluded hideouts — and, with the help of well-wishers among the mountain people, getting ample supplies of food, clothing, and ammunition — the fugitives passed the next few weeks in comfort and comparative safety.

Then, in mid-September of 1892, came their next bloody brush with the law. At that time the two were hiding out in the vicinity of Simpson Flat, a remote mountain meadow that could be reached only by steep, winding trails. This was familiar country to both men, for in the past they had often prospected in the area and had staked out a number of claims there. One day — according to the rambling account of their adventures later dictated by Evans — they had set out for the cabin of one Jim Young, on the top of Pine Ridge, where they had gone "to get a warm meal, for we had been eating cold hash for a long time."

Young was absent, but soon a second mountaineer, a young man named Mainwaring, appeared and accommodatingly prepared a meal for the bandits. Unknown to the three, however, those directing the hunt had stationed a man nearby — charged with keeping an eye on the cabin. Having seen the pair enter, he had hurried away to summon reinforcements. To Evans and his partner, the first intimation of danger came when Mainwaring, glancing up from his cooking, saw a mounted posse coming down the trail. Panic-stricken, the youth called the others' attention to them and asked what could be done.

"Get into the garden and up to the spring for a bucket of water or I'll blow the top of your head off!" shouted Evans. Mainwaring needed no further urging; seizing a bucket, he set off on the double-quick, while the outlaws, guns in hand, peered through the windows at the approaching horsemen. Recalling the moment later, Evans made it clear that they regarded their situation as a desperate one. "There we were, penned in a small cabin which had only one way of getting out, and that by the front door. Escape was impossible. We were cornered and had to fight."

The posse, numbering half-a-dozen men, held a brief parley outside the gate. Then two of their number dismounted, let themselves through the gate, and strode toward the cabin. The bandits waited until the pair were "within fifteen or twenty feet of the door," then thrust the muzzles of their shotguns through the windowpanes and pulled the triggers. As the victims fell, Evans and his partner dashed out the door, firing first the remaining shells in their shotguns, then their rifles, into the group at the gate. This sudden onslaught threw the posse into confusion, those who had not been struck putting spurs to their horses and fleeing down the mountain trail.

Two of their number, however, failed to join in the flight. These were a brace of Indians who had been much in the newspapers since the man hunt had begun. Heralded as re-nowned scouts, they had been brought up into the moun-tains from their native Arizona in the expectation that, with the traditional cunning of their race, they could pick up and follow the trail of the fugitives. Evans made it clear, how-ever, that in the affair at Young's cabin it had seemed these scouts had signally failed to live up to their advance billing.

> The Indians meantime had taken to the rockpile at the left of the gate and were fighting in true Indian fashion. We did not mind them much. . . . [They] simply thrust their rifles above the rocks and blazed away without taking aim. . . . Pretty soon I made it so hot for them that they dashed away down the road.

However, while the bandits, profiting by their surprise attack, were routing the group at the gate, danger developed from another quarter. For at the moment the Indians had fled and the battle seemed over, shooting broke out again. Evans later reported:

> Sontag suddenly dropped his right arm and cried out that it was broken, while a bullet sped past my right eyebrow. . . . Whirling about, we saw that McGinnis [one of the two men

who had entered the gate] had revived and had turned over
on his back to fill us both with lead from his Winchester.
. . . I was compelled to put another bullet into him.

That was the end of the carnage. Silence fell over Young's
cabin and — Evans having bound a handkerchief about his
partner's arm, which proved to have only a superficial flesh
wound — the pair made their way unmolested back to their
retreat higher in the mountains. Behind them lay the bodies
of two of the posse: Vic Williams and Andy McGinnis.
With Oscar Beaver, slain in the Evans yard at Visalia, the
bandits' score had reached three in the space of a little more
than a month.

This lethal encounter much intensified the already high
public interest in the man hunt, and from then on virtually
all the leading California newspapers, as well as the news
services, kept men permanently assigned to the story. These,
haunting the sheriffs' offices in Fresno and Visalia or trailing
along with the posses in the field, forwarded daily dispatches
later prominently displayed on Page One. For the next several weeks these contained little in the way of exciting news,
being in the main routine accounts of the ever-widening
hunt, of the rugged nature of the mountain terrain, together with prophesies that, now that winter was about to
set in, there was little likelihood that further contact with
the bandits would be made before the coming of spring.

Then, on the morning of October 7, 1892, readers of the
San Francisco *Examiner* — which thirty-year-old William
Randolph Hearst had recently taken over — were startled
to find virtually its entire front page given over to what purported to be an interview with the robbers at their mountain hideout. The story was promptly branded a hoax by

the law enforcement officials, and by the *Examiner's* com-
petitors. But a reading of the interview — which was signed
by Henry Bigelow, the paper's star reporter — convinced the
public at large that it was authentic. For "Petey" Bigelow's
narrative contained such a wealth of realistic detail, including columns of direct quotations in which the bandits gave
their version of the events of recent weeks, that few doubted
the reporter had in fact visited the outlaws at a secret hideaway and got the story at first hand.

The precise means by which the debonair Bigelow carried out this assignment has long been a matter of debate.
One version is that when he left San Francisco he carried
in an inner pocket of his London-made jacket five hundred
dollars of the *Examiner's* money, that he went direct to the
Evans cottage in Visalia, made himself and his errand known
to the bandit's wife, exhibited the five hundred-dollar bills,
and offered to turn them over to her if she would arrange
the hoped-for interview.

That, however, was too prosaic a theory to win wide ac-
ceptance; the commonly accepted story was much more romantic. This — which was so often repeated that it became
a part of the folklore of the area — has the dapper little
reporter slipping unobtrusively into Visalia and day by day
lounging about its bars and hotel lobbies, where he confided
to whoever would listen that he wished to arrange a meeting
with the hunted men and later present in his paper the
robbers' side of their long-standing feud with the railroad
corporation.

This, the story continues, went on for several weeks, while
the reporter's fine raiment daily grew more bedraggled and
his once neatly trimmed beard became matted and unkempt,
and still nothing happened. Then at last came the hoped-for

break. One evening a stranger slipped into a chair beside him in his hotel lobby, listened to his then familiar story, and at its end instructed him to appear at a certain hour the next night at a rendezvous on the edge of town, and to come prepared for a long, hard ride into the mountains.

Whichever version is correct is immaterial; the important point is that Bigelow did in fact join the hunted pair at their Sierra hiding-place and get his interview. He followed his first *Examiner* story with another the next day, in which he told something of his trip into the mountains. His account, however, was a model of vagueness, for, as he pointed out, he had given his word that he would divulge no information as to the hunted men's hideout that would prove useful to their pursuers. "I am," he wrote, "not at liberty to describe definitely the position which the fugitives now consider their stronghold." But he made it clear that it was cunningly concealed and that to reach it from the valley involved a tortuous and exhausting journey.

> I set out [he stated] for the vicinity of the Kings River. This is a broad territory and seemed to me to consist chiefly of rugged mountains about 6,000 or 7,000 feet high.

Although he prudently refrained from stating whether or not he had had companions on this trip, it became clear from his narrative that he had traveled in company with a group of the outlaws' friends. He had, it also developed, joined a party carrying supplies to the pair. Evidently it was a considerable caravan that wended its way via unfrequented mountain trails to their lofty lair.

> The last of their winter stock of provisions [wrote Bigelow] was being got in on the backs of tiny burros . . . Being

forced into service, I was compelled to act as driver to two of the animals, and I can confidently say that Evans and Sontag have an excellent supply . . .

The arduous ascent ended, according to the reporter, about noon on October 4. The meeting place — one of several of the outlaws' hideouts — he described as "a small house standing in a tiny gulch that overlooks the great Fresno plain." The interview took place in the bedroom of the two-room cabin, with the reporter seated companionably between the two bandits on the bed. While he was assuring the pair that the entire West was following the man hunt with close interest, the reporter looked about. What mainly impressed him was the array of weapons they kept close at hand. "Against the wall to the right," he wrote, "leaned a Winchester rifle and a shotgun; opposite and next to Sontag was another Winchester of newer make than its fellow." In addition, each had strapped to his hip a .44-caliber revolver.

This led to a discussion of armaments and the pair gave their opinions of the merits of their various weapons. Evans' favorite firing-piece, it developed, was a "No. 12 laminated steel breech-loading shotgun," which he carried on a hook attached to a strap beneath his right arm — a position that permitted him to bring it into action with a minimum of delay. "The two barrels exhausted," added Bigelow, "he takes to the rifle."

There was, however, stated Evans, one point in connection with his shotgun on which the public had been misinformed, and as a conscientious craftsman he welcomed this opportunity to set the record straight:

"There is an impression," he said, "that I use wire cartridges. I only did once; that was on Oscar Beaver." He continued judiciously: "I don't think they are any good except to make a big hole in one spot. For my part I prefer this little recipe I am using at present. I load my brass shells with a dozen buckshot, and while they do considerable scattering, yet they are very useful in a pinch."

These, however, were mere preliminaries. The main body of the interview was given over to the bandits' own story. In it, they stoutly denied that they had had any hand in the train robberies and that, given an opportunity, they could present abundant evidence to prove their innocence. Then followed their version of the shooting at the Evans house — which they claimed had been brought on by boorish conduct on the part of the railroad detective — and of subsequent clashes with their pursuers. All this, and much more, "Petey" Bigelow took down, and in his follow-up story he told of the outlaws' determination to fight to the finish, and of the widespread sympathy for them expressed by residents of the little mountain communities. He summed up thus:

> I think the capture of the fugitives will be a difficult, if not an impossible, task. They are well supplied for the winter and they have quarters that are extremely comfortable, as well as almost inaccessible. Besides, the entire district is with them. I don't think there is a man, woman or child within a radius of fifty miles who would not give them all they wish of eat and drink. This may not have been the condition of affairs for a week or two after the train robbery, but when the posses began to spread themselves around Mill Creek Valley, Squaw Valley, Pine Ridge, and Simpson and David flats, the trouble began.

Bigelow was of the opinion that while this friendly attitude sprang in part from the almost universal distrust of the railroad dating from the Mussel Slough tragedy, it was primarily the behavior of the searching parties that had alienated the mountaineers. Residents of the remote ranches and isolated Sierra villages were a clannish lot and quick to resent the influx of hordes of strangers from the lowlands who, careless of rural amenities, left gates unclosed, permitting livestock to stray, trampled on gardens, and rode roughshod over growing crops.

These, however, were not the mountaineers' only grievances against the law. For the men directing the hunt, Sheriffs Kay and Overall, of Tulare and Fresno counties, and "Big Bill" Smith, chief of the railroad detectives, although they were frequently at odds among themselves over how to conduct the search, were uniformly high-handed in their treatment of those whom they suspected of being in touch with the bandits and of furnishing them with supplies or information.

One sufferer from these unwelcome attentions was a well-known resident of the area named Clarke Moore, whom Detective Smith had kept under constant surveillance and had once threatened to arrest as an accomplice of the fugitives. To Bigelow, Evans stoutly denied that he and his partner had ever received any help from Moore. On the contrary, he stated, it had been on Moore's urgent appeal that the lives of several of the man hunters had been spared.

"We met accidentally on a pathway at Pine Ridge one night," he recalled, "and were ready to commit general havoc in the midst of a stupid posse of detectives. Moore vehemently implored us not to kill anyone unless we were first attacked, and through his intercession we spared their lives."

Bigelow's interview was, of course, a sensational news beat, and the *Examiner* made the most of it. "Nothing," it stated on October 8, "ever surprised the town half so completely as that graphic story."

But it is clear, too, that the paper had some difficulty deciding just what attitude it should adopt toward the outlaws. Admittedly the problem was a knotty one; public interest was high, with opinion so sharply divided that to take a strong stand one way or another involved the risk of alienating hundreds of readers. The journal, though, was equal to the emergency, prudently adopting a middle-of-the-road course calculated to offend no one:

> Strange as it may seem [it commented] the pursual of the remarkable interview has awakened a certain amount of sympathy for Evans and Sontag. It is the first time their side of the blood-stained story was heard. While few people who expressed an opinion put any stock in their denial of the train robbery, yet when Evans spoke of his pursuers as blood-hungry, his readers saw it in that light for the first time.

End of the Evans-Sontag Saga

Predictions that the pair would be able to elude capture throughout the winter of 1892–1893 proved well founded. They lived snugly at their mountain hideaway — which they called Fort Defiance — during the season of deep snows, and as month succeeded month the opinion was freely expressed that, because of their intimate knowledge of the region, plus the friendship of the mountain people, they could remain at large indefinitely. This feeling seems to have been shared by the bandits themselves, with the result that they were presently led to take an unnecessary and, as it proved, highly injudicious chance.

In early June of 1893, some nine months after the encounter at Young's cabin, the pair made their way down to the valley — bound for Visalia, where Evans planned to visit with his wife and children and pick up some articles needed to make life in the mountains more comfortable. The latter part of this program was never carried out. For the railroad detectives and sheriffs' men somehow got wind of their movements and laid their plans accordingly, posting men at strategic points along the route they would be most likely to follow.

That maneuver paid off. On the morning of June 12, the bandits cautiously approached a spot in the foothills known as Stone Corral, where they made their way to a pile of straw, intending to hide their sawed-off shotguns before continuing on to the town. From their points of concealment four deputy sheriffs brought their guns into action, firing at point-blank range and bringing down both men. Sontag received a wound from which he died several weeks later; Evans, however, though struck in the head and wrist, managed to make a temporary getaway, only to be picked up a few hours later at a nearby farmhouse to which he had fled.

To all appearances the drama was over; such, however, was not the case. Both men were lodged in the jail at Fresno, charged with train robbery — a capital offense in California — and murder. Sontag presently died of his wounds, leaving Evans to face the music alone. Some five months passed before he was brought to trial, and in the interval a new development served to keep the public's interest high. Ostensibly as a means of raising funds for the surviving bandit's defense, a group of San Francisco newspapermen hit on the plan of producing a play based on the Evans-Sontag epic, and — a stroke of pure genius this — of casting Evans's pretty seventeen-year-old daughter Eva in the role of heroine. The play, *Evans and Sontag; or, The Visalia Bandits* — a four-act melodrama in which the robbers and the courageous Eva invariably bested the villainous railroad detectives — opened at San Francisco's National Theater and, despite the protests of local clergymen, who denounced it, played to capacity audiences for several weeks.

As a consequence, when the trial opened in the Fresno County Superior Court on November 20, 1893, the accused man was represented by a brace of able trial lawyers, G. G. Goucher and S. J. Hinds. These used every wile to arouse in the jurors sympathy for the prisoner and neglected no opportunity to heap ridicule on the soulless railroad corporation which they maintained was responsible for his plight. However, opposing counsel was able to present overwhelming evidence that the pair had slain three law-enforcement officers, and at the end of the weeks-long trial the jury brought in a verdict of first-degree murder — with a recommendation that the sentence be one of life imprisonment.

Evans was thereupon returned to the Fresno jail to await sentence, and there a few days later occurred the next in the long series of sensations. This was a cleverly engineered scheme by which the condemned man regained his freedom and again fled to the mountains. Evans himself is generally credited with plotting his escape and, from his cell in the Fresno jail, directing every phase of the carefully planned coup. He had, of course, confederates on the outside, including his wife and daughter Eva. His chief co-conspirator, however, was a young ex-jailbird named Edward Morrell, an ardent admirer of the train robber. Morrell was then working as waiter and dishwater at a restaurant near the jail, and one of his duties was to carry trays of food to the prisoners, including the bandit.

The Evans women were frequent patrons of this restaurant and it was no difficult task for Eva to persuade the hero-worshiping Morrell to join in the planned escape. However, Evans and his fellow plotters recognized that his chances of fighting his way out of the well-staffed jail would be slim indeed, and accordingly an ingenious scheme was worked out designed to draw elsewhere most of the men normally stationed there. The result was that as the year 1893 neared its close a young man aboard a train en route from Porterville to Fresno approached the conductor and, showing signs of extreme nervousness, confided that he had recently become acquainted with a group of free-spending strangers in a Visalia poolhall; that he had been persuaded to join up with them, and that the gang planned to hold up the train on its return to Porterville that evening.

The youth, who claimed to have had a change of heart about embarking on a career of crime, told his story so convincingly that the conductor on reaching Fresno reported the matter to the railroad officials, who in turn got in touch with the sheriff's office.

When the Porterville train pulled out of the Fresno station that evening it had on board four deputy sheriffs, all armed to the teeth and determined to thwart the expected holdup.

Accordingly when, half an hour later, young Morrell appeared as usual carrying a tray bearing Evans's supper, there was but a single guard on duty at the jail. This guard, not bothering to lift the napkin covering the meal, opened the door to Evans's cell and let Morrell enter. Presently, the

prisoner having finished his ample meal, the waiter summoned the jailer to unlock the cell so he could carry the
tray back to the restaurant. As the door swung open, the
officer found himself looking into the muzzles of revolvers
in the hands of both Evans and Morrell. With the jailer, his
hands aloft, leading the way, the trio marched down the
front steps of the jail and across the street to the courthouse
square, where a buggy and team of horses had been posted
for their use in making their getaway.

Thus far the plot had gone smoothly and exactly as
planned. Now, however, came several unlooked-for complications. On their progress toward the buggy they chanced to
meet a prominent Fresnan, an ex-mayor of the town. Fearing that he would promptly give the alarm, Evans ordered
him to raise his hands and join the jailer. The augmented
party continued down the street to the point where the team
was tied — and here the escapees were confronted by a new
emergency. For standing on the sidewalk directly opposite
the vehicle two men were conversing, one of whom was
John Morgan, the Fresno city marshal.

Thereupon, the impetuous Morrell, who had hurried on
ahead to untie the horses, complicated the situation by making a quite unnecessary show of force. For whereas, as Marshal Morgan later stated, the two fugitives and their hostages
could, under protection of the gathering darkness, have
climbed into the buggy and driven away unmolested, Morrell chose instead to confront the officer and, revolver in
hand, order him to pass over his own weapon.

This the marshal, caught by surprise, was forced to do;
however, as Morrell turned to search Morgan's companion
— who was unarmed — the officer sprang on Morrell, pin-
ioning his arms to his side. At that juncture Evans hurried

up, ordered the marshal to release Morrell and, after the other had done so, raised his revolver and shot him, the bullet entering the officer's side and dropping him to the sidewalk. The report of the weapon frightened the getaway team, which reared back, broke the halter by which it had been tied, and dashed off down the street.

Deprived of that means of escape, the pair thereupon ran down an alley to the next street. There they commandeered a horse and cart belonging to a boy who had been delivering newspapers, whipped the animal to a gallop and rumbled out of town, headed for the mountains.

With the marshal wounded and most of the sheriff's deputies on the train to Porterville, there was a considerable delay before a posse could be assembled. The consequence was that the fugitives were able to make their way unmolested into the high Kings River country that Evans knew so well.

There is no point in recounting here the details of the new man hunt that promptly got under way. Suffice it to say that throughout the month of January, 1894, determined groups of sheriff's deputies, stung by the ridicule heaped upon them and their chief because of their having fallen for the train-robbery ruse, patrolled the icy Sierra trails, while others ran down rumors that the fugitives had been sighted at various points throughout the state. Meantime — the escape having rekindled interest in the exploits of the bandit pair — the Evans-Sontag melodrama was hastily revamped and put on the road again, with Eva Evans once more playing the lead.

Not until February 4 was the first contact with Evans and Morrell made. On that date two deputies, Timmins and

Boyd, were driving up a road that wound steeply up a canyon some miles to the south of Simpson's Flat. On coming to a point where the grade was particularly steep, Timmins climbed down from the cart and Boyd proceeded on alone. At the top of the ascent stood a mountain cabin belonging to a man named St. Clair, and as the horse and cart appeared, Evans himself stepped out of the cabin's door and, rifle in hand, ironically called out to the deputy to "Come in and be sociable."

Boyd's reply was to reach for his own weapon on the floor of his vehicle, whereupon Evans put his rifle to his shoulder and fired, the bullet striking the seat of the cart. As Boyd whipped his horse to a gallop, Morrell ran from the cabin and sent a second shot after the officer, this one hitting a wheel. Meantime, Timmins, who had approached near enough to see what was going on, himself opened fire on the pair, thereby diverting their attention long enough to permit his fellow deputy to make his escape.

The officers thereupon made their way to headquarters farther down the mountain, got re-enforcements, and resumed the hunt. Next day the augmented party picked up the pair's tracks in the snow and, following them, presently came in sight of a little shack well hidden by trees and thick underbrush. One of the officers, spying Evans on the lookout outside the shack, fired a single shot — which grazed the bandit's head, tearing off a tuft of hair — whereupon the two fled and their trail was lost in the darkness. The cabin was found to be well supplied with food, clothing, weapons and ammunition, and for a time — the bandits being now without these necessities, and the weather being extremely cold — hopes for their capture were high.

Once more, however, the wily Evans — whose acquaintance with the mountains was far more complete than that of his pursuers — managed to elude them. The law thereupon resorted to a new means of bringing them to book.

Toward the middle of February a man named Brighton, with his wife, appeared at the Evans cottage in Visalia and announced that they were looking for a place to rent. Both Mrs. Evans and Eva were absent with the barnstorming theatrical company, and the young children of the family were being cared for by a relative who lived next door. A deal was thereupon made by which the Brightons rented the house and agreed to look after the Evans offspring. Later it developed that the strangers were in reality detectives who had been placed there either by the Fresno County sheriff or by the railroad officials.

The trap was then ready to be sprung. Somehow a message was transmitted to Evans in his mountain hideaway stating that one of his children was ill and wished to see him. The result was that a night or two later the bandit, accompanied by Morrell, made his way down out of the hills and stole into the cottage. On receiving word of their arrival the sheriff, having stationed his men about the place, sent a message to Evans demanding his and his partner's surrender. After an exchange of notes, the pair, realizing that the jig was up, admitted the officers, turned over their weapons, and, handcuffed together, were marched off to the town jail.

Next day they were transferred to Fresno, where the same judge who had presided at Evans's first trial sentenced him to life imprisonment at Folsom penitentiary. A week later, Morrell, after a brief trial, was likewise found guilty and sent to the same prison.

The aftermath can be briefly told. During his incarceration Evans proved a model prisoner, and when, some seventeen years later, Hiram Johnson — himself a bitter enemy of the railroad — became governor of California he released the bandit on parole. Evans, then sixty-four years old and in broken health, lived the remaining six years of his life with his family in rural Oregon. He died there on February 9, 1917, bringing to a final close the long-drawn-out mountain saga, the memory of which is still fresh in the minds of a few elderly residents of the high Kings River country.

VIII

Home on the Range

The Ancient and Benevolent Order
of E Clampus Vitus

By AND LARGE, life in the Sierra diggings during the first few years was no bed of roses. Of this we have abundant evidence in the letters, diaries, and reminiscences of those who had first-hand knowledge of the situation. Moreover, so many of the participants felt impelled to put on paper a record of their adventures and misadventures that today the gold rush is generally acknowledged to be one of the best-documented mass movements in history.

And what was it that the forty-niners wrote about? There were, to be sure, a few who made occasional passing references to the larger significance of the enterprise, commenting on one phase or another of its social, economic, or political implications, or on the odd behavior of their fellow Argonauts who had been drawn from many parts of the world and from all walks of life.

Reflections of that type were, however, few and far between. When the typical gold-hunter dipped his pen in ink it was, nine times out of ten, to tell the folks back home of the manifold hardships of his lot: of the discomfort of standing knee-deep in the icy waters of the Sierra streams, of the back-breaking labor of scooping up and washing the gravel in the hope of finding a trace of color in the bottom of the pan. And almost invariably he made some mention of the isolation of his surroundings, its complete lack of the comforts of home or of facilities for recreation during his occasional hours of leisure.

This last complaint, however, was mainly from those marooned in the more remote of the camps, and then only during the early days of the rush. For the forty-niners were in general a highly resourceful breed and it was seldom long before means had been provided for combatting the loneliness of their lot. The first and most obvious of these were, of course, the saloons and gambling resorts, where they foregathered before the bars or gaming tables in a determined effort to escape the harsh realities of their daily existence.

But not all were attracted by such diversions, and even those who were soon came to feel the need of a more varied social life. The result was that throughout the Sierra towns and camps the miners presently organized themselves into groups, forming debating societies, political or literary or dramatic clubs, and — quite early — establishing chapters of the fraternal orders they had known at home. Thus the Odd Fellows, Masons, and half a dozen others came into being in numerous mountain communities in 1850 and 1851, and some even earlier.

Among such groups was one which seems to have made an irresistible appeal to the amusement-starved populace of the camps. This was E Clampus Vitus, an order having a ritual that broadly burlesqued those of other lodges, and the primary purpose of which was to foster the miners' taste for uninhibited humor. One theory as to its origin and swift rise to popularity is that it offered those who for one reason or another were not eligible for membership in the other lodges the facilities for social relaxation, and at the same time presented an opportunity to poke fun at the pretensions of the rival orders.

In any event, the Clampers — as they called themselves — from the first laid much stress on the democracy of their organization, emphasizing that immediately upon his election every member became, not only an officer, but "Chairman of the Most Important Committee." This broad satire was carried out, too, in the names conferred on the dignitaries, the presiding officer being the Grand Noble Humbug and others bearing such titles as Clampatriarch, High Honorary Humbug, and Noble Grand Chiseler.

Terming itself a benevolent order, the primary objective of which was the relief of the community's widows and orphans — "but more particularly the widows" — its initiation ceremonies were in keeping with that high purpose. Members were summoned into executive session whenever two or more applications for admission — known as "poor blind candidates" — could be rounded up, the signal being ear-splitting blasts from a ten-foot-long horn called the "hewgag." In the early days considerable pressure seems to have been brought to bear on local residents to take out membership in the mystic order, one historian of the movement stating that "no merchant could hold his customers, no drummer could make a sale, no man was safe from social ostracism until he had joined . . ."

Much of the early history of the order is now obscure, for no official records of the numerous chapters that flourished in California throughout the 1850's and later are known to have survived. The reason for this, according to one old-timer who had been a member of one of the Sierra groups during his youth, was that no records were ever kept. "The trouble was," he explained, "that during the meetings none of the brothers was in condition to keep any minutes, and afterwards nobody could remember what had taken place."

Later research seems to indicate that the order had its beginnings back in "the States" during the early 1840's, its probable originator being one Squire Ephraim Bee, a frontier sage who operated a blacksmith shop and tavern in a mountain community of West Virginia, which bore the picturesque name of Meat Horse Fork of Middle Island Creek. Positive evidence that it existed in pre-gold rush days is contained in a handwritten document entitled "Ancient and Honorable Order of E Clampus Vitus, Division No. 110," now preserved in the Huntington Library at San Marino, California. There can be little doubt, however, that it was in the towns and camps of the Sierra that it enjoyed its brief but hilarious heyday.

The California town that has the distinction of having sponsored the first Far-Western chapter has long been a matter of debate. References to the order have been found in the files of gold rush newspapers as early as 1850, and an issue of the *Sonora Herald* for the month of December, 1852, carried a notice of a forthcoming meeting there, which was signed by "P. BROWN, *Noble Grand Humbug.*" Lodges are known to have been active at a number of points in the northern mines by the middle of that decade, among them "Balaam Chapter No. 107,402" at Sierra City — founded in 1857 — and one at Yreka a year earlier.

At any rate it spread rapidly from camp to camp the entire length of the Sierra, and for an excellent reason. For, in the words of George E. Dane, who collected much material relating to the order's early days:

It existed principally for the purpose of taking in new members, and for the entertainment and refreshment thereby provided for the old members at the neophyte's expense. By the time he had sat in the *Expungent's Chair,* passed through the *Cave of Silence,* ridden the *Rocky Road,* experienced the *Elevation of Man,* taken the fearful oaths, endured the *Obliterating Obfuscation,* received the *Staff of Relief,* and seen his initiation fee converted into liquid assets and consumed by the assembled Clampers, he was under no misapprehension as to what had happened to him. He had indeed been "taken in," and he was as eager as the other brothers to find another sucker, so that he might get even.

With the gradual scraping dry of the area's placers and the resultant sharp drops in population, the Clamper lodges — like many other features of the Sierra boom towns — went into a profound decline, and for the better part of a century they were all but forgotten. It was not until the early 1930's that a group of Californians, intrigued by references to the organization in pioneer newspapers and diaries, decided to revive and reactivate the order. Fortunately, the sponsors of E Clampus Vitus, Chapter Redivivus, had the advice of ninety-two-year-old Adam Lee Moore, who had been a member in good standing of the Sierra City Chapter in the early 1860's.

As had been the case some eight decades earlier, the burlesque order, affording as it did an outlet for bawdy humor and high spirits in general, has found a ready welcome among history-conscious Californians, and during recent years a number of other chapters of Clampus Redivivus have been formed, both in the cities of the coast and in the Mother Lode towns. With one or another of the lodges acting as host, the present-day Clampers assemble from time to

time at historic spots throughout the state, dedicate plaques
in commemoration of events, heroic or bizarre, that happened there, take over the towns by the sheer weight of their
numbers and, at the sound of the hewgag, repair to a neighboring hall or other convenient spot for the initiation of
"poor blind candidates," followed by a banquet. Thus today's Californians strive to keep alive something of the spirit
of the pioneers in its more untrammeled aspects and at the
same time find an outlet for their own exuberance.

It is all good — and moderately clean — fun.

High Trip, Burro Trip, Knapsack Trip

Although, during its first California incarnation, the activities of the Ancient and Benevolent Order of E Clampus
Vitus were mainly confined to the towns and camps of the
Sierra, it cannot properly be termed an association of mountaineers. That distinction, in so far as these mountains are
concerned, belongs to another organization — the Sierra
Club — and the story of how it came into being is an interesting one.

As has been indicated, the Californian's attitude toward
the great range that parallels the eastern border of his state
has over the years undergone a series of changes. During
the gold rush and for some years thereafter it was looked on
as a bulky, awkward, and inconveniently high barrier shut-
ting off the state from the rest of the nation, over which one
could make one's way only with the expenditure of much
time and effort and, not infrequently, with a certain degree
of peril. Later, safe and reasonably speedy means of transmountain travel having been provided, first by wagon roads

and then by the railroad, the public came to look on the range from a new viewpoint; that is, as an area possessing certain resources useful to the economy of the rapidly growing state. Thus was ushered in a period lasting several decades during which these resources were exploited to the full, with little thought being given to what the ultimate result might be.

To be sure there were a far-sighted few who, as early as the 1860's, deplored this reckless waste and urged that steps be taken to withhold certain areas from spoliation by private interests and so preserve them in their natural state for the enjoyment of future generations. Accordingly, the first step in that direction was taken in 1864 when a bill, introduced by California's Senator Conness, was passed by Congress transferring title to the Yosemite Valley and the Mariposa Grove of Big Trees to the state, with the proviso that they be held in perpetuity for the use of the public.

After that beginning, however, for more than a quarter-century, little further was accomplished in the way of setting aside other scenic areas of the range. It was not until 1890 that, as we have seen, Congress passed an act creating the Yosemite National Park, an area of lofty peaks and picturesque mountain lakes and canyons embracing some 12,000 square miles and completely surrounding the state-owned Yosemite Valley. The passage of that bill caused concern to many Californians, particularly to sheep owners, lumbermen, and miners, and considerable pressure was brought to bear on Congress to repeal the act, or, failing that, to make drastic reductions in the size of the park. By then, however, a movement looking toward the preservation of the nation's natural resources had gained adherents all over the country, and in California members of that group

were considering plans of how best to combat efforts to have
the act rescinded or modified.

The result was the organization in the spring of 1890 of
the Sierra Club, with John Muir serving as its first president. Its purposes, according to its Articles of Incorporation,
were: "To explore, enjoy and render accessible the mountain regions of the Pacific Coast; to publish authentic information concerning them; to enlist the support and co-operation of the people and the Government in preserving the
forests and other natural features of the Sierra Nevada."
The club's first act was to wage a vigorous and ultimately
successful campaign to defeat the bill then before Congress
that would have reduced the area of the Yosemite National
Park by more than half. Next it undertook to bring about
the formation of other national parks and forest reserves,
and in this it was so successful that during the next few
years a number of other large areas were set aside, both in
the Sierra and elsewhere on the Pacific Coast.

During its first few years, another of the club's prime objectives was to make the scenic attractions of the range more
widely known, and to that end steps were taken to encour-
age the building of roads and trails by which the public
could reach great areas of the back country that had previously been closed to all but the hardiest mountaineers. In
order to further that aim, the club in 1901 inaugurated
what has ever since been its best-known and most widely
popular activity; that is, its sponsorship each year of summer camping trips into the high Sierra. During the first few
seasons base camps were set up at spots within easy reach of
existing roads, and from such points parties visited places
of interest in the areas, scaling the neighboring peaks or setting off on two- or three-day camping trips.

Presently, however, this plan was modified, the annual outings becoming itinerant pilgrimages during which the parties made extensive tours of the remote upper sections of the range, establishing new camps each night. Such trips, lasting a month or longer, served to introduce the wonders of the high Sierra to thousands and, in nearly every case, made ardent mountain-lovers of them. The annual excursions took in many points of interest in the most rugged and picturesque parts of the range; that is, the area that lies between Mount Whitney on the south and the Yosemite National Park, including the lofty peaks and chains of mountain lakes and meadows in the upper reaches of the Kings and Kern rivers, as well as numerous other spots equally spectacular.

So popular did these mountain treks become that by the late 1930's they had grown to an unwieldy size and a new policy had to be adopted. Accordingly, now three separate excursions are offered each summer; namely, the High Trip, the Burro Trip, and the Knapsack Trip. These still visit different areas of the mountains and, as their names indicate, offer different modes of travel. On the High Trip, pack animals carry food and supplies to one or another of a series of camping grounds, at each of which stops of from two to five days are made, the members proceeding from one camp site to the next at whatever pace suits their fancy and, on arriving, finding their meals prepared for them by commissary crews. These are commonly the most numerous groups — some joining up for a two-week period, others remaining the entire four or six weeks — but in recent years a limit has been placed on the number of High Trippers to avoid overtaxing grazing facilities by too many pack animals.

On the Burro Trips — normally limited to twenty members — the campers for the most part shift for themselves, learning the art of loading the little beasts that carry their supplies, and each in turn taking a hand at preparing meals for the group. These excursionists maintain a far less rigid schedule than those who take the High Trips, for both the route followed and the camping places are chosen by the members themselves, the only restriction being that, because of the burros, they must stay on or near the established mountain trails.

So far as freedom of movement is concerned, however, the third of the series, the Knapsack Trip, is supreme. For on these the members dispense with pack animals entirely, carrying their personal belongings — sleeping bag, extra clothing, toilet articles, and the like, to a limit of twenty or twenty-five pounds — strapped to their backs, and progressing by whatever routes they choose to the designated camping sites, at which caches of food have been deposited in advance. There the vacationists remain for some time, cooking their own meals and visiting points of interest in the vicinity until their food supply runs low, then moving on to the next cache, and so on to the end of their tour.

Both men and women take part in these annual Sierra trips, and of all ages from high school youths to those of sixty or over. For the amount of energy expended is largely up to the individual, the less active spending his — or her — time lounging about the camps or taking short rambles to nearby points while more strenuous members range farther afield, exploring the canyons or lakes of the area or scaling its lofty peaks. However, because of the high altitudes encountered on all trips, those who take part are expected to be in sound health, and the club requires that applicants undergo a physical examination on joining up.

During the more than six decades of the Sierra Club's existence the steadily growing popularity of the range as a recreation center has necessitated certain modifications of its original objectives. On its founding its announced purpose was, as stated, "to explore, enjoy and render accessible the mountain regions of the Pacific Coast" — and in particular the lofty Sierra Nevada Range, which was then *terra incognita* to all but a few Californians. With the passage of time, however, the entire area was thoroughly explored and mapped, while the building of roads and the advent of the automobile made easily accessible many districts that formerly could be reached only by those who traveled on foot, carrying supplies on their own backs or on those of pack animals.

While this steadily growing number of visitors at all seasons of the years — campers, fishermen, and mountain climbers during the summer months, and devotees of skiing and other winter sports when deep snows blanket the upper areas — is convincing evidence that the Sierra's facilities for recreation have come to be widely recognized, it has also posed serious problems. The chief of these, and one which Sierra Club members view with growing concern, is that the area of unspoiled wilderness grows smaller year by year. Thus during the past several decades the club's major effort has been directed toward discouraging the building of roads, inns, or like "improvements" in such districts, thereby keeping them in their natural state for the enjoyment of present and future visitors. To that end it has worked closely with the National Park Service, with the result that extensive areas in the most majestic parts of the range have been set aside, to be permanently preserved in their untouched, primeval state.

Some Sierra Ladies

The pioneer groups who first established towns deep in the Sierra canyons were, of course, predominantly men, and during the first year or two the presence there of a white woman was enough of a novelty to win her a permanent place in the annals of the town. That condition, however, lasted only a short time. For, following closely on the first waves of miners, came parties of women — from the East Coast, the Middle West, the countries of South and Central America, and elsewhere — who made their way into even the most remote of the mountain settlements, some to join husbands, fathers, brothers, or other close relatives and to occupy themselves with prim domestic duties, and others to follow more worldly pursuits.

But whatever the reason for their coming, there is ample evidence that they found life in such isolated communities far from easy. More or less typical of those who left written records of their experiences are these words set down in the spring of 1850 from a camp near the headwaters of the Yuba by a young woman who signed herself C. Berry:

> Oh! you who lounge on your divans & sofas, sleep in your fine, luxurious beds and partake of your rich viands at every meal know nothing of the life of the California emigrant. Here are we sitting on a pine bench, a log or a bunk; sleeping in beds with either a quilt or a blanket as substitute for sheets, (I can tell you it is very aristocratic to have a bed at all) & calico pillowcases on our pillows. Our fare is very plain, consisting of meat & bread, & bread & meat, with some stewed fruit, either apples or peaches, now and then (as a great delicacy) some rancid butter that had been put up in the Land of Goshen and sent around a six months

cruise by Cape Horn, for which we at times have given the moderate sum of $2 per pound; now it has fallen to $1.50. Everything in the way of provisions is remarkably high. Flour during the winter was $1 a lb., potatoes the same, also pork. Fresh beef is now 35¢ per lb., sugar .75 & coffee .50 . . .

"For a bottle of pickles that will last on our table one meal, $2.25. dried fruit, always about $1 per lb., molasses $4 to $5 per gallon. We have during the winter eaten as much as $5 worth of potatoes at dinner & then none of us had more than a decent taste. I have not seen an egg or a drop of milk since I have been in the country.

This observer, however, was by no means oblivious to the natural beauty of her surroundings, for in the same letter quoted above she wrote:

There is one point on which I must say the writers from this country have told the truth and that is respecting flowers. It is emphatically the "Land of Flowers" — the surface of the earth is a gay pasture, every hill, every vale and rill speaks the beautiful language of flowers.

Of the women who left personal accounts of their stay in the Sierra towns during the early days, none had a more observant eye or wrote with greater facility and charm than Louise Clappe, who, as wife of a pioneer physician, spent the period from September, 1851, to September, 1852, at Rich Bar, a camp high in the gorge of the Feather River. In a long series of letters, which she signed "Dame Shirley" — and which were later published in one of California's first magazines, appropriately named the *Pioneer* — she presented a vivid picture of the manner of life lived in the high Sierra diggings during their brief heyday.

Because Rich Bar lay deep in the mountains, in a district so rugged that more than half a century was to pass before it could be reached by any means save circuitous, rocky trails, Dame Shirley's account of her journey there sheds light on the hardships and hazards of early-day Sierra travel. Of the first phases of her long trip, from the valley town of Marysville to Bidwell's Bar, she wrote:

> On Monday the eighth of September [1851], I seated myself in the most excruciatingly springless wagon that it had ever been my lot to be victimized in, and commenced my journey in earnest. I was the only passenger. For thirty miles the road passed through as beautiful a country as I had ever seen. . . . On one side rose the Buttes, that group of hills so piquant and saucy; and on the other, tossing to Heaven the everlasting whiteness of their snow wreathed foreheads, stood, sublime in their very monotony, the glorious Sierra Nevada.

As the journey continued, however, the passenger grew less interested in the scenery. "Ten miles this side of Bidwell's Bar," she continued, "the road, hitherto so smooth and level, became stony and hilly. For more than a mile we drove along the edge of a precipice, and so near, that it seemed to me, should the horses deviate a hair's breadth from their usual trace, we must be dashed to eternity. Wonderful to relate, I did not oh! nor ah! nor shriek *once,* but remained crouched in the back of the wagon as silent as death. When we were back again in safety, the driver exclaimed in the classic *patois* of New England, 'Wall, I guess yur the fust woman that ever rode over that are hill without hollering.' He evidently did not know that it was the intensity of my *fear* that kept me still."

Dame Shirley's husband had come down from the hills to meet her at Bidwell's Bar, and, that being the end of the road, early the next morning the pair set off on muleback

on the long trek up to Rich Bar. That journey, at best an
arduous one for a girl unused to the hardships of the frontier, proved in this instance a particularly trying one. For
the doctor presently lost his way on the winding, poorly de-
fined Indian trail they were following and, far off their
course, they spent the next several days wandering over the
high ridges and through the deep canyon of the North Fork
of the American River. At length, after two nights in the
open without blankets or food, the exhausted pair had the
good luck to meet a prospector — the first human being
they had seen since leaving Bidwell's Bar — who directed
them back on their course. "This joyful news," wrote Shirley, "gave us fresh strength, and we rode on as fast as our
worn-out mules could go."

Having made their way to a mountain cabin called the
Berry Creek House and there enjoyed their first real meal in
three days and rested overnight, the pair pressed on. Some
twenty-four hours later their little caravan at last approached
its destination:

> But what a lovely sight greeted our enchanted eyes, as we
> stopped for a few moments on the summit of the hill lead-
> ing into Rich Bar. Deep in the shadowy nooks of the far
> down valleys, like wasted jewels dropped from the radiant
> sky above, lay half a dozen blue-bosomed lagoons, glittering
> and gleaming and sparkling in the sunlight, as though each
> tiny wavelet were formed of rifted diamonds. It was worth
> the whole wearisome journey, danger from the Indians,
> grizzly bears, sleeping under the stars, and all, to behold this
> beautiful vision.
> While I stood breathless with admiration, a singular
> sound and an exclamation of "A rattlesnake!" from F——
> [Dr. Clappe] startled me into common sense again. I gave

one look at the reptile, horribly beautiful, like a chain of living opals — as it corkscrewed itself into that peculiar spiral, which it is compelled to assume in order to make an attack, and then fear overcoming my curiosity — although I had never seen one of them before — I galloped out of its vicinity, as fast as my little mule could carry me.

Although the camp toward which they were heading was then in sight, to reach it involved one of the most exciting — and hazardous — parts of the entire journey, as this passage makes clear:

The hill leading into Rich Bar is five miles long, and as steep as you can imagine. Fancy yourself riding for this distance, along the edge of a frightful precipice, where should your mule make a misstep, you would be dashed hundreds of feet into the awful ravine below. Every one we met tried to discourage us, and said that it would be impossible for us to ride down. They would take F—— aside, much to my amusement, and tell him that he was assuming a great responsibility in allowing me to undertake such a journey. I however insisted upon going on.

About half way down, we came to a level spot a few feet in extent, covered with sharp slate-stones. Here, the girth of my saddle — which we afterwards found was fastened only by four *tacks,* gave way, and I fell over the right side, striking on my left elbow. Strange to say, I was not in the least hurt; and again my heart wept tearful thanks to God; for had the accident happened at any other part of the hill, I must have been dashed a piece of shapeless nothingness, into the dim valleys beneath.

F—— soon mended the saddle-girth, I mounted my darling little mule, and rode triumphantly into Rich Bar, at five o'clock in the evening. . . . Many of the miners have told me that they dismounted several times while descending . . . I of course feel very vain of my exploit, and glorify myself accordingly; being particularly careful all the time not to inform my admirers that my courage was the result of the know-nothing, fear-nothing principle; for I was certainly entirely ignorant, until I had passed them, of the dangers of the passage.

Having become a member of a community where mining was the universal occupation, it was inevitable that Dame Shirley should try her hand at wresting a fortune from the icy waters of the stream that flowed through the camp; namely, the East Branch of the North Fork of the Feather River. In a letter dated November 25, 1851, she thus described the experience:

> Nothing of importance has happened since I last wrote you, except that I have become a *mineress;* that is, if the having washed a pan of dirt with my own hands, and procured therefrom three dollars and twenty-five cents in gold dust (which I shall enclose in this letter), will entitle me to the name. I can truly say, with the blacksmith's apprentice at the close of his first day's work at the anvil, that "I am sorry I learned this trade;" for I wet my feet, tore my dress, spoilt a pair of new gloves, nearly froze my fingers, got an awful headache, took cold and lost a valuable breastpin, in this my labor of love. After such melancholy self-sacrifice on my part, I trust you will duly prize my gift. I can assure you that it is the last golden handiwork you will ever receive from "Dame Shirley."

Women of Shirley's type were, however, a rarity in the early-day Sierra camps, most of her sisters there being of a quite different stamp. For news of promising new strikes anywhere in the range invariably set off not only a horde of prospectors eager to share in the profits but, close on their heels, a group of entrepreneurs able and willing — for a price — to provide the miners with facilities for whiling away their leisure hours. Thanks to the widely read stories of Bret Harte and his imitators, the mining-town gambler, bland and inscrutable, beneath whose impeccable frock-coat often beat a heart of gold, presently became a stock figure in American fiction. Although there is evidence that the John Oakhursts and Jack Hamlins of Harte's tales had but few counterparts in the Sierra towns, the records of the Argonauts make it clear that their bars and gaming-tables offered almost the only means of entertainment. Almost, but not quite. For few of the camps, particularly those enjoying a period of flush times, were long without their quota of ladies of joy, euphemistically termed "fandango girls."

Following the conventions of the time, the editors of mining-town newspapers usually maintained a discreet silence on this aspect of community life. Sometimes, however, inmates of the brothels, or their customers, became involved in gunfire, stabbings, or other forms of violence, and on such occasions brief items in the local journals listed the names of the victims, the nature of their injuries, and usually pointed out to their readers the folly of frequenting such resorts.

Some towns, to be sure, held out no welcome to the fandango girls, the citizens turning them away on their arrival, or, if they had already established themselves, sending them and their exploiters packing, bag and baggage. The result was that the ladies, on making their way into a new camp, were never quite sure what kind of welcome might await them. Thus one party of five girls, accompanied by their madam, upon approaching Durgan Flat, high on the North Fork of the Yuba, were so nonplussed at seeing the entire population of the camp rush out to extend them a hearty welcome that one maiden fell in a faint, convinced that this howling mob was bent on lynching them.

Some years later, in 1860, an event of a quite different

nature transpired, this one arousing much indignation throughout the northern mines. The story, preserved in the *Illustrated History of Plumas, Lassen, and Sierra Counties,* published in 1882, relates that a settler named Ransom Griswold, having been attracted by the daughter of a west-bound emigrant passing through the Honey Lake region, proposed to the father a trade for the girl, offering in exchange two ten-gallon casks of whisky. His offer being accepted, Griswold took the girl — who was only fourteen — to live with him; then, having grown tired of connubial ties, he presently sold his child-spouse to a man named Jim Bradley. This mountain saga, however, had a happy termination, for Bradley promptly married the girl and according to all reports the two, in the best storybook manner, lived happily ever after.

Perhaps the most celebrated of all such *affaires d'amour* to take place during the period when women were still a novelty in the Sierra towns revolves about one Juanita, reputedly a fair but frail Mexican girl, who plied her trade in a Downieville fandango hall in 1851. A number of different versions of how Juanita came to her end exist, but all agree on one point: that as an aftermath of a community celebration on July 4 of that year, Juanita and one of her friends, an Australian named Jack Cannon, had a quarrel during the course of which the fiery Mexican girl drew a knife and stabbed the other, with fatal effect.

In Downieville there seems to have been a good deal of sympathy for the hot-blooded Juanita, particularly in view of the fact that Cannon had addressed her in abusive and insulting language, terming her, among other things, a whore. However, the Australian, too, had friends in town and the latter refused to let the matter drop. The result was that an impromptu court was set up, a judge and jury chosen, and Juanita was held to answer on a charge of murder.

The trial that followed occupied the undivided attention of the entire community during the next two days while counsel for the prosecution and defense presented their evidence and made their pleas. While the spokesmen for Juanita had of necessity to admit that she had indeed stabbed her victim to death, they maintained that his behavior had been such as to constitute justifiable homicide; moreover, a local physician, C. P. Aiken, was called to the stand and testified that the girl was pregnant — a statement that she herself indignantly denied. However, despite these and other eloquent pleas in her behalf, the jury found her guilty and the judge sentenced her to death, a decree that was promptly carried out by hanging her from a bridge that spanned the Yuba River in the middle of the town.

Sending a woman to the gallows was an all but unprecedented occurrence in the 1850's, and when the news got about it caused international reverberations, no less an authority than the *London Times* denouncing it as a travesty on justice and a shocking example of the lawlessness of the American frontiersmen. In vain the Downieville citizens tried to stem the tide of criticism and abuse by pointing out that this had been no extemporaneous lynching bee; that the prisoner's trial, conviction, and execution had been in strict accordance with accepted principles of law. Nevertheless it was many years before the little town ceased to bear the stigma of having hanged a woman. To that extent Juanita had her revenge.

Literature and Such

During the final third of the nineteenth century the writer whose name was most closely identified with the Sierra was, of course, Bret Harte. For from the middle-1860's to 1900 literally hundreds of California stories flowed from his active pen, most of which were laid in the towns or camps of the Mother Lode.

In view of this, there is an element of irony in the fact that Harte's personal acquaintance with the locale of his best-known tales was extremely sketchy. So far as is known, his firsthand knowledge of the area was limited to a few weeks in the summer of 1855 during which he worked an unproductive claim on the lower reaches of the Stanislaus River, plus an even briefer period the following year when he may — or may not — have served as an express agent on stages plying between towns in the same region.

Notwithstanding his limited experience in the diggings, however, Harte's fiction must be accorded a place, and a by no means insignificant one, in the literature of the range. For his tales, despite their often hackneyed themes and late-Victorian sentimentality, gave readers a graphic and in the main true picture of early-day inhabitants of the gold camps and of what sort of lives were lived there. Many of his host of fictional characters had their counterparts in real life, men who walked the resounding board sidewalks of the foothill towns, washed gold from the beds of its streams, and spent it freely at the bars and gambling resorts that constituted the region's only centers of conviviality.

Nor did Harte invariably romanticize the sturdy miner; on occasion he took off his rose-tinted glasses and wrote of them with steadfast realism. Thus — to cite a single example — in a sketch called *A Night at Wingdam,* written when he was only twenty-four — he pictured the plight of a frail gentlewoman, a Boston-educated schoolmarm, married to a brawny innkeeper and daily working herself to the point of exhaustion at menial tasks about the "Wingdam Temperance Hotel." It was a devastating commentary on the Ingomar-Parthenia theme, one that pointed up the hard realities of life in the raw gold towns, its backbreaking toil and all but complete lack of those redeeming features to be found in longer-established communities.

Several years later, in commenting on this tale, Harte thus wrote a friend:

> Let Corydon marry Phillis, and Chloe, Strephon, but let the Greek patrician maiden have a Greek patrician husband that can keep her fingers from getting red, and her graceful figure from growing bent. . . . [For, he added] The curse of California has been its degrading, materialistic influences which have reduced men and women to the lowest working equivalents.

Strange words for the man who, above all others, has been accused of casting a glow of specious romanticism over the lives of the Argonauts!

Another — and greater — literary figure whose name has in some degree come to be associated with the Sierra is Mark Twain. Twain's acquaintance with the range, like Harte's, was far from extensive and — again like Harte — it was mainly confined to its lower levels. During the early 1860's, as he records in *Roughing It,* Twain tried his luck in several mining camps on the eastern flank of the range and, as stated earlier, spent idyllic interludes on the shores of lakes Tahoe and Mono, the first-named of which he pronounced "the fairest picture the whole earth affords."

Of the range itself, and of California's mountains in general, Twain was considerably less enthusiastic. While admitting that the Sierra's peaks were "imposing in their sublimity and their majesty of form" when viewed from a distance, he felt that on closer acquaintance they lost much of their charm. In particular he deplored what he termed "a sad poverty of variety in species" in the Sierra forests, the trees being, he complained, "chiefly of one monotonous family — redwood, pine, spruce, fir":

> . . . and so, at a near view there is a wearisome sameness of attitude in their rigid arms, stretched downward and outward in one continued and reiterated appeal to all men to "Sh — don't say a word! — you might disturb somebody!" . . . There is a ceaseless melancholy in their sighing and complaining foliage; one walks over a soundless carpet of beaten yellow bark and dead spines of the foliage till he feels like a wandering spirit bereft of a football.

Not content with that heresy, Twain went on to comment that even the mountains' open spaces, their celebrated upland meadows, left much to be desired:

> Its grass blades stand up vindictively straight and self-sufficient, and are unsociably wide apart, with uncomely spots of barren sand between.

Clearly Mark cannot be counted among those who have written eloquently of the unparalleled beauties of the Sierra.

A year or two later, Twain spent a brief period in another part of the sprawling range, this time on its western slope in the decaying mining towns of the Tuolumne area. Having gone down from the Comstock and got work on one of San Francisco's then numerous newspapers, he had, according to legend, had a difference with the local police that made it prudent for him to absent himself from the city until memory of the affair grew dim. He accordingly retired to the southern mines, where he shared a cabin at Jackass Hill with Steve Gillis, a former co-worker on the Virginia City *Territorial Enterprise.*

> We lived [Twain later recalled] in a small cabin on a verdant hillside, and there were not five other cabins in view over the wide expanse of hill and forest. Yet a flourishing city of two or three thousand population had occupied this grassy dead solitude during the flush times of twelve or fifteen years before, and where our cabin stood had once been the heart of the teeming hive, the centre of the city.

Twain's none-too-energetic essays at mining were no more remunerative than had been his earlier attempts on the far side of the range. However, during his stay at Jackass Hill he chanced to hear a miner's yarn that for him was to prove a veritable bonanza. This was, of course, the story of Jim Smiley and his celebrated jumping frog, a tale that had been told and retold in those parts for well over a decade, the first printed version having appeared in the *Sonora Herald* on June 11, 1853. Twain at once recognized the yarn's humorous possibilities, and when his version, much expanded and with a wealth of cogent detail, appeared in the New York *Saturday Press* in 1865, the country at large got its first intimation that a fresh new talent had arisen in the West. Hence the Sierra — of which, as we have seen, Twain was a none too ardent admirer — served to launch him on his spectacular career.

Thus, while it may be said that the range supplied both Harte and Twain with the material they used on their entry into the literary field, and although one of the pair — Harte — continued industriously to work that vein for many years, neither can be regarded as among the true interpreters of the great uptilted chain. That distinction belongs to a group of writers who appeared on the scene a few years later. We have mentioned one of the first of these, both in time and in the extent and quality of his contribution — John Muir. Born in Scotland in 1838, Muir, after having spent his youth on a farm on the Wisconsin frontier, reached California in 1868 and headed at once for the Yosemite. During the next forty years he devoted himself to exploring the range and, from the mid-1870's onward, to making its attractions known to the public in a steady flow of magazine articles and books. Of the latter, perhaps the best known today are *The Mountains of California* and *My First Summer in the Sierra,* published in 1894 and 1911 respectively, and both frequently reprinted.

Second only to Muir in spreading abroad a knowledge of the wonders of the range was the energetic New Englander Clarence King, whom we have described in connection with Mount Whitney. In 1863, he joined a field party of the California State Geographical Survey and during the next three or four years explored large areas of the range, from Mount Shasta and Mount Lassen on the north to Mount Whitney far to the south. The result was a series of papers which, after having first appeared in the *Atlantic Monthly* in 1871, were published in book form the following year as *Mountaineering in the Sierra Nevada.*

This work, reissued two years later in an expanded edition, played an important part in making the Sierra better known.

For King was an entertaining writer and, although it presently grew clear that some of his mountain climbing feats were far less difficult and dangerous than he had made them out to be, he had a none the less real appreciation of the beauty and scenic grandeur of the range and succeeded better than most in communicating these qualities to others.

Another publication of the 1870's that added to the growing renown of the region was *Ramblings through the High Sierras*, an account of a six-week camping trip through the Yosemite-Mono-Tahoe area made in company with a number of his students by Joseph Le Conte, Professor of Geology and Natural History at the University of California. Le Conte's informal narrative, picturing as it did the pleasures of that carefree outing amid the region's lofty peaks and lake-strewn meadows — "we had no tent but slept under trees with only the sky above us" — undoubtedly inspired others to follow his example, and so added to the Sierra's growing popularity as a vacationland.

Prominent, too, among those who first publicized the wonders of the range was James M. Hutchings, of the Hutchings hospitality we have met earlier. Hutchings was one of the earliest permanent residents of the Yosemite Valley, where, besides for a time presiding over its first hotel, he published a number of books and pamphlets dealing with the area — its geology, history, scenic attractions, and other features of interest to visitors. The most ambitious of these was *In the Heart of the Sierras*, first published in 1886 and several times reissued during the next few years.

Among other publications in this field may be cited *The Alps of the King-Kern Divide* by David Starr Jordan, first president of Stanford University, which appeared in 1903; Stewart Edward White's *The Pass* (1906), that then widely popular writer's account of a summer's camping trip; and, coming down to more recent times, George and Bliss Hinkle's *Sierra-Nevada Lakes* (1949). In addition, a vast amount of material relating to the range has appeared in the more than fifty-year run of the *Sierra Club Bulletin,* in the annual reports of the Yosemite Valley Commissioners covering the years from 1866 to 1904, and in those of the superintendents of the Yosemite and Sequoia national parks from 1891 to 1915.

Of early-day accounts of Sierra travel, one of the most dramatic is that of Helen Hunt Jackson, author of *Ramona,* who, in 1872, made a horseback trip from the floor of Yosemite Valley to Gentry's Resort, by way of Indian Canyon and the old Mono Trail, in company with a grizzled guide named John Murphy. Of their climb up out of the valley over a newly built trail that zigzagged up the sheer face of the cliff she wrote: "On our left rose a granite wall . . . so piled up in projecting and overlapping masses that, mountain as it was, it seemed as if it might topple at any second. On our right hand — space! nothing more. . . . I turned, dizzy, shuddering, and found the threatening rocks on the left friendly by contrast." More than twelve hours after setting off, during which a badly flooded stream proved unfordable, necessitating a long detour, the courageous woman and her companion reached Gentry's long after nightfall.

Gregory Summerfield Gets His Comeuppance

One of the most curious of all contributions to the literature of the range is a now all-but-forgotten story called *The Case of Summerfield,* which on its first publication in a San

Francisco weekly in 1871 created something of a sensation on the West Coast, where many readers, failing to recognize it as a work of fiction, accepted it as an account of an actual happening. Its author was a San Francisco attorney, W. H. Rhodes, who made an avocation of writing and, under the pen-name of "Caxton," contributed a series of bizarre, pseudo-scientific stories to the California newspapers and magazines of the period.

The Case of Summerfield professed to be a factual account of a tragic happening on the mountain division of the newly completed Central Pacific Railroad. As an eastbound overland train was rounding Cape Horn, where the roadbed occupied a narrow shelf high above the American River, one passenger was heard to suggest to a companion that they step out on the platform so as to get a better view of the spectacular scenery visible at that spot. The two men did so and a few moments later others on the train were horrified to see one of the pair plunge over the cliff into the abyss below, a sheer drop of some 1700 feet. The train was stopped briefly but, since it was clear that the victim had been killed by his tremendous fall, and because there was danger of a collision if the cars remained long at that point, it got in motion and proceeded to the next station, where the dead man's companion, who was suspected of having pushed him over the precipice, was put under arrest.

The main body of the story purports to be the survivor's account of the tragedy and of the events that led up to it. He identifies himself as Leonidas Parker, a San Francisco attorney, and his late companion as Gregory Summerfield. Summerfield, whom Parker had known earlier in Texas, was described as an elderly man of eccentric but brilliant mind, with a thorough knowledge of the science of chemistry. By

Parker's account, Summerfield had recently visited him at his office and, having sworn the attorney to secrecy, confided that he had discovered a substance that on coming in contact with water decomposed it into its component parts and caused it to burn fiercely.

Parker, assuming that the other had come to him for the purpose of taking out a patent on his process, started to congratulate him on his ingenuity when Summerfield cut him short. With the gleam of a fanatic in his eye he announced that the vial in his hand made him master of the fate of the world, that with it he could ignite the oceans and destroy the planet, adding that only by the payment of a round million dollars would he refrain from carrying out that design. When Parker remained unconvinced, the older man had the doubter procure a bowl from the washstand and place it on his desk. Into it Summerfield poured a small amount of water and added a single pellet from the vial. Thereupon "a sharp explosion took place, and in a second of time the water was blazing in a red, lurid column, half way to the ceiling." When the water was consumed and the flames had died down, the badly shaken attorney asked: "To whom, sir, is this tremendous secret known?" "To myself alone," the other responded. "And now answer me a question: is it worth the money?"

Parker, convinced that his visitor had indeed hit on a means of destroying the world, thereupon set about trying to raise the huge sum demanded. By interviews with wealthy San Franciscans, and by demonstrations to them of the awesome nature of Summerfield's discovery, he succeeded in getting pledges for approximately half the amount. But the city was then in the grip of a depression and, it having grown clear that the entire sum could not be raised there, he suggested to Summerfield that the balance be sought in New York City. "To this proposal," Parker added, "Summerfield ultimately yielded, but with extreme reluctance."

The attorney's account continues thus:

> It was agreed in committee that I should accompany him thither, and take with me . . . evidences of the sums subscribed here; that a proper appeal should be made to the leading capitalists, scholars and clergymen of that metropolis, and that, when the whole amount was raised, it should be paid over to Summerfield, and a bond taken for him never to divulge his awful secret to any human being. With this, he seemed to be satisfied, and left us to prepare for his going the next morning.

On his departure from the room, one member of the committee, a bishop, arose and stated that such action was "childish and absurd"; that there was no reason to believe that the demoniac Summerfield would carry out his part of the bargain. He went on to state that in his opinion it would be no crime to deprive the other of "the means of assassinating the whole human family," and that for his part he was in favor of dooming the "diabolical wretch" to immediate death. The other committee members having unanimously concurred in that opinion, various plans for making away with Summerfield were discussed.

> It was finally resolved [continues Parker] that the trip to New York should not be abandoned, apparently; that we were to start out in accordance with the original programme; that during the journey some proper means should be resorted to by me to carry out the intentions of the committee, and that whatever I did would be sanctioned by them all, and full protection, both in law and conscience, afforded me in any stage of the proceeding.

He goes on to state that he accepted the assignment only after an hour of deep meditation, during which he considered the various factors involved: on the one hand his natural revulsion at the thought of taking a human life and, weighed against this, the knowledge that should he refuse, "the destiny of the globe itself might hang on the balance." Once he had made his decision and announced it to his fellows, he began preparations for carrying it into effect.

> Having [he continued] passed over the line of the Pacific Railway more than once, I was perfectly familiar with all its windings, gorges and precipices. I selected Cape Horn as the best adapted to the purpose, and . . . the public knows the rest.

Then followed his concluding paragraph:

> I am conscious of no guilt; I feel no remorse; I need no repentance. For me justice has no terrors, and conscience no sting. Let me be judged solely by the motives that actuated me, and the importance of the end accomplished, and I shall pass, unscathed, both temporal and eternal tribunals.

The story, persuasively developed and with a wealth of realistic detail, attracted wide attention on its publication, with, as stated, many readers being convinced that it dealt with an actual happening. Later, it having come to be recognized as fiction, the delicate ethical question it posed made it for months thereafter a favorite conversation piece in cabins and bars and parlors all over the West.

Index

Index

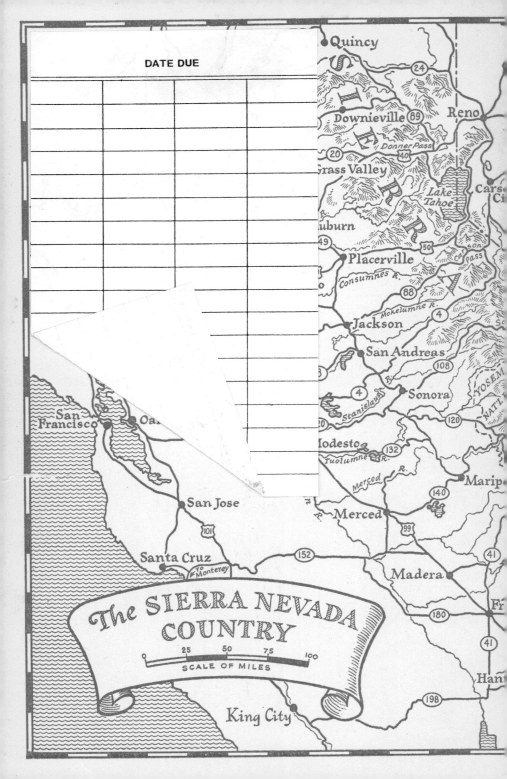